New York Stories

The Best of **The City** Section of

𝔗𝔥𝔢 𝔑𝔢𝔴 𝔜𝔬𝔯𝔨 𝔗𝔦𝔪𝔢𝔰

EDITED BY

Constance Rosenblum

NEW YORK UNIVERSITY PRESS
New York and London

NEW YORK UNIVERSITY PRESS
New York and London
www.nyupress.org

Library of Congress Cataloging-in-Publication Data
New York stories : the best of the city section of the New York Times /
edited by Constance Rosenblum.
p. cm.
ISBN 0–8147–7571–3 (acid-free paper) —
ISBN 0–8147–7572–1 (pbk. : acid-free paper)
1. City and town life — New York (State)—New York—Anecdotes.
2. New York (N.Y.)—Social life and customs—Anecdotes.
3. New York (N.Y.)—Biography—Anecdotes. 4. New York (N.Y.)—
Social conditions—Anecdotes. I. Rosenblum, Constance.
F128.55.N48   2005
974.7'04'0922—dc22   2004028961

New York University Press books are printed on acid-free paper,
and their binding materials are chosen for strength and durability.

Manufactured in the United States of America

c 10 9 8 7 6 5 4 3 2
p 10 9 8 7 6 5

CONTENTS

Part II Moods and Mores

Part IV City Lore

ACKNOWLEDGMENTS

THIS book exists because of the generosity of a lot of people. The New York Times was kind enough to grant the necessary permissions so these articles and essays, along with the accompanying photographs and illustrations, could be collected in book form. Susan Chira, former editorial director of book development at The Times, endorsed this project from the beginning, and her successor, Alex Ward, was equally supportive as it moved through the pipeline. All my colleagues in the City section played a role in helping birth these pieces and easing their journey into book form; I'd especially like to thank Sarah Weissman for her help with the images and C. J. Satterwhite for handling myriad technical tasks. If it weren't for Eric Zinner, editorial director of New York University Press, these articles would still be moldering on yellowing newsprint (or tucked away in an electronic archive). Most of all, I'm grateful to the writers who allowed their works to be included in this collection. It was an honor to publish every one of them.

Introduction

IT was not long after European settlers touched down in Manhattan in the early 17th century that they began putting pen to paper—or quill to parchment—in an effort to describe the glories, frustrations and peculiar appeal of their new home. To pick just one writer and one excerpt at random: in a document published in London in 1670, the beguiling English essayist Daniel Denton wrote of the island: "Yea, in May you shall see the Woods and Fields so curiously bedecked with Roses, and an innumerable multitude of delightful Flowers, not only pleasing the eye, but smell, that you may behold Nature contending with Art, and striving to equal, if not excel many Gardens in England."

The centuries that followed would produce a torrent of writing inspired by the city, not only by legendary figures like Walt Whitman, Herman Melville, Hart Crane and F. Scott Fitzgerald, but also by less celebrated individuals who found their muse on the city's streets and byways. As Phillip Lopate points out in his marvelous anthology, "Writing New York," few cities have inspired as much great writing as this one, noting that the literature of the city is unmatched in its variety and sheer volume.

These rising voices—personal, urgent, idiosyncratic, eloquent, astute —capture the essence of one of the world's extraordinary places. Or try to. New York, like an exquisite but elusive butterfly, is famously hard to pin down. That, of course, is part of its charm.

For the past few years, readers of The New York Times have been hearing some of these voices by way of the City section, a part of the Sunday paper that is distributed to readers in the five boroughs (and via

1

the paper's Web site to the rest of the world). The section was started in 1993 as a counterpart to the weekly sections that served Connecticut, New Jersey, Long Island and Westchester County, the four sprawling regions surrounding the city. While the paper has, of course, always cared deeply about the town whose name it bears—never more so than in recent years—the City section offered a unique opportunity to shine a white-hot light on that place and that place only, to tease out and explore the many aspects of the city that might slip through the netting of regular news coverage.

At the time of the section's birth, the city was reeling from a welter of ills, from drug-fueled crime and dysfunctional schools to filthy streets and subways and a pervasive malaise that was discouraging non–New Yorkers from making their homes here and forcing even longtime New Yorkers to reconsider their decision to remain. Living in New York seemed to require a special grit and resilience. In response, the City section in its early years focused on helping New Yorkers cope with a myriad of challenges and navigate an often daunting urban landscape. But as New York became a city in ascendancy, as it grew cleaner, safer, more vital, more enticing, the section's mission evolved from helping people master an unruly setting to allowing them to savor, through the eyes of quintessential New York writers, its ever-changing texture.

The number of such writers was growing. As New York flourished like a robust plant, the number of nonfiction books about the city, both past and present, rose steadily. According to Bowkers Books in Print, which keeps track of such things, there were under 800 such titles in the 1980's; by the 1990's there were nearly 2,000, not including biographies of notable New Yorkers. This is hardly a surprise, because unlike books about most other places, those about New York are often considered national books and reach readers around the country, sometimes the world. The audience is an ever-widening group that includes not only natives and tourists but also newcomers eager to learn about their adopted home.

In a tragic irony, the events of September 11, 2001, hastened this evolution. As the city reeled, mourned, rebuilt, and rebounded, both those who lived here and those who simply cared about New York were forced to examine what it was that made the place so precious, so essential. The city's vulnerability helped the world appreciate New York as never before.

Unfortunately, the City section arrived too late on the scene to offer up work by the likes of Whitman and Crane. But there is no lack of late

20th- and early 21st-century chroniclers who can cut through the ca-
cophony of seemingly endless news reports and make sense of the city on
a more personal, more lyrical level. We like to think that these writers let
us present a deeper New York, a city that is more profound, more nuanced, than the one typically offered through the necessary day-to-day
headlines.

Many contributors to this book need no introduction. Writers like
Phillip Lopate, Vivian Gornick, Richard Price, Jerome Charyn, André
Aciman and Tom Beller are among the most eloquent observers of our
urban life. Others are relative newcomers, among them Jim Rasenberger,
whose gripping City section portrait of the high-steel workers who built
the world's greatest skyline became the basis of a book on the subject;
and Adrian Nicole LeBlanc, who discovered that the borough that inspired her prize-winning book, "Random Families: Love, Drugs, Trouble, and Coming of Age in the Bronx," was an integral part of her own
roots. Still others, like Field Maloney, a member of the editorial staff of
The New Yorker, who wrote of his summer idyll in Rockaway, and
Katherine Marsh, who explored the near-crippling claustrophobia that is
the ultimate urban ill, are not household names, but we suspect you'll be
hearing about them one day.

What distinguishes all these pieces is the presence of a powerful voice.
New York itself is a city of voices—sophisticated and street-smart, wise-
guy and nostalgic, loud and soft, subtle and over the top. The City section is distinctive in that it has been able to cultivate these distinctive
voices. Inspired by New York's rich cultural and geographic diversity,
these essayists and stylists present a passionate and well-written portrait
of the city in all its facets.

There are a million stories one could write about New York; eight million, if you believe the old saw. This collection contains 40, falling into
four general categories. The essays in "A Sense of Place" bring to vivid
life some of the city's quintessential locales, among them a Greenwich
Village basketball court where pathos and humor bounce about with as
much abandon as the ball; an Upper East Side Starbucks where dramas
large and minute play out around the clock; and the exquisite townhouse
on West 11th Street—"the little house on heaven street"—that was destroyed in 1970 when young radicals accidentally set off a bomb inside.
The essays in "Moods and Mores" seek to capture the city's peculiar
rhythms and rituals by examining a few of those eternal questions: Why
are New York sports fans so whiny? Why is New York life so random?

(Or is it?) Can soccer dads ever escape? (No.) Why do we adore "Law and Order"? Is New York a writer's graveyard? (David Leavitt says it is; we, of course, disagree.)

The section called "New Yorkers" offers a bouquet of indelible profiles. We meet Sonny, the beloved panhandler of the F train; Alan Campbell, who ruled the subway slug like a Godfather; and Lodovico, the dashing young 16th-century aristocrat who lives in the Frick. The pieces in "City Lore" excavate slices of the city's rich and endlessly fascinating past: the mysterious treasure ship sunk beneath Hell Gate and one man's quest to drag it ashore; the plane that crashed into Park Slope, Brooklyn, more than half a century ago (and the nurse who cared for the child who for a single, sad day was its lone survivor); a baseball encrusted with myths and memories, some of which were even true.

In the five years I've been editing the City section, we've published an increasing number of these essays. To someone like me, who grew up in a small town outside the city, moved here as soon as I could, and never had the slightest desire to leave, it's been a joy to present these pieces to readers of The Times. We hope their words will appeal both to existing New Yorkers, new and entrenched, and to the countless people who savor the city from afar.

Constance Rosenblum

September 2004

Part I

A Sense of Place

The blast scene. (Librado Romero/The New York Times)

The House on West 11th Street

Three Decades After Young Radicals Blew Up an Elegant Brownstone in Greenwich Village, Echoes of the Blast Linger.

MEL GUSSOW

THE cross streets off lower Fifth Avenue just north of Washington Square are among the most historic and quietly residential in Manhattan, a haven in a city that thrives on its hyperactivity. Writers and artists as varied as Mark Twain, Leonard Bernstein and Thornton Wilder once lived and worked here. Even those less famous have prized this neighborhood for its classic beauty and its privacy. Eleventh Street between Fifth Avenue and Avenue of the Americas is one of the choicest streets, with brownstones evoking an atmosphere resonant of the last turn of the century.

For three years in the late 1960's, my wife, Ann, our son, Ethan, and I lived on the second floor of a brownstone at 16 West 11th Street. The house was owned by Joe Hazan and his wife, Jane Freilicher, the painter. The parlor floor was occupied by Dustin Hoffman, his wife, Anne, and their daughter, Karina. Mr. Hoffman had become a movie star but partly because this was West 11th Street had continued to live a relatively secluded life. The street seemed destined to remain a kind of sanctuary, until just before noon on March 6, 1970, when the house next door, at 18 West 11th Street, exploded. The explosion, which became front-page news and sent a shock wave through the city, was caused by the accidental detonation of dynamite in a subbasement bomb factory. Young radicals from the Weathermen were making bombs to destroy property, beginning with the main library at Columbia University.

Three bomb makers, Theodore Gold, Diana Oughton and Terry Robbins, were killed. Two others, Kathy Boudin and Cathlyn Wilkerson, escaped and remained fugitives for more than a decade. The first was the daughter of the civil liberties lawyer Leonard Boudin, the second the daughter of James P. Wilkerson, the owner of the house at No. 18.

During the years since, I have thought about the explosion often: every March on the anniversary, and on other occasions; when Cathy Wilkerson resurfaced in 1980 and was tried and convicted, and served a brief prison sentence; when Kathy Boudin took part in a 1981 robbery in which two police officers and a Brinks guard were killed. She was tried, convicted, and sentenced to serve her time at Bedford Hills Correction Facility in Bedford, N.Y. Every time I walk by the house that was built on the site, I am ineluctably drawn back to memories of when it was a place of destruction.

In the interim, children have grown up and married. The Hoffmans were divorced, and married other people. The surviving bombers are in their 50's, and they have refused to talk about the explosion. Yet 30 years later, the event still shadows those affected by it.

Houses have personal histories. As they pass between owners, they become carriers of family chronicles. The house at 18 West 11th Street and those surrounding it, beautifully matched four-story town houses of Federal design, were built in the 1840's by Henry Brevoort Jr. and were known as the Brevoort Row. Early in the 20th century, No. 18 was owned by Charles Merrill, a founder of Merrill Lynch & Company. His son, the poet James Merrill, was born there.

In 1930, Charles Merrill sold the building to Howard Dietz, a successful Broadway lyricist and a movie executive. Merrill followed up with a note saying that he hoped the new owner would enjoy "the little house on heaven street." Dietz lived there lavishly with each of his three wives. When he gave a party, sometimes for as many as 250, all the furniture was placed in a van, which was parked on the street until the guests finished "dancing in the dark," as Dietz phrased it in his most famous song.

James Wilkerson, an advertising executive, bought the house in 1963 and moved in with his second wife, Audrey. He continued the high style of living to which the house had become accustomed. The dwelling had 10 rooms, including a double-size drawing room, a paneled library, where the owner kept his valuable collection of sculptured birds, and a sauna. He restored antique furniture in the subbasement workroom. The house still had the original mantles on its fireplaces and was filled with Hepplewhite furniture. In the garden was a fountain with a mirror behind it.

In 1964, Mr. Wilkerson celebrated his 50th birthday with a masked ball for 90 people, dancing to an orchestra until 2 a.m. Among the guests were two daughters from his first marriage, Ann and Cathy. Several times my wife and I came home from the theater and saw the Wilkersons welcoming guests in formal attire.

•

At 11:55 on Friday morning, March 6, 1970, Anne Hoffman was coming home and the cabdriver accidentally drove past her house. As she got out of the cab, No. 18 exploded. If the cab had stopped at No. 16, she and the driver might have felt the full brunt of the explosion. She rushed into her apartment, where she found her frightened baby sitter with the family's terrier. Back outside, she was met by a wall of flame.

At the moment of the explosion, my wife was at Fifth Avenue and 11th Street with our son, whom she had just picked up at nursery school. Leaving him with a friend, she ran toward our house.

Arthur Levin, who still owns the building at No. 20, was at home at the time of the explosion. At first, he thought it had occurred in his house; when he went outside, he realized that it was next door. He immediately telephoned the police.

Further down the street, Susan Wager, a neighbor, was in her kitchen. "I felt my house tremble," she said. "It was like an earthquake."

She rushed to No. 18 and saw two grime-covered young women coming out of the downstairs door. One (Cathy Wilkerson) was naked. The other (Kathy Boudin) was partly clad in jeans. The assumption was that their clothes were torn off in the blast.

Mrs. Wager took them back to her house, gave them fresh clothes and offered them the use of a shower. Then she went back into the street to see what was happening. By the time she returned home, the two women had left, one wearing Mrs. Wager's favorite boots and coat. She never saw the women again. "I thought they were in an accident," Ms. Wager said. "I never thought they could have been responsible."

By the time I arrived, the street was swarming with firemen, policemen and sightseers. Seeing the smoke pour out of No. 18, we felt that our house would also be destroyed. That afternoon, each tenant in our building was allowed to make one quick trip inside and rescue items of property. In our apartment, the walls creaked, as if a ship had been torpedoed and was about to sink beneath the sea. None of the tenants of No. 16 ever spent a night in that house again.

On the evening news, there was a picture of a red tricycle and the suggestion that a child might be missing in the explosion. It was Ethan's tricycle. It had been in the lobby of the building and the fireman had put it outside. Our upstairs neighbor, a playwright, rescued his tax forms, a Picasso drawing and a tin of truffles. His top hat and tails, worn for openings at the opera, were never recovered.

Devastated by the explosion, the splendid house at No. 18 had been reduced to shattered walls and windows. Mr. Hoffman's living room wall had a huge hole torn in it. His desk had fallen into the rubble next door.

Late that day he stood in the street with his daughter. It was her fourth birthday, and he was trying to reassure her.

"Don't worry, Karina, everything will be all right," he said to his daughter, and then said it again. She looked up at him and replied, "If everything is going to be all right, why are you shaking so hard?"

On Saturday, we were allowed to go up and retrieve a few more things. What we did not know was that buried in the rubble were 60 sticks of dynamite, lead pipes packed with dynamite, blasting caps and packages of dynamite taped together with fuses. An F.B.I. report later determined that "had all the explosives detonated, the explosion would have leveled everything on both sides of the street."

When the Wilkersons returned from St. Kitts, where they had been on vacation, the police took them and the Hoffmans to a warehouse on the Gansevoort Street pier. Mr. Hoffman remembers seeing huge mounds of debris, five feet high, the remnants of the Wilkerson house. His wife tripped over a blue coat; thinking it might be hers, she went through the pockets. She found a penciled map of the underground tunneling system at Columbia University. Most chilling to her was that her father was the head librarian at Columbia and would have been at work had the explosives been detonated in Butler Library.

Later, the police—or was it the F.B.I.?—showed the Hoffmans photographs of Weathermen and the remains of the three victims. In some cases, Mr. Hoffman had difficulty even recognizing the body parts.

Several years ago, in pursuit of long buried facts, my wife and I went to Washington and looked at sections of 10,000 pages of once secret or classified F.B.I. documentation on the Weathermen and at papers of the New York Police Department dealing with the investigation. Several things seem evident, even as other mysteries linger.

Kathy Boudin and Cathy Wilkerson were deeply committed to civil protest against what they saw as injustices, in particular the war in Vietnam. They met in 1964 when both were arrested for protesting against segregated schools in Chester, Pa. The F.B.I. had followed them for years.

Cathy Wilkerson had often stayed at her father's house when she was a college student and had asked to stay there in March 1970 while the Wilkersons were in St. Kitts. Mr. Levin, who was often on the street walking his dog, remembers once seeing people carrying boxes from a car into the house. Later he surmised that the boxes contained explosives.

●

As time passed, the explosion faded into history, but for some of us, it remained a vivid memory. During the last few years, in search of questions, if not answers, I talked to some of the key figures in the event. One was Mr. Wilkerson, who was living near Stratford-on-Avon in England. Sipping tea in a Stratford hotel, he reluctantly drew himself back to the experience.

"Talking to you about this subject is like talking to somebody about a bad case of poison ivy that I had many years ago," he said at one point. "I survived it, and I'm fine, and thoughts don't well up in my mind about it, because either consciously or subconsciously I put them out of my mind."

"Possessions are fine, but when the chips are down, they're not all that important," he added. "We were concerned about our daughter Cathy."

Before the explosion, his house had been up for sale. His wife was English and they had been planning to move to England. They simply left earlier than intended.

Mr. Wilkerson said that for 10 years he did not hear from his daughter. Then in 1980, her younger sister got in touch with him to say that Cathy was about to surface. She was tried and convicted on charges of illegal possession of dynamite. She served 11 months in Bedford Hills.

"I keep repeating, what my wife and I lived through, what you lived through, what Cathy lived through, so many other people have lived through worse experiences, and survived," Mr. Wilkerson said. "People have children killed in automobile accidents and houses burn down every day of the week. Human nature keeps you going. You forget the bad things. Here I am, no visible outer scars." He paused, and added, "I'm sure there are some inner ones."

Had he ever asked his daughter why she was involved in the bomb making? "Never," he answered. "And she never offered."

Audrey Logan, Cathy's mother, also preferred not to discuss the subject.

"I understand what it must have done to you," she said by phone from her home in New Hampshire. "I can't begin to tell you what it's done to me." She paused. "My daughter has so much integrity and has tried to reconstruct her life. She's made a constructive life for herself and for her child." As to whether the explosion was simply a thing of the past and no longer mattered, she responded: "It matters. In some ways, it seems like yesterday."

In contrast to the Wilkersons, the Boudins were often in the political spotlight. Leonard Boudin was on the front line fighting for civil liberties and human rights. His wife, Jean, was a poet; Jean's sister was married to I. F. Stone, the liberal journalist. Kathy grew up surrounded by activists and artists. Her social consciousness came naturally. As Mr. Boudin said at his daughter's trial, "We are responsible in a large sense for our daughter's views on life: the prelude to a long prison sentence." Leonard Boudin died in 1989, his wife in 1994.

As an inmate, Kathy earned a master's degree in education and has been active as a teacher and in counseling other prisoners. Her activities formed the basis for her petition to Gov. Mario M. Cuomo for clemency, which was rejected in 1994.

Next to the Wilkersons, the Boudins and the Weathermen themselves, the people most affected by the explosion were the owners and residents of the adjoining buildings. The landlords of Nos. 16 and 20, Joe Hazan and Arthur Levin, were faced with repairing their houses. Mr. Levin, who publishes a health newsletter, said the bombing "was a seminal event in a very turbulent period."

He added: "It was an interesting kind of victimization. Here I have good politics and I'm still getting blown out of my house."

Looking back on the explosion, Mr. Hoffman said it was a life-changing and philosophy-changing experience. Before it happened, he said, he was "in a chrysalis," away from reality.

"It remains an abstraction until it happens to you," he added. "Since then, we've seen killings of abortion doctors, killings by Christian fundamentalists. At a certain point, the radical left and the radical right merged. They shook hands."

Mateo Lettunich, a writer who lives in California, lived on the top floor of No. 16 at the time of the explosion. Recalling his Greenwich Village days with affection, he seemed to have no angry feelings about the explosion. "I'm afraid I never dwelt on the sociological side of it all," he said. "The Weathermen were a sign of the times, which ended, or fizzled, not too long after, only to be replaced by much worse: the violence of the 90's."

Gino Sloan, a textile designer who lived in the garden apartment, suffered the most damage to his home. His floor collapsed and his bedroom caved in. He lost all his clothes except for a polyester suit he hated. Although he was appalled by the explosion, he feels that it offered him an immediate freedom. An avid collector of books and other objects, he felt suddenly liberated from his possessions. "I felt as light as a feather and free and unencumbered," he said, except for his concern about his pets.

He finally found his orange cat in a closet, terrified and turned pitch black by the fire. When he brought the cat outside, the crowd greeted him with a cheer. But Leona the Lion Head Goldfish did not survive; too much sediment had fallen on her aquarium.

Mr. Sloan moved to another apartment in the Village and has again surrounded himself with possessions. An odd thought enters his mind: perhaps he needs a metaphorical bombing to simplify his life once more.

Catless, he now has a dog that he walks daily along 11th Street. He says the dog "makes a statement" by habitually relieving itself in front of No. 16 and never in front of No. 18, perhaps out of some atavistic canine memory. Mr. Sloan says politically he felt kinship with the Weathermen, and "except for the bombing," would have been on their side.

•

At the time, the explosion had a profound effect on my life and family. I had recently started a new job and was awaiting publication of my first book. Our son was not yet 4, and for a time everything was "before" or "after" the explosion, as in a reference to a toy "I used to have before the explosion."

We were without a home, moving from a hotel to a sublet to a friend's house and back to a hotel. The objects we had rescued were kept in storage. When finally reclaimed, they were still heavy with smoke. Years

later, we would occasionally open a book or drawer and be met with the
lingering smell of the fire. It was a long time before my wife or I could
speak about the explosion without tears. After a year, we moved to West
10th Street, where we live today.

When all the rubble was gone at No. 18, a fence was erected in front
of the property. There was a door in the fence, and one day I opened it.
Behind the door was a bombed-out war zone: ashes, rubble, broken
beams and the charred remains of a book, "Catch-22."

Eventually, Hugh Hardy, the architect, and Francis Mason, then an
executive at Steuben Glass, bought the land. Mr. Hardy designed a startlingly modern structure. After considerable debate, the radical design
was finally approved by the Landmarks Commission. The Hardys and
the Masons planned to turn the new house into a two-family dwelling.
But as time passed, the two couples changed their minds and put the
property back on the market.

For eight years, the plot remained vacant. Then, in 1978, it was sold
to David and Norma Langworthy, a wealthy Philadelphia couple. They
used Mr. Hardy's design for the exterior, with a facade jutting out toward the street. They moved in the following year, and Mrs. Langworthy
remained after her husband's death in 1994.

Inside, the new one-family house has 10 levels, with perspective-
distorting angles and open spaces allowing for dramatic views. The former bomb factory is now a laundry room. Nowhere is there a hint of the
building's past.

The signature touch is a Paddington bear in the jutting window. Its
costume is changed according to the weather. On rainy days, Paddington
wears a raincoat. During a storm, he switches to snow wear. For the first
day of school, he is decked out in his schoolboy outfit. By special request,
one day two bears appeared in the window dressed as a bride and
groom; on cue, a neighborhood doctor fell to his knees on the sidewalk
and proposed to his girlfriend.

Every March 6, people place flowers around the tree in front of the
building. One day in the early 1990's, Francis Mason invited James
Merrill and his mother, Hellen Plummer, to see the house that had replaced their former home. After her son's death in 1995, Mrs. Plummer,
then 95, reminisced about the original house at No. 18. She had lived
there when she was first married 70 years before. Her son spent his first
five years in the house and went to Sunday school at the Church of the
Ascension around the corner.

"We were happy there," she said. About returning to the site, she added: "It didn't feel like our old house. It was totally different architecture. But it was soothing to us that someone cared enough to put something else on the property."

It is not surprising that a poet would have made one of the most moving statements about the house. After the explosion, James Merrill wrote a poem titled "18 West 11th Street," mourning the memory of his birthplace. He writes about the "dear premises vainly exploded." Later, he observes:

> Shards of a blackened witness still in place.
> The charred ice-sculpture garden
> Beams fell upon. The cold blue searching beams.

March 5, 2000

(*Editor's note*: Kathy Boudin was released on parole in September 2003.)

A legendary music store on 116th Street. (Rebecca Cooney/The New York Times)

2

Spanish Harlem on His Mind

As Latinos From Many Lands Stream Into New York, Puerto Ricans Watch, Remembering a Time El Barrio Was Theirs Alone.

ED MORALES

EL Barrio. In my childhood its mere mention conjured all kinds of feelings, from a kind of reverence for proud beginnings to my parents' wariness of its slow descent into hard times. It was a magic Spanish phrase that fell easily from my father's lips, a reference to a place that curiously seemed to belong to us, even though New York didn't belong to us. As more of us moved to various corners of the Bronx, El Barrio increasingly became the source of authenticity, like the bacalaitos (codfish fritters) on 116th Street that were the closest thing to what you could get on the island.

As I grew older and the neighborhood's mean streets became even meaner, I was still in awe of its self-assured Latin style. Even in my feeble Santana fan worship I knew that what "Oye Como Va" talked about ultimately went back to Tito Puente and the streets of El Barrio.

Sharkskin-suit-wearing mambo men spinning leggy lace-draped women at the Park Palace on 110th and Fifth Avenue lurked in my subconscious. Multicolored Latin men standing their ground against turf invaders, wearing T-shirts and pegged pants, with an angry curled lock of defiance spilling onto their foreheads, haunted me in my exiles in the Bronx, New England and the Lower East Side. I could almost hear the slow boleros from rooftop parties, the anomalous screech of roosters on fire escapes, holding me in the grip of the peculiar alchemy created by tropical people shivering in poorly heated tenements.

The late theater director and promoter Eddie Figueroa, who lived in the projects at 114th and Lexington Avenue, once declared that wherever he called home was the embassy of the Spirit Republic of

Puerto Rico, and for the first time I understood El Barrio as a sanctuary of an idea, an identity. It was an imaginary homeland that I shared with countless other displaced souls, U.S.-entrenched Puerto Ricans in search of being Puerto Rican.

Today, although Puerto Ricans are still the city's most populous Spanish-speaking group—of the 2.2 million Latinos, 830,000 are Puerto Ricans—we can sometimes feel like an afterthought in the Latin New York we all but created.

•

When the Metro-North trains come rumbling like massive conga drums out of the Park Avenue tunnel at 96th Street and toward the northern viaduct, they draw attention to one of the enduring symbols of racial and class division in New York. It's as if they're saying: Welcome to East Harlem, where hip-hop and salsa trump classical, and prime real estate gives way to inner city. The architectural necessity of the viaduct, built in the 1840's, is the primordial source of the real estate mantra: "Manhattan below 96th Street."

But now, whispered buzzwords of gentrification like Upper Yorkville, Carnegie Hill North and SpaHa (for Spanish Harlem) are creeping up from the south. The specter of new luxury high-rise developments with tony names like the Monterrey and Carnegie Hill Place are pushing back the ghetto flavor. The Spanish Harlem of the mind, dotted with the world's greatest cuchifrito stands (fried Caribbean snacks), stickball clubs and old-school piragueros, men who sell flavored ices from push-carts, is threatened with extinction.

The changing face of East Harlem is due not only to the real estate charge from south of 96th Street, but also to a surge of Latino immigrants. That new presence is personified by Valente Leal, a 14-year-old immigrant from Mexico who has lived in East Harlem for the past eight years.

Valente has a bushy, spiked punk haircut, likes hard rock bands like Korn and Slipknot, is an occasional painter and wants to be a doctor. And Valente's got a theory about why so many people from south of 96th Street are moving in. "Ever since 9/11 there's all these people from downtown around here," he said, wide-eyed. "I think they got scared or something."

So, as the strip on Lexington between 104th Street and 96th morphs from Barrio to boho periphery, a loose confederation of mostly Puerto Rican politicians, activists and residents is trying to make a stand to preserve the area's Latino identity. Rafael Merino, a graphic designer who grew up on the Lower East Side and recently moved from Williamsburg, thinks what's happening uptown is bigger than mere nostalgia.

"It's not about Latinos losing El Barrio, it's about New York City losing El Barrio," said Mr. Merino, who lives on 116th Street. "This is one of those diverse gems that makes the city what it is."

•

All of this flux, all of these questions—about gentrification, about the future, about whom El Barrio truly belongs to—sent me back to the neighborhood's streets, where the ambivalent dance of development is played out.

For me, the son of Puerto Rican parents who came to Manhattan during the late 1940's, East Harlem, or El Barrio, as we called it, stirred mixed emotions. It was where my parents suffered the early indignities of American dream-searching, a grimy tenement-land they escaped for the relatively pastoral Castle Hill in the Bronx in the 1960's. But even as I left the Bronx for the East Village and, finally, Brooklyn, El Barrio had an undeniable allure for me.

I craved the memories of the smells and sounds of then-exotic Caribbean vegetables at La Marqueta, the indoor market at 115th Street and Park Avenue, and the salsa jams throbbing from the Casa Latina record store on 116th Street. Six years ago, when I went to the funeral for my uncle Angel Luis, one of the last of my relatives to still live there, I felt as if I had a claim to El Barrio's mythology.

The Barrio of bodegas, botanicas and bomba y plena (traditional Puerto Rican folk music) came into being in the 1950's, when the Puerto Rican migration peaked. The neighborhood went into a steep economic decline and depopulation in the 1970's, and East Harlem's Latino identity began to take on an ephemeral quality.

"Some of us, if they were lighter skinned, gravitated to a white identity," said Aurora Flores, a publicist and community activist. "Those who were darker gravitated to a black identity, so it's become important to us to define our identity."

Ms. Flores is the M.C. of a weekly Thursday gathering called Julia's Jam, held at the Julia de Burgos Cultural Center at 105th and Lexington Avenue. Recitations by single mothers and schoolchildren take precedence over slam poets, and the evening culminates in a free-form jam session by the bomba y plena group Yerba Buena.

Administered by the arts organization Taller Boricua, the de Burgos Center is part of a "cultural crossroads" envisioned by a Taller co-founder, Fernando Salicrup, a painter and a Barrio homeowner. Born and raised in the neighborhood, Mr. Salicrup is a mentor to an emerging group of young artists, writers and musicians who are moving back to the neighborhood. "I learned to be Puerto Rican in this community," Mr. Salicrup said. "I didn't learn it in Puerto Rico."

On any night, El Barrio, a true cultural crossroads, comes alive. And while it still holds on to a Puerto Rican identity, it is also infused by new blood.

As I tool around Lexington, I can run into Erica González or Melissa Mark-Viverito, co-founders of Women of El Barrio, a political group, or Mariposa, a poet, scribbling away in her notebook. When I slide into a booth at La Fonda Boricua (Boricua is an affectionate name for a Puerto Rican) on 106th Street, surrounded by paintings by Latinos, and feast on rice and beans, I feel as if the Latino renaissance that could have happened in the East Village 15 years ago is happening here.

But Tato Torres, a founding member of Yerba Buena and conscience of the area's cultural renaissance, warns me: "This art thing is a double-edged sword. It's easy to become the exotic Latino-flavored thing and make the place chic for outsiders. There's already been some animosity between Barrio natives and recent arrivals like me."

I ponder his words, and remember how artists were the leading edge of a rent escalation that displaced thousands of Puerto Ricans east of Avenue A as I head further down Lexington, to the intersection of the new and old East Harlem, to Galeria de la Vega, run by a local artist.

James de la Vega is a hybrid between a street kid and an Ivy League-educated guerrilla performance artist. He surfs among the personas of mayor of the block, eccentric artist and entrepreneur with relative ease. Because he has run tours of El Barrio for outside agencies, scrawls incendiary slogans on the sidewalks and occasionally flaunts a huge Afro wig and black leather pants, he is the focus of some controversy.

"I have a love-hate relationship with this place," said Mr. de la Vega, who grew up in the neighborhood the son of Puerto Ricans. "Some of the things I write on the sidewalk are a little tough for the people here." And he admits that he likes to provoke people with phrases like "We walk amongst each other in a deep dream committing small acts of violence against one another."

Some people in the neighborhood have taken such offense to Mr. de la Vega's act that they have painstakingly defaced most of his murals scattered around East Harlem. "As much as I like to promote the concept of this being Spanish Harlem, I also feel that we have to connect with the world in a bigger way," he said. "But there's an element here that doesn't feel I'm doing the right thing, so I'm forced to rethink myself sometimes."

A quick stroll west, under the stone arches of the northern Park Avenue viaduct and through the projects on Madison, brings me to El Museo del Barrio, which has been challenged by a local group called Nuestro Museo Action Committee that feels the museum, founded by local Puerto Rican activists in 1969, has neglected the neighborhood to focus on the high art of Latin America.

Tony Bechara, the museum's chairman and a painter from Puerto Rico but not El Barrio, gave me a thorough tour, beaming with pride about a recent wildly successful show of the Mexican painters Frida Kahlo and Diego Rivera and the permanent exhibition about the Taino Indians, the ancient indigenous people of Puerto Rico.

"Our direction has been toward inclusivity," he said, explaining that the museum's limited space restricts the number of community artists they can show. Next up was the Puerto Rican artist Rafael Tufiño, but the Nuestro committee continues to lobby for local representation on the board.

Tato Torres of Yerba Buena had recently sent an e-mail message to committee members including a Web page from Citysearch.com, which listed El Museo with the pull quote (since changed): "This little museum isn't just for Boricuas anymore." It seems a harmless sentiment, but it represents an attitude that makes Puerto Ricans angry. In the larger world of Latinos we (and to an extent Dominicans, who dominate Washington Heights) are underdogs in the Latino identity game, easily marginalized by swanky displays of cultural capital that Mexicans and South Americans can summon.

But, as Mr. Torres says, El Barrio's Mexicans don't necessarily profit from Kahlo chic, and are crucial to the future of the neighborhood: "In El Barrio we have to find those threads that bind. We have to find what will unite us, whether we're Colombians, Mexicans, Dominicans or Puerto Ricans."

•

My father, who lived on First Avenue near 114th Street in the early 1950's, likes to tell the story of a friend from his hometown in Puerto Rico who came to visit him after immigrating to Chicago. "He adopted some of the Mexican customs they have over there and came to New York wearing a flashy zoot suit," he said. "He was late, so when I went to check on him, I found him bloodied in the hallway. The Italians had beaten him up."

Forty years later, the Mexicans truly began arriving, and after enduring their own beatings from local groups, they settled in to become hardcore residents of El Barrio. The main drag of 116th Street offers several Mexican restaurants, record shops blaring mariachi and rock en Español, and a store filled with fútbol jerseys.

Leaders of both the Puerto Rican and Mexican communities fall all over themselves to express solidarity, but there is little overt interaction.

On the surface, the differences are clear: the jukebox in El Paso Taquería favors Mexican corridos and cumbias over salsa and merengue, and the street kids align themselves in camps that prefer the Mexican rockers Jaguares or the Puerto Rican rapper Fat Joe. But in the public schools, the teenagers are creating a new Latino melting pot. Alberto Medina, a Puerto Rican classmate of Valente Leal's, says: "I play soccer. I eat tacos, my uncle married a Mexican and my other uncle married a Dominican."

The Mexicans bring such a feeling of new energy that they give some locals the incorrect impression that they are the new majority Latino population, though they are third after Puerto Ricans and Dominicans, with a population of 196,000. The neighborhood also contains sizable populations of African-Americans and Italian-Americans.

Mark Alexander, who runs Hope Community, a development corporation that manages 1,400 housing units and oversees $125 million worth of real estate, points out that "many of the Latino residents of the past have moved out."

"Last summer we had six free concerts in our garden," Mr. Alexander said. "The biggest hits were mariachi bands."

Although many of Mr. Alexander's tenants are Latinos and his organization has commissioned work by local muralists like Mr. de la Vega, he doesn't see a Latino-centric future for East Harlem. "Gentrification is happening, regardless of what we do," Mr. Alexander said.

So, whose casa will El Barrio wind up being?

The political activist Erica González insists that "unless you actually make a commitment to create a permanent home here, you're looking at being pushed out." But these good intentions, coupled with the untamed forces of real estate, could displace even more people in the end.

Perhaps the sprawling projects, which literally slice and dice the neighborhood, will make it hard to gentrify, and buy time for East Harlem to reshape itself in a way closer to its self-image: a place where conga drums and commerce can coexist. But it's going to take awhile, and the current economic slowdown will only reinforce what everyone in El Barrio knows, that things move a little more slowly in their neighborhood.

Maybe these are just the ramblings of a nostalgia-obsessed migrant of the new Latino diaspora. But when I sit at a table at La Fonda Boricua with a plate of bistec encebollado (onion steak) with fried plantains, I feel as if I have found the center of my universe. And as I make fleeting eye contact with new and old acquaintances, and total strangers who look like cousins, aunts and grandfathers I've never met, I know I'm part of something that will never completely disappear.

El Barrio is where strangers will still say hello to you on the street, where people are trying to hold onto a sense of melody and rhythm that has defined them for half a century. I can hear it echoing on these streets —it's a song that calls me back, like a sailor to his old home port.

It's the song of Harlem, Spanish Harlem.

February 23, 2003

An apartment house of memories. (Chester Higgins/The New York Times)

3

The Old Neighbors

Who Lives Where We Live? Who Sprinted Down
This Hall, Smelled Spring From This Window?
In a City Where the Past Is Ever Present,
Tracing the Footsteps of Those Who Came
Before Is a Haunting Journey.

JIM RASENBERGER

LATELY, I've been getting to know some of the old neighbors in our apartment building. I mean the really old neighbors. There's Mr. Hirschfeld, the Berlin-born maestro who conducted several light operas back in the 90's—that would be the 1890's—and Mrs. Hiller, the wealthy butcher's daughter, and Mr. Washburne, the candy maker whose "Garden Gems" were so popular after the Depression. And those old lovebirds, the Baumans; they celebrated their 63rd wedding anniversary here in the fall of 1934.

My favorite old neighbor is Robert S. Heilferty. A bluff, ancient fellow with a white mustache, Mr. Heilferty was born just a few blocks away, on West 108th Street and the North River, as the Hudson was known in those days. Morningside Heights was farmland, and Broadway was a wide dirt lane.

Before moving into our building at 238 West 106th Street, near Broadway, Mr. Heilferty spent most of his long life in the neighborhood. He left just once, at 16, to fight in the Civil War. One day, in City Point, Va., he found himself face to face with Abraham Lincoln.

"You are pretty young," said the president, putting his hand on Robert's shoulder. "How old are you?"

"Going on 18," Mr. Heilferty replied.

"You're all right, my boy." Lincoln smiled, then gave Mr. Heilferty a slap on the back. "How do you like war?"

"War's all right," he replied. "I just don't like the shooting!"

That dialogue comes from Mr. Heilferty's obituary, published in The New York Times in October 1942. It's one of the remarkable slices of biography I've recently discovered about former tenants of my modest little building.

I never had the opportunity to meet Robert Heilferty—we moved in 50 years too late—but I sometimes stand amid the faded glory of our marble and gilt-trimmed lobby and conjure him up, an old stooped figure shuffling by in uniform, passing the great oak table and stained-glass windows that are no longer there, then resting in the long-gone armchairs by the electric fire that once crackled in the false fireplace.

You don't have to practice parapsychology, or even be especially imaginative, to feel the presence of the dead in New York. For all the development this city has sustained over the last several hundred years, much of New York remains old, by American standards anyway. Half our compatriots live in homes built since 1970, but 90 percent of New Yorkers live in homes built before that year, according to the Census Bureau's New York housing survey. More remarkable, more than 40 percent of us live in homes constructed before 1930, and nearly 18 percent in homes built before 1920.

Wherever we live, others have probably lived before us. They ate their dinners in our dining rooms, slept in our bedrooms, read the newspaper in our living rooms. They gave parties, listened to the radio on winter evenings, worried about the latest stock market crash, or war. They invented strange new candies and tallied their inheritances and celebrated their anniversaries.

Our relationship to these people is complicated. On one hand, we share intimate space with them, trespassing where their most private moments occurred, removed from them by a few thin coats of paint. On the other hand, they are dead strangers.

If we know them at all, it's by the clues they left behind. Like the yellowing life insurance policy that Kevin Casey, our downstairs neighbor, found when he opened the wall safe in his apartment. Or the ticket stub that David Thompson, a neighborhood realtor, told me he uncovered when he renovated his apartment a few years back. The ticket was for a movie theater on the East Side; the price of admission was 10 cents.

"We live here in the traces of others' lives," said Richard Rabinowitz, president of the American History Workshop, based in Brooklyn. "It can be a great kick to imagine the people who preceded us. It's the way great literature works, in that it lets you project yourself into multiple possibilities."

New Yorkers may be especially prone to this sort of projection, not only because we tend to live in homes that cater to historical reveries, but also because many of us come from someplace else.

"People have a tremendous interest in connecting themselves to sites that have human histories that one can almost appropriate," Mr. Rabinowitz said. "Over time, they become part of that history." Mr. Rabinowitz has coined a term to describe the study of how buildings and sites pass through time: "the genealogy of place."

•

I trace my interest in the genealogy of our place to an October night shortly after we moved in. Until this moment, I'd given little thought to our predecessors, except to disparage their taste in bathroom tile and kitchen linoleum. I'd painted the walls and had turned my attention to scraping the dining room radiator, which I'd detached from the steam pipe.

My handiwork notwithstanding, the apartment was remarkably unchanged from its 1909 design. Most of the fixtures were original, including the oak and maple French doors. The previous owners had carried out one structural renovation: they'd cut a small door between the master bedroom and their young son's bedroom. He was afraid of ghosts, they explained, and the door was for midnight rescues. Maybe we should have taken this as a warning.

The October night we received our own ghostly visitation the temperature dropped suddenly and the heat came on. We woke at 3 a.m. to find the apartment filled with a stifling white vapor. The sheets were clammy, the walls dripping with moisture. A strange rushing noise came from the hall. By the time we figured out that the open radiator pipe was spewing steam into the apartment, the damage was done.

Over the next several days, the dampness peeled and bubbled my freshly applied latex off the walls, and then peeled off some additional paint for good measure. The white vapor seemed to carry a message from beyond the grave, something about the vanity of renovation. "Paint all you want," it seemed to say, "but we were here first." Which begged the question: Who was here?

•

Developing a fascination with the history of an apartment building is one thing; satisfying it is another. Buildings tend to leave brief and insipid paper trails, a ledger of code infractions and property assessments. The New Building Dockets, stored in the Municipal Archives, did provide some useful information: the architect of our building—christened Raymore Court—was George F. Pelham, and construction was completed May 19, 1910.

While at the archives, I studied the tax photo of our building taken in the 1930's. I noticed that several cornices had been removed from the roof, an interesting architectural detail but not what I was searching for. I wanted faces in the windows; some sign of human history.

I already knew a little about the human history of our building simply from talking to people who lived here. Estela Boggio, who moved to Raymore Court as a newlywed in 1952, recalled the four sisters, spinsters all, who lived in our apartment at midcentury. Proper and cultured ladies, the Cribben sisters, as everyone knew them, kept a grand piano in the living room, a feat given the room's modest dimensions. When television arrived in the 1950's, the sisters fell in love with Lawrence Welk. They eventually donated the piano to Ascension Church on 107th Street, but the television, and Lawrence Welk, they kept for themselves.

Conor Fitzgerald passed on a piece of building lore he heard from his grandparents, in whose former apartment he now lives: that Babe Ruth once rented in 3-A. Another piece of building lore has it that Jack Dempsey kept a mistress in 4-C. Both accounts are as tantalizing as they are unverifiable. But neither is as remarkable to me as the discovery I was about to make.

It would be nice to attribute my breakthrough to dogged research illuminated by flashes of insight. The truth is, I owe it to advanced technology and good old-fashioned dawdling. I was sitting before a computer in the main reading room of the New York Public Library acquainting myself with ProQuest Historical Newspapers, an electronic subscription service that had recently made available the entire run of The New York Times from 1851, when the paper began publishing, to 1999. Users can search the digitized pages of the paper, all 3.4 million of them, by word or phrase. On a whim, I typed in the address of my building.

Astonished, I began to browse. Many of the hits were classified or display ads. Under the heading "High Class Apartments," a small notice from 1910 announces Raymore Court as "Just Completed," with annual rents of $600 to $1,100. A few years later, another ad promises "an elevator apartment house of the highest class; the very newest in apartment house construction."

More informative were wedding and probate announcements and obituaries, which provided a number of details that accumulate into a portrait of middle-class respectability. In 1924, Mr. and Mrs. Benjamin Cahn saw their son, a doctor, married to Miss Marjorie Alter of 875 West End Avenue. A few years later, Mrs. Linda Hiller's father, who got rich in the butchery business, died and left her $10,000 and land in Saratoga Springs. In November 1934, Mr. and Mrs. George Bauman celebrated their 63rd anniversary with a "family dinner." A year later, Mr. Bauman, 88, died of pneumonia.

If none of these notices are earth-shattering, they do provide glimpses of the people who once lived here. In some cases, they provide a good deal more. The riches-to-rags-to-riches story of James M. Washburne would be inspiring even if it had not played itself out at my address.

In the 1920's, according to his obituary, Mr. Washburne ran a profitable chain of candy stores. Then the Depression struck. The candy stores closed, leaving Mr. Washburne destitute. Determined to start over, Mr. Washburne, now in his 70's, concocted a new kind of candy by mixing honey and "vegetable matter" from spinach, beets, corn, carrots and peas. He called them Garden Gems.

Every morning, too proud to tell his wife, Mr. Washburne traveled down to Times Square to sell his candies from a street corner. He was still doing this in 1937, when a candy tycoon heard of him and decided that Garden Gems were exactly what the American sweet tooth required. He set Mr. Washburne up as president of the James M. Washburne Candy Specialty Corporation, and Mr. Washburne spent his remaining prosperous years in our building on West 106th.

James Washburne, the candy maker, would have known Robert Heilferty, the Civil War veteran. Their tenancies here overlapped. Like Mr. Washburne, Mr. Heilferty was already old when he moved in; phone book records indicate he arrived in 1936.

For most of his career, Robert Heilferty worked as a storekeeper at the Customs House, but the defining moment of his life occurred in 1864, when he was 16 and bluffed his way into the Fourth New York Heavy Artillery. He fought in several of the bloodiest engagements of the Civil War before his vivid meeting with Lincoln.

Heilferty's name, and our address, appeared in the paper over a dozen times in the late 1930's and early 1940's. Patriotic fervor ran high in New York in the early days of World War II, and the nonagenarian veteran was frequently trotted out at flag-waving celebrations. Indeed, with the possible exceptions of Babe Ruth and Jack Dempsey, Robert Heilferty was as close as we've come to a celebrity in the building. On April 4, 1942, after reviewing the Army Day parade, he told reporters how America should defeat the enemy: "It is my belief that we gather all those who are able to shoulder a gun—secure ships enough to send them over in a body—and then rip the life out of them. That's the way we used to do in the Civil War."

Robert Heilferty died in his apartment on Oct. 16, 1942, at the age of 95. Mayor Fiorello H. La Guardia and a thousand others attended his funeral. James Washburne died two months later.

The building nearly disappeared from the newspaper after 1942. It did earn a melancholy mention in 1948, when a resident named Emma Vidder checked into the Narragansett Hotel on Broadway and jumped from an eighth-floor window to her death, nearly landing on a blind woman. There is no suggestion of what drove Mrs. Vidder to jump or why she went to the Narragansett to do it. Perhaps our six stories were not high enough for the deed, or maybe she just wanted to spare her neighbors the trauma.

After 1948, there were no mentions of our building for another 30 years. As it happens, The Times's silence corresponded to a rough patch in the building's history. The neighborhood fell into a steep decline in the 1960's, and Raymore Court suffered with it. The furniture in the lobby was stolen, the stained-glass windows defiled. A derelict landlord virtually abandoned the building after a fire gutted several apartments in 1974. Eventually, the city took possession of the building for nonpayment of taxes.

The Times may have been silent during the building's decline, but it was back to cheer its renaissance. A 1979 article tells how a young teacher named Felix Polanco—he still lives here, a school principal now —organized residents to acquire the building under the city's Tenant Interim Lease Program. They brought the building up to code and bought it from the city.

Today, Raymore Court is a well-kept and genial place. Its residents are a colorful array, both ethnically and professionally. We are teachers and store owners and entrepreneurs. One of us is a street preacher who goes out on the corner of Broadway every evening to shout "Hallelujah" at the top of his lungs. Whenever we pass him in the lobby, he assures us that Jesus loves us. There are worse things a neighbor could say.

As for the really old neighbors, they are mostly forgotten now, even our semi-famous Robert Heilferty. I tried to track down his offspring a few months ago and found a man in Vermont who thinks he is related to the Civil War veteran but isn't sure how.

The truth may be that those of us who live here today know the old neighbors better than anyone. We know the room they woke up in every morning and the way the morning sun moved across the dining room wall and then vanished. We know something about the lapse of taste that allowed them to paint the transom windows. It's not much, but it's enough to remind us that our presence here is just another episode in the long life of this place.

Future residents of our apartment may wonder why the pane of glass in the French doors is missing (a 2-year-old swatted it with a bat) or how that hole got into the bedroom wall (a 4-year-old kicked it with a boot) or what we were thinking when we put that absurd blue linoleum on the kitchen floor (we weren't). Maybe they'll find a ticket stub to "Kangaroo Jack" and marvel at a time when movies cost a mere $10. If they find a MetroCard with $21.50 remaining on it, I'd like that back, please.

March 9, 2003

4

Everyone Knows This Is Somewhere, Part I

An Englishman Finds Himself in the City of His Childhood Dreams, a Strange, Lofty, Urgent Presence, Beckoning Westward.

GLYN MAXWELL

(Lars Leetaru)

SINCE I came to live in New York in September, I've been trying to remember what my future was like. When I was 9 or 10 in my quiet English suburb, I had a little slide show of mental images that represented what was to come. As with any boy of that age, there were glimpses of a racetrack, a winner's rostrum, heroic orations or, later, bright lights and record-album covers; but all these faded in time.

It didn't matter what I ended up good at—there had to be something —what mattered was where I'd be when it happened.

There was one constant backdrop. I didn't appear in this image as a sports hero or film star or writer or any kind of functioning grown-up, but as my child self, seated calmly by a tall window against a vista of countless high buildings brightly lighted at night.

It was a glimpse of loftiness and space and strangeness, distant from the familiar so it couldn't be London, that dreary glow 20 miles south, but it was also an image of welcome, of warmth. The vision was without anxiety. I belonged where I was. I seem to be here now, with my child self right beside me.

There are thousands of reasons to be here now, in New York. Mine are not economic, political, social or even professional. I can write here —silence isn't hard for poets to find—but that's not the reason. Something about this city, some blueprint or template, seems to have existed in my mind for as long as pretty much anything.

If life begins with dreams and ends with memories, perhaps there comes a point in the middle where the two impulses are somehow balanced and neutralized, where the past is a manageable parade, and the future has been fed enough of our daylight to be sated for a while. One is confronted, faced, nailed, by the urgency of the present. These are the moments when we are doing what we dreamed of, or what we know we'll remember always, yet they are moments with no time for looking forward or back.

Coming from the place I do, in the time it takes, with the language I speak, at the middle age I am, New York simply feels like the present: glittering, breathtaking, with its back to the past, its horizons heaped too high to see far. Something very young in me—or do I mean old?—always wanted to spend the present with people from everywhere, at a great meeting place in the center of the world.

But it's beyond childish; it's a deeper layer than that. The only comparison that springs to mind is with an earlier visitor, King Kong, who, in his terrible panic, for a still bewitching second of film, believes the cityscape is the rocky peaks of his island home. It reminds him of simplicity; it reminds him of safety; he sets off for the summit. And of course that sad, flickering denouement was the first glimpse of this metropolis that millions of 20th-century children had on my own little native island. New York City reminds this primate, too, of something far away, something lost and found, some improbable yet necessary next step.

Wonder is a privilege of any new arrival, but perhaps an Englishman's view has special resonance. We are the old country, the reason for flight, the bygone: our journey to America is a journey in time and space and the English language.

We've been the controlling parent, the rejected patriarch, we've been proud and ashamed, the forgotten ancestor—we, not the Scots or Irish, but the English, are perhaps as invisible as foreigners get. And as the land stretches out dizzyingly westward, our own language drifts from us, its quaintnesses all ours now, and New York, the gate through which the European mind passes to contemplate America, is a day away, a constant tomorrow, a handhold on the future. When we English move here and speak to those we miss, they are five hours ahead; we have five more hours to sunset, and they might just be the five hours when we make our mark on the earth.

Drawing maps of imaginary cities was a persistent habit of my childhood. I didn't realize I was sketching the future. Each place had a strongly defined sense of the compass: my inhabitants could never mistake east for west. Each city was within reach of the sea and not so far from the wilderness. There were zones of threat and zones of comfort. There was often a scary wood in the middle, because a scary wood was called for and it needed to be handy.

Streets were straight and logically numbered, so I could remember where I'd put things. Where the streets curved and had curious names was the place to go at night, south, to the labyrinth, where you weren't to be found, to the regions where the plot advanced, where the face was glimpsed or the secret told. By morning you'd be back on the grid, telling your east from west, gazing for miles in sunlight down the endless avenues. And each new city was bigger than the last, packed more densely, built higher, crayoned in more fiercely, as if the wax itself could lift from the page's horizon, be a landscape in a third dimension.

Perhaps what draws me to New York is that, alone among the great cities, it looks created, not over politely differing centuries by emperors or kings or presidents or committees, but somehow all at once on a rainy afternoon. And not so much created as made up, by a child open-mouthed and drooling with concentration, numbering the streets to save time for later, carefully using a ruler for the avenues, marking a big green oblong in the center, dotting it with lollipop trees and calling it Central Park. Calling the middle of town Midtown; the river to the east East River; and the island to the east, the one that disappears off the page, Long Island.

And then, when it all looks too neat and systematic, fetching an eraser, swiping a fat diagonal white path down the island, and starting to color the place in with names that tell stories: Hell's Kitchen, the Battery, the meatpacking district. Names that recall other worlds: Little Italy, Chinatown. Making childish compounds full of secret meaning: SoHo, NoLIta, TriBeCa, Dumbo.

The more I know about New York, the more its form really does seem a blossoming of childlike dreams and fantasies: the Flatiron Building, Coney Island, Brooklyn Bridge, the Chrysler Building, the Great White Way, the Empire State Building, still lit up nightly as a little boy would have it, always in color. All those inanely grinning picnickers poised on iron girders, kids given superpowers for one day only. At Thanksgiving, the town is roped off to make way for gigantic toys, as if it is these that have to be thanked in all dreams. But then nightmares come too, jealous, puerile, sickened by the breadth and dignity of humanity prospering.

When the new map is colored and completed and named, what is left to its maker to do but to lower himself gently into its streets, and people the place with stories? And to walk the blocks of New York is to experience a warm anonymity. I've lived in the kingdom of the smirk and the chuckle, I've passed through the town of the sneer and the village of the snarl—we all have—but I'm at home now, in the city of the shrug. It's not the shrug of not caring, but the shrug of having cared, the shrug of acceptance that so many have come, so many have suffered, so much has happened. The Maker, the real one, would be greeted with a shrug here —He probably is, every day, somewhere near Port Authority—yet, speaking as a child who made up cities and wanted to live in them, I suspect that would be absolutely fine by Him.

April 27, 2003

5

Everyone Knows This Is Somewhere, Part II

He Journeyed From the Frozen Wastes of the Great Plains in Search of New York City Cool. He May Have Found It.

CHUCK KLOSTERMAN

(Lars Leetaru)

THERE is nothing inherently remarkable about how I ended up in New York. Like most people who live here, I just got out of a cab one afternoon and there I was. That's pretty much the whole story. And it all seemed completely normal to me—until I started talking to people and telling them where I was from. Only then did I realize that I am an absolute alien here, akin to the likes of Yao Ming, Tony Blair and/or Chewbacca.

I came to New York from Akron, Ohio (pop. 217,000), which is where I lived after relocating from Fargo, N.D. (pop. 91,000), which is the only metro area within an hour of my hometown of Wyndmere, N.D. (pop. 533), which was five miles from my parents' farm (pop. 9). This (apparently) qualifies me to write about my "personal journey," the assumption being that I must have myriad insights and askew observations about New York.

This is what people assume about you when you come from a place where it's totally acceptable to leave your car running—with the keys in the ignition and the doors unlocked—in the middle of the night.

People in North Dakota do this because it falls to 40 below zero in January and the wind regularly blows in excess of 40 miles an hour, and those climatic conditions cause the fluid in a car battery to freeze into a brick. This makes it impossible to drive home from the bar. Consequently, everyone leaves their automobiles running when they're in public, sometimes for up to five or six hours. People in rural North Dakota don't steal cars, and people in New York find that strange.

In fact, people in New York seem to find everything about rural North Dakota strange, almost to the point of not believing such a place exists. But that's good, because if they did believe North Dakota was a real place, I'm sure they'd tell me it was over.

In the 10 months I've been here, I have learned only one thing: Absolutely everything is no longer relevant. Every rock band, every film, every book, every restaurant, every street, every emotion, every newborn baby, every religion, every species of antelope, every over-the-counter cough medication, every style of affordable trousers and every future moment is completely over. Moreover, I fully realize that pointing out how "everything is over" is also over, so this essay is completely tired and clichéd. It was over before I started.

Like many young American idiots, I moved to New York because I wanted to be cool. New York rewards coolness; in fact, I have met at least 17 people in this city who apparently make a living by being cool full time, a vocation that requires its adherents to (a) never actually work, yet still (b) wear stylish neckties. Unfortunately, I can't seem to make this lifestyle work, and my problem is semantic. In North Dakota, the words "cool" and "trendy" are interchangeable; if you're cool, you're also trendy (and vice versa). This is not the case on the coasts.

In New York and Los Angeles, these two terms are antonyms: "trendy" means doing what everyone else is doing, while "cool" means doing what no one else is doing. People in L.A. put a premium on being trendy, so no one there is cool; meanwhile, New York is more focused on coolness than on trendiness. Granted, there are trendy people here, too, but they're uncool (usually, they're just inexplicably rich).

Now, these people would have been cool if they had done what is now trendy before it was widely recognized as popular, but because they did-n't, they are completely over. Of course, even the cool people are kind of over, because they inevitably congregate with other cool people, and their coolness becomes a localized trend. That's trendy, which is not cool. It's a wicked game.

As far as I can tell, being cool in New York requires you to do something totally and wholly random. These actions include (but are not limited to) walking around your neighborhood with a toucan on your shoulder; wearing an eye patch and a Dekalb Seed cap; drinking hemlock recreationally; and/or smashing a banjo on the L train in the hope of getting spare change.

I'm not necessarily claiming that any of these schemes will work, but you may as well try (it's always 50/50). And being cool is certainly worth the gamble. This is the best place in the universe to be socially desirable, since we all know that New York is supersaturated with beautiful people. (Please note that I am using supersaturated literally: the air around Manhattan actually contains more attractive people than it has the potential to hold under normal atmospheric conditions.) While walking home from work one afternoon, I decided to count how many people I would classify as physically desirable; over 18 blocks, the number was 204, and that included one homeless woman who wore tin foil on her forearms and was talking to an invisible minotaur. New York has got to be the only city on earth with foxy homeless people.

The main thing I've noticed most about New York is that people who live here have no idea how anyone else in America lives, thinks or manages to survive. They seem to assume rural Americans mostly sit in barren 12 x 12 aluminum rooms and stare at mounted elk carcasses.

However, it's worth noting that the rest of the country has the same confusion about New Yorkers, particularly in regard to their level of general rudeness. It has been my experience that strangers in New York are exceedingly friendly, almost to the point of being weirdly insecure.

I've noticed that if you stand at the top of a subway platform and appear even mildly baffled, someone will immediately ask you if you need directions (and they seem almost disappointed if you don't). I suspect this is because just about everyone here is ultimately from somewhere else, and they all adore recalling the bygone days when that disconcerting displacement was still new and electrifying and vaguely dangerous.

New Yorkers love reliving the New York experience. For example, my apartment in Midtown recently had a mouse; what I did not realize is that at one time or another every apartment in New York has been plagued by vermin. So whenever I mentioned this mouse problem at a social function, every other person in the room would insist on telling me his or her own personal mouse story. "The glue traps don't work," they would say, "so I bought a cat to eat the mouse, and then I had to get a dog to take care of the cat problem, and then I had to buy a wolf to eat the dog, and then I had to sue my landlord for not allowing my wolf to install an air-conditioner. It was a nightmare."

That's how all New York anecdotes seem to end: "It was a nightmare."

Clearly, living here is not easy. Everything costs too much; getting anywhere is a hassle; most people are profoundly lazy and nobody is willing to admit to being wrong about anything. I constantly find myself fighting my Midwestern impulse to stop conversations in mid-flow to tell people: "You're lying! And we all know you're lying!"

It's maddening to live here. But it's also amazing to live here. It's impossible to deny that this city is where all the good stuff is, and all that stuff can still be purchased at 3:50 a.m. That only happens here, and I will never live anywhere else. And I always make sure I tell people that whenever they ask, "So what do you think of New York?"—a question I get at least five times a week. I always say I will stay here forever, because I know what that question really means: "I'm going broke and I'm feeling alienated and I'm trying to make it and I'm failing horribly, but I desperately need you to tell me that living here is still worth the effort."

And I always tell them it is, because it's probably true. New York may be terrible, but it's as good as it gets. Besides—the rest of America is so over.

April 27, 2003

John Seravalli Park. (Joyce Dopkeen/The New York Times)

6

Nothing But Net

The Basketball Court Was Just a Patch of Asphalt in a West Village Playground, an Empty Page in the Urban Landscape. It Needed Players to Give It Meaning.

THOMAS BELLER

ONE day last fall, when the weather had cooled and summer seemed to be over, I went down to my local basketball court, on Hudson Street between Horatio and Gansevoort Streets, where I've been going for seven years. The court, which is wedged between the West Village, where I live, and the meatpacking district, is on the loose circuit of courts upon which Players, as it were, like to play. But it looked a little emptier than usual. The players there were mostly those diehards whose compulsion to play basketball is somehow suspicious.

Basketball junkie. There's a phrase you don't hear much anymore. It's a bit morbid, but there is some truth to the formulation.

I played a few games and then, after nearly everyone had gone home, I lingered to shoot around in the strangely early dusk.

The trance of the court, into which I had fallen so happily all summer long, was broken. I saw from the inside how the place must look from beyond the chain-link fence that surrounds it: a wide swatch of asphalt in the middle of the city, with dented hoops, a playground at one end, a softball diamond at the other, the whole thing populated by dog walkers, bench sitters, kids, parents, some derelict types and guys in baggy shorts playing basketball, all in a space officially known as John Seravalli Park.

Just then the person I have come to call the Crazy Lady approached me, with an unusual expression on her face.

"Will you take one of these?" she said, handing me a flier. "It's really important."

The Crazy Lady, whose name, I later learned, is Lana, was not, in fact, crazy. She was just very brave, but the two qualities sometimes blur. I started thinking of her as the Crazy Lady when I arrived at the court one afternoon and found her at the center of a mob of basketball players, defending her kids and their friends against what are normally understood to be the laws of playground.

The issue, as is so often the case, was real estate. There is a point in the afternoon when a critical mass of players have arrived, and the half-court games move over to the full court. Lana's kids were shooting on the full-court basket when they were suddenly overrun by the players, all of them itchy to get their hands on the ball.

Lana has frizzy gray hair, wears sandals and jeans, and smokes cigarettes. Her face often registers a "What in God's name is next?" expression that I associate with city parents. The day of the turf war I arrived to find her standing in the middle of the full court, a cigarette in one hand, a cellphone in the other and, like Gandhi, refusing to move. Words were exchanged. Voices were raised. Finally, a half-court basket was secured for the kids and, like refugees given a new homeland, they were ushered to their basket before Lana yielded the full court to the mob.

This autumn day, however, she approached me with a stack of fliers in her arm and an odd look on her face. According to the flier, the Parks Department was considering a proposal to tear up the playground, resurface it with artificial turf and turn it into a private softball field. The nearby Xavier High School would help pay for the renovation. The gates would be padlocked, the ground green, and there would be soccer practice by day and Little League games by night. Who could argue with that?

Quite a few people, apparently. But the tenor of the flier, and the fact that a community board meeting had been arranged to discuss the proposal, suggested that, unknown to us, wheels had been turning for some time. All summer we had been involved in the drama of our playground while, just like a horror movie, a huge monster was almost upon us.

•

Now it's spring. On the first nice day I went down to the court. There was a game in progress at each of the three half-courts, and a crowd of people waiting to play.

Arriving at a basketball court is a seemingly casual thing, but who actually gets to play is determined by a number of Byzantine rituals involv-

ing such things as how well known you are to the regulars, how well respected your game is, how you look, what color you are (and there is a
very wide range of colors), how you dress, walk, talk.

These rules are not written down. They are implicit. They incorporate
the rules that pertain to the world outside the playground—the rules en-
forced by the police, for example—but there are variations, additions
and deletions, and no one on hand with a clipboard and a whistle to en-
force them.

This is not gym. One of the more important rules is that, in certain
circumstances, there are no rules.

That first day, everyone was in an unusually friendly mood. I slapped
people five. Vague communications were made, along the lines of "How
you been?," answered by various words and noises that equated with
"Good."

I saw a guy I recognized go by on a bike, a fiercely quick, whippet-
thin kid the color of Turkish coffee whom I have privately nicknamed
the Assassin, in part because he is so lethal on offense and in part because he usually wears the expression of someone who is prepared to kill
you. Most basketball players exist in a state of mild irritation, like magi-
cians who cannot get a certain trick to go just right. Street ball elevates
this irritation to a style, and a lot of people on the court sport a home-
boy version of the Travis Bickle line "You talkin' to me?" as though they
are just waiting for someone to tick them off.

"You been playin' ball this winter?" someone asked the guy on the
bike.

"Yeah," he replied. "In a way."

The reply was so conversational that I had a hard time equating it
with the nasty style he had on the court, where he often wore a white
doo-rag that made him look like a member of the hip-hop division of the
Foreign Legion. This day, on his bike, he seemed like a sweet guy only a
few years past teenagerdom.

Glancing around the playground, I realized I knew a lot of the guys
there. I know if they are good in the clutch or if they choke. I know how
they smile when they mean it, and how they smile when they are faking
it, and how they look when they are trying desperately not to smile because they just made a great move but don't want to make it look like a
big deal. I know what it takes to stop them and what they'll do to stop
me. What I don't know is their names, other than a first name or nickname. I don't know how old they are or how they make a living.

I came to appreciate the strangeness of this dynamic a long time ago, in the events surrounding a guy named Rich. He was a longtime regular at the court I grew up playing on, in Riverside Park at 77th Street. Rich used to arrive in a shroud of silence, carrying a big shoulder bag. He was very fat. Upon arriving, he would stake out a considerable amount of asphalt (a shade of gray as distinctively New York as a yellow taxi) and elaborately change into a pair of immaculate white tube socks. Then came his game sneakers.

Once he got changed, he always made sure he was a captain so he could pick his team. He did this as judiciously as any N.B.A. general manager. The thing about these street games is that if you win, you play again. If you lose, you watch. Considering the time and effort involved in getting to the playground in the first place, there was a lot at stake in winning. Rich wanted to win. Therefore he always refused to put me on his team.

Rich was a trash talker. He wore a plastic mouth guard, like a football player, but spent half the game with it sticking halfway out of his mouth as he did his running commentary. The commentary was usually about the ineffectiveness of the man guarding him. He would use his bulk to bounce you out of the way and get room for his shot. After it went in, he would remove his mouthpiece and tell you how useless you were.

It takes no effort for me to recall how Rich's body felt when I banged into him in a game. The sound of his voice, the way he ran, the speed with which he shifted from being caustic to being, if the word can be applied to basketball, sweet: all that comes to mind easily. He's a perfect example of how, on the basketball court, you can know someone intimately and not know him at all.

One day I went to the court and Rich wasn't there. I didn't notice his absence until I heard some guys talking about him. "When they showed his picture on the late news, I didn't recognize him," one said. "Then I switched to Channel 11 and saw their picture."

It took me a few seconds to realize I had seen Rich that day, too. I'd stopped at a newsstand to stare at the picture of a dead body lying in a pool of blood that was on the cover of both The Daily News and The New York Post. In spite of the smudgy image, there had been something disturbingly intimate about the picture. Now I knew why.

Rich, it turns out, was a token booth clerk at the West 145th Street subway station. He earned $30,000 a year. He worked a 6 a.m.-to-2 p.m.

shift, which meant that all those years I had seen him shortly after he got off work.

Meanwhile, nothing changed at the court. The culture of street ball in New York is like the city's population. Some people are fixtures as permanent as a tree. Others show up out of the blue and then, after a week or a month or a couple of years, disappear without explanation, though usually for reasons less tragic than those that explain the disappearance of Rich.

•

My game got under way. I had on my team Monsieur M, a skinny man who had arrived not long ago from Haiti and speaks hip-hop with a French accent. He can jump to the moon, but he has not yet learned not to smile. He doesn't use his smile as a weapon of contempt.

Then there was the Laughing Man. Only a month earlier, he had suffered a dislocated thumb. "I broke my thumb!" he called out, and, in a continuation of the play, ran right out of the playground toward St. Vincent's Hospital. A month later he was back, with white tape around his injured finger, in his irrepressibly good mood.

The Laughing Man has one of those iron-hard upper bodies (he usually plays without a shirt), and he can jump quickly; he's like a socially well-adjusted Dennis Rodman, with a touch of Karl Malone. The Laughing Man is also a father. A little girl who was standing near him one day as he changed into his sneakers and socks announced loudly, "Daddy, those socks stinky!"

Our third member is a young man named D. He has the baggiest shorts on the court and, when he can bring himself to shoot it, a nice jump shot. But in games, with the pressure on, D tends to, shall we say, withdraw. The painful disparity between the basketball opera in his head and the game on the court makes him sullen. He's probably the only guy about whom one could say, "He doesn't shoot enough."

The fourth member of my team is me. At 6 foot 5 1/2, a high school and Division III college career behind me (Vassar!), I am, in my own way, a basketball poster boy. In every basketball poster there are two essential components: the first is someone flying through the air in the middle of some amazing, gravity-defying move, usually a dunk. The second is the person, often partially obscured, being dunked on. I fulfill the latter role.

We won our first game. Monsieur M was the star of the show, skying for rebounds and hitting his jump shot. The team we beat comprised guys about whom I could give thumbnail sketches, quick scouting reports and some essential details about personality, and whose names I hardly knew.

The next team was a tough athletic squad that comprised longtime locals, among them the Litigator. His real name was Dennis, but he was the Litigator to me because he was always manipulating the score and arguing calls. Once, when I referred to him as the Litigator out loud, a guy on the sidelines said: "What are you talking about? He works in a bodega."

My team had no litigator. None of us could argue, least of all me. On the court, I am mute. What words I do say hardly count as language; a transcript would sound vaguely pornographic: "Yes, yes! That's right! Give it to me! Here! Come on!"

We played hard in our second game. Monsieur M! I loved him! His jump shot looked like a shot put; he'd take two massive dribbles, lift off with both feet and throw toward the rim, but the shot was falling. The Laughing Man rolled to the hoop, bruising everyone around him, I had my rebounds and short jumpers. Then Monsieur M unleashed a series of his funny jump shots, and we won. I wandered off, exultant. Then, for the first time since last fall, I saw Lana.

●

Over the autumn and winter, the outlook for the court had gone from bleak to cautiously sunny.

A meeting had been called by Community Board 2 to discuss the fate of the court. The day of the meeting was a spectacular Indian summer day, and the court was mobbed. Each of the half-court baskets had two teams waiting to play, the full court was packed, and no one was paying attention to the fliers about the meeting that had been taped here and there around the park.

But as 6 o'clock approached there was a giant mood swing. Some of the regulars said they were going, and at the last moment a large contingent of sweaty guys in shorts headed for a cramped room in an N.Y.U. building, where the meeting took place.

"It was immediately apparent that this was an incredible turnout for a Community Board 2 parks and recreation committee hearing, possibly the best-attended hearing the committee had ever seen," a friend e-mailed afterward. The plan to privatize the court and resurface it was abandoned in the face of community opposition.

As Lana and I chatted, I noticed the new hotel, the W Hotel, that was rapidly rising on a former parking lot across the street from the court. Some of the rooms will have a view of the meatpacking district, others of the West Village and still others of Chelsea. Some guests will look out and see, right across the street, a big stretch of not very pretty asphalt on which people are jumping around in baggy shorts, playing basketball. If they see that, they'll know they're in New York.

It was a rosy dusk. The court cleared. I practiced some dunks. I bounced the ball in a trance, vowing to get skinny, to be strong, to move around the city and play at other courts, so that the whole fluctuating but familiar family of basketball junkies who go to Horatio Street doesn't get too familiar. I promised myself not to disappear too far down the rabbit hole of street basketball, walked in circles bouncing the ball and took foul shots in the soft and almost gauzy darkening heat. I was wretched, sticky, dirty, thirsty, thrilled. Finally, I went home.

May 18, 2003

The Great Lawn. (Ruby Washington/The New York Times)

7

New York's Rumpus Room

For Nearly 150 Years, Central Park Has Been the City's Endlessly Changing, All-Frills Heart. It's Hard to Imagine New York Without It.

WITOLD RYBCZYNSKI

I CAN'T imagine Manhattan without Central Park. Without the park, meadows and lakes would be miles away, instead of just behind the Metropolitan Museum. Without the park, taxis couldn't take those east-west shortcuts that are like sudden short drives into the country. Columbus Circle would be simply a circle, like Piccadilly Circus, instead of an arc opening onto a generous green wood. I would never see the top of the Dakota sticking up out of the trees like a spooky Transylvanian castle.

Without the intervening park, the Upper East Side would blend into the Upper West Side—unthinkable. Without its enchanted setting, Tavern on the Green would be just another tourist eatery, and the site of the Bethesda Fountain would be simply an ordinary street corner. New York City without Central Park would be like Chicago without the lake, San Francisco without hills or Los Angeles without sunshine.

I've always liked Napoleon's description of the Piazza San Marco in Venice as "the finest drawing room in Europe," a somewhat ingratiating remark since he had just conquered the city. A decorous Parisian park could be described as a sort of salon, with nothing more strenuous going on than a game of pétanque; a London park is more like a comfortable living room, with people dozing in scattered deck chairs. Central Park is like neither; it's too informal to be a drawing room, and too sweaty and boisterous to be a living room. On any given day, you can see dog walkers and bird watchers, bicyclists and joggers, horseback riders and folk dancers, soccer and baseball teams, and yes, pétanque players. Central Park is the city's outdoor rumpus room.

Most urban parks reflect the style of their cities. Parisian parks and gardens exhibit a Gallic sense of good order and neat urbanity; London parks are casual and elegant, like London buildings and streets. Central Park, which officially got its start 150 years ago yesterday, when the proposal to create the park went to the New York State Senate, is different. The uniform Manhattan grid was laid out for the convenience of real-estate subdivision and traffic flow, just building lots and streets. No frills. Pragmatic, standardized, commercial, artless—and largely treeless —the grid represents an urbanism that only a surveyor could love.

The creators of Central Park turned their backs on this mercantile diagram. They made the park all loopy curves; even the streets crossing the park lose their straightness. Despite its matter-of-fact name, Central Park is romantic, nonstandardized, uncommercial, artful—and full of trees. It is all frills.

It was Edmund Burke who first coined the famous description of parks as "the lungs of the city," but Central Park is also New York's heart. Without Central Park, New York would risk becoming as callow and mercenary as many of its critics maintain it is. The park is part of New York's better nature.

Whenever I walk down Fifth Avenue next to the park, and I am not in a hurry, I get drawn in. I can't resist. Maybe it's all those shady trees, or the glimpse of sparkling water, or the sinuously curved path that disappears behind a clump of bushes. Before I know it, I am in another world.

It's easy to forget what a distinctly odd world it is. Generally, urban parks are conceived as large public gardens with gravel paths, flower beds and manicured lawns. Central Park is a swath of Adirondack landscape—woodland, rocky outcroppings, lakes and all.

City and park meet at a simple, rugged stone wall. On one side of the wall, a sidewalk, women in frocks, traffic, and the bustle of the city; on the other, a dark, silent primeval forest. Jay Gatsby meets Natty Bumppo. The abruptness of the change—from man-made to natural, from natural to man-made—is so absolute, it almost takes my breath away. Even though I know that the park is as much an artifact as the surrounding city, like any work of art, it's what it makes you feel that's important.

Above all, Central Park is horizontal, in the most vertical city in the world. The contrast is underlined by the looming cliff of skyscrapers that encloses the park like an architectural frame. The experience of any urban park is always the experience of temporary escape, but in

Central Park the distant view of tall buildings is a constant reminder of the city.

Paradoxically, this heightens the experience of retreat and lends a particular zest to everyday, ordinary occurrences. That's why so many memorable movie scenes have been filmed in the park: romantic carriage rides, park-bench conversations, harrowing chases, echoing steps in a shadowy underpass. There is always that delicious and slightly unsettling sense of dislocation, of being in the city—and not. A walk in Central Park always makes me feel that I'm playing hooky.

•

The bill that authorized the construction of the park followed three years of cantankerous public debate. It was not a straightforward decision—this was New York City, after all—since there were two competing sites. The affair was settled in the courts, and the "central" site prevailed.

The southern section of Central Park opened to the public in the winter of 1859, about two years after the competition for the design of the park was held. Can one imagine such speed today? Surely not. New Yorkers immediately took to skating on the frozen lake. In the summers they went boating in rented skiffs, and later cruised silently in electric launches, or lounged in one of several Venetian gondolas, listening to the singing boatmen.

The park had an elaborate system of bridle paths and carriage drives, an elm-lined mall for promenading, a ball ground for games, and a parade ground (today, the Sheep Meadow) for military exercises. There were rustic arbors and the Belvedere viewing platform, but the only building was a genteel watering hole, the Ladies' Refreshment Salon. In all, Central Park was a mannerly place, mirroring the high-minded ideals of William Cullen Bryant, an early advocate, who hoped that a park in New York would promote "good morals and good order."

Frederick Law Olmsted and Calvert Vaux are often praised for the farsighted vision of their design, but one thing that they did not anticipate was how popular Central Park would become. By 1865, before the park was complete, there were already more than seven million visits a year, at a time when the city's population was about half a million (today there are more than 20 million visits annually).

From its opening, and ever since, Central Park played catch-up, trying to adapt itself to the various demands of its voracious clientele. Vaux added a boathouse at the head of the lake, a dairy that served milk to children, and a spa pavilion that served mineral water to adults. The 1880's saw a welter of new outdoor activities in the park: roller-skating, bicycling, baseball. There was a craze for tennis, and more than a hundred grass courts were set up in the South Meadow.

Olmsted introduced free concerts to the park as early as 1859, and these proved so popular that an ornate bandstand was built beside the Mall. Nineteenth-century concerts were decorous affairs; people were not allowed to sit on the grass. For many years, parks commissioners, notably Robert Moses, who ruled from 1934 until 1960, had a strict notion of which recreational activities were appropriate, and that did not include large public gatherings.

Paradoxically, it was Moses who was responsible for creating the 90-acre Great Lawn on the site of the filled-in Lower Reservoir. The flat open area turned out to be the perfect place for outdoor concerts. In the summer of 1966, 75,000 people gathered on the Great Lawn to hear the New York Philharmonic, led by Leonard Bernstein, and the following year 135,000 people listened to Barbra Streisand.

It took sanitation workers three days to clean up the trash, raising the question, not for the last time, of whether the park should be open to mammoth crowds. Nevertheless, more concerts followed, culminating in the reunion of Simon and Garfunkel, who played to nearly half a million people in 1981.

Musical concerts have a long tradition in Central Park, so it is easy to forget that the park has also served as a place for mass demonstrations. This is a relatively recent development, for during the 19th century, political meetings were not allowed in the park.

That changed on Suffrage Day in 1914, when a group of suffragists marched down the Central Park Mall. "The crowd was as large as that drawn by a municipal band concert," marveled The New York Times. In the early 1930's, during the Depression, a group of unemployed homeless men built a so-called Hooverville on the site of the planned Great Lawn to protest federal policies; the 200 temporary shacks remained in place for two years.

What is still the largest recorded public gathering in Central Park's history took place in the Sheep Meadow on Oct. 27—Navy Day—in 1945, when an estimated one million people listened to President Harry S. Truman give a foreign policy address. Photographs show an attentive crowd, seated on orderly rows of wooden folding chairs.

The 1960's included a variety of distinctly disorderly public events—love-ins, be-ins, kite-ins. The park continued to be a magnet for political causes: rallies for and against the Vietnam War, protests against nuclear weapons and apartheid, celebrations of Gay Pride and Earth Day. Such events would have surprised Olmsted and Vaux, who imagined the park as a contemplative retreat, not a public forum. But each generation of New Yorkers has redefined the meaning of Central Park to suit itself: a place to promenade, a place to listen to Sousa, a place to demonstrate, a place to Rollerblade. Whatever.

Central Park was conceived with a very specific function, but it has not been static. It is a historical place, but it is also a place with a history, a changing history. It took long time before the park was open at night, for example. A hundred years ago letting automobiles use the carriage drives must have seemed like a good idea; today it feels, and sounds, like an imposition.

One day, no doubt, we will further restrict the use of cars, and not only on weekends. (One group, Car-Free Central Park, advocates barring cars permanently from East and West Drives.) But that does not mean that there is a "correct" way to use the park. Uses come and go, users jostle each other, sometimes the odd elbow is thrown. Central Park is often described as a democratic space, but it is really a democratic arena, where there is no fixed consensus, just a constant conversation whose tenor rises and falls with the times.

•

Olmsted had foreseen that the time would come when Manhattan Island would be covered by "rows of monotonous straight streets, and piles of erect, angular buildings" and there would be "no suggestion left of its present varied surface, with the single exception of the Park." But I'm not sure if even he could imagine just how precious its 843 acres would be to a city grown unimaginably large and dense.

Mayor Bloomberg, in a rare burst of eloquence, once described the park as "our picnic spot, our playground, our nature preserve, our band shell, our field of dreams." Not only dreams, memories. There's something about parks that makes people want to fill them with commemorative statues. It must be the tranquil surroundings—I always think that if he were able, William Tecumseh Sherman would leap his horse over the yellow cabs that circle Grand Army Plaza, and find himself a quiet spot overlooking the Pond.

He would have plenty of company. There are now more than 50 fountains, monuments and sculptures in the park, though there is no memorial to Calvert Vaux, who deserves one, and Olmsted, who disliked flowers, is honored by, of all things, a flower bed.

The monuments are a decidedly odd mix. The men on plinths reflect the city's various ethnic groups (Simon Bolívar, Columbus, the Polish king Jagiello), celebrate famous artists (Beethoven), notable New Yorkers (Alexander Hamilton), largely forgotten New Yorkers (the newspaperman Arthur Brisbane) and adopted New Yorkers (John Lennon). There are hallowed authors like Shakespeare and Sir Walter Scott, and literary characters like Mother Goose. My favorite statue is Balto, the heroic Alaska sled dog, whose bronze surface is rubbed bright by the stroking of innumerable tiny hands.

New York is a city relentlessly driven by change, with one eye always cocked on the future, the latest fashion, the next new thing. Yet Central Park looks obstinately backward. It is a repository of the past; other peoples' pasts (Cleopatra's Needle) as well as our own. Perhaps that's why the park, picnic spot and playground that it is, is also, at times, a sort of shrine. It is where New Yorkers go to remember, to commemorate and to grieve. When George Harrison died, bouquets piled up in Strawberry Fields, which also serves as the site of an annual memorial for John Lennon.

The day after the attacks of Sept. 11, the Great Lawn was one of the important places people gathered spontaneously, simply to feel the warmth of each other's companionship on that mournful day. On the first anniversary of the attacks, the park was a major place where flickering candles marked an evening vigil.

No one is buried in Central Park, but those little brass plaques on the park benches that memorialize loved ones—privately famous people, as opposed to the public variety—have always seemed to me as moving as gravestones. Here they once sat, the plaques testify, doing not much of anything, taking a break, listening to the birds, reading a book, eating a sandwich, watching the children play, hearing the hum of traffic far away, daydreaming, convivially alone. In the park.

June 22, 2003

8

Manhattan '03

The Attacks of September 11 Prompted People Around the World to Articulate How Much New York Means to Them.

JAN MORRIS

(Rodica Prato)

55

FIFTY years ago I arrived in Manhattan, for my very first visit, on board the Cunard liner Mauretania—not the elegant four-funneled Mauretania of maritime legend, but its successor, built in 1939 with twin smokestacks that were set, for my tastes, too close together.

Never mind, it got me there, on a sunny day in 1953, and I have come back every year since—sometimes several times in a year. I have loved the place always, but with a love that has varied in intensity.

I have experienced the city in curiously varied circumstances, too, for halfway through my acquaintance with Manhattan, in the 1970's, I did the then unthinkable and changed my sex, so that I can claim to have observed the island's own half-century with both a male and a female eye. Not many people, I suppose, can boast of such a relationship; but Manhattan being Manhattan, it has never even been noticed.

If I never surprised the city, though, the city certainly surprised me, and for years astonishment was a leitmotif of my Manhattan experience. Throughout my early visits, direct from a shabby postwar Europe, I seem to have been in a condition of constant wonder—I would say stupefaction, were it not wonder of a marvelously vibrant kind. The color of the cars, and the size of them! The babel of languages, the bluntness, the old-school courtesy, the crime, the opulence, the martinis! The pride, fun and self-satisfaction of it all, and the grape jelly for breakfast—ugh, the grape jelly.

I wrote my very first essay about any city during my original stay in Manhattan, and it still revives for me those exhilarating sensations. Who did not feel like Ginger Rogers or Fred Astaire, I thought then, on a brilliant, windy day on Fifth Avenue?

Was there anywhere else on earth where the poorest of the poor, the loneliest immigrants, would so earnestly declare their faith in the grand dream that was their city?

Several mantras from those early years sound in my ears to this day. One was, "Are my seams straight?" Another was, "Say, do those lords push you around much over there?" I can still hear the old waiter assuring me that there was nothing, nothing that the Waldorf-Astoria couldn't offer me for my dinner. I can still recite the ambiguous advice on the railroad ticket: "Let us know if you can't keep this reservation, it may be required by a friend or a business acquaintance of yours"—a perfect encapsulation, it seemed, of midcentury Manhattan capitalism.

But I still hear, too, like a voice from another age altogether, the reply of an elderly gentleman standing one evening at the head of a long Park Avenue taxi line. I was in Manhattan on a lecture engagement with Edmund Hillary, who was flushed with fame after his first ascent of Mount Everest that summer. Being young and excited, and perhaps having had difficulty in tying our black ties, we were horribly late for some celebratory banquet, and I asked the old gentleman with my best British diffidence—frightfully sorry, awful cheek, do forgive me, etc.—if he could possibly allow us to jump the queue and take the next cab.

"Sir," declared that courtly Manhattanite, that survivor of still older times and manners, "Sir, for Hillary of Everest it will be at once a pleasure and a privilege."

That first Manhattan essay of mine was largely about walking. I soon discovered that this was the walkingest city on earth, with its convenient grid pattern and its relaxed attitude toward jaywalkers. I walked nearly everywhere, and have done so ever since, frequently applying to Manhattan my own Smile Test. This consists of grimacing ingratiatingly at everyone I pass in the street, and recording how they react: more than anywhere else on earth, my research shows, this city's responses depend upon the weather.

Manhattan does not resent familiarity in strangers—on the contrary, it rather expects us to know which is north, which south, and how best to exploit the subway system. Everyone here was a foreigner once, after all, if only a few generations ago, and almost every time I come, a new ethnicity seems have taken over the cabs, the fruit stalls and the newsstands. One year you are misunderstood in Korean, the next in some variety of Afghan.

•

I suppose nobody is familiar with the whole of Manhattan, but over the years I have come to know discrete bits of it well. For a time my life's love and I, being indigent, innocent and happy, frequented a modest restaurant called the Original Joe's. It was on Third Avenue, somewhere in the 30's, I would guess, and I recall it always as part of the world of the Elevated Railroad. The street outside was dark with the shadow of the tracks above, or dappled with evening sunlight shining through, and, in my mind's eye, I still see the elaborate wooden staircases, galleries and waiting rooms, stove-heated, fret-boarded and jumbled like something in India, through which we clambered to our train when we had finished with the pasta.

Then, at a time of crisis in my life, I was invited to take refuge in a friend's house in the lovely enclave of Turtle Bay. I had my own suite at the top of the house, and from there I could look upon the gardens below, frequented by littérateurs and actresses, with parties happening sometimes where famous faces gossiped, and my host was to be seen merrily accepting his fourth martini of the evening.

For a time I had my own apartment on the edge of the Village, and spent lots of my time drinking in small bars, and lots watching the chess players in Washington Square, and praying for closing time when kind friends took me to hear eminent jazz musicians in clubs. I rented a Midtown apartment once, from a dubious importer of Italian marble, and one on the Upper East Side, from a Russian violinist, and for a couple of months I lived at the Mayflower Hotel on Central Park West, which endeared itself to me by cheerfully accommodating animal guests.

I was digging myself into Manhattan, you see, getting to know it. By the 1970's, on the day before a night flight home to Wales, I felt myself sufficiently at home to saunter into the offices of this very newspaper, to which I had contributed from time to time, and ask if they could fix me up with a sleeping pill, to ease the coming long hours of travel. "One enough?" was all they said. But I suspect it may have been a placebo, anyway.

A glory of the Mayflower Hotel is its position directly overlooking Central Park, and as a walker I regularly made circuits of what New Yorkers consider a botanical masterpiece. I disliked the park from the start, and still do. Nothing seems natural about it to me. Its foliage is gloomy, its fauna largely verminous, its plan pompous, and my heart used to go out to the distracted polar bear pacing round and round his miserable quarters in the zoo. I often wrote about the place, never very festively, and I was once filmed by a Welsh television crew jogging despondently around it before breakfast.

One day in 1968, at home in Wales, I was invited by Austin Tobin, then director of the Port Authority, to come over and write a book about the port. Of course I accepted, and immediately stuck a big aerial photograph of New York Harbor on my study wall. "See that port?" I used to say to visitors. "That port's mine."

The impertinence of it! But it was true that my initial astonishment at the presence of Manhattan, my growing familiarity with the island, was maturing into a sense of possessiveness. I liked to tell people I had one foot in Manhattan and the other in Llanystumdwy. ("Llanystumdwy, unreal," said Americans, who didn't believe there could be such a place. "Manhattan, where's that?" asked the Welsh, but they were only joking.)

Working for the Port Authority, if only as a sort of court poet, did give me a temporary place in the civic structure, and as I pottered around its wide demesne, in helicopters and small boats, on foot or in the big black limousines that the Authority preferred, I certainly acquired an intimate grasp of the seaport and its meaning. How lyrically mysterious those foggy dawns beyond the Narrows, when the Sandy Hook pilot took me out to meet an incoming vessel. I added to my Manhattan mantras a macabre phrase from a harbor policemen, discussing the watery suicides on his patch: "Floaters is everywhere."

•

By the 1980's, something had changed for me. It was not just that I was getting old. The city had aged, too. Who would have thought it? Manhattan, that universal symbol of youth, energy, bubble and chutzpah, actually getting old. But so it was, and it began to remind me of a Colombian poet's remark that he loved his native city much as he loved a favorite pair of old footwear. Yes, a well-worn, comfortable pair of leather boots was what Manhattan suggested to me now.

It rarely astonished me any longer. Many a foreign city seemed more modern, and even more flashy. Many could claim to be The City That Never Sleeps. My sense of possession was becoming a sense of almost aunty affection. I was taken to one of the city's famous old clubs one evening, and was persuaded to try its celebrated in-house cocktail, which was served in a silver tankard. "When I was a little boy," said my host, "I used to be brought here by my father, and he always let me have one."

How touchingly Old New York, I thought: the indulgent Daddy, the boy in his best suit, the avuncular servants, the happy sense of continuity and complicity—for the boy's mother, I'm sure, would never have approved. Unwisely accepting a second tankard, I staggered out into the street feeling decidedly mawkish about the city (and realizing that, as usual, Mother had been right).

I made a television film in Manhattan one winter, and the scarf-wrapped, woolly-hatted, gloved and earmuffed island seemed then more old-fashioned than ever—the Smile Test had long before assured me that New Yorkers are nicest in the snow. Policemen were almost stagily considerate. Youths helped old ladies across intersections murmuring: "It's a pleasure, ma'am. Mind how you go." We filmed in a bus one day, and only two passengers rejected the general bonhomie and refused to talk to the camera—an old lady who was too busy reading the poems of Terence in Latin, and a chalk-faced youth in shades.

Of course there was always friendship—another constant of my Manhattan years. A citizen once told me that American friendship was misleading to Britons. On the surface, he said, your average American was friendlier than the Briton; one layer down, the Briton was more sincere than the American; but to the American sensibility there was an extra, more profound layer of friendship, summoned from the inherited challenges and sacrifices that were the national experience.

I have found this to be perfectly true of Manhattan. Friends I made at the start of my five Manhattan decades, not invariably at first sight, have remained my friends to this day.

And now, after 50 years of it, how do I feel about dear old Manhattan? My astonishment has blended into familiarity, my familiarity into possessiveness, my possessiveness into nostalgia, my nostalgia into— what? People in Europe always ask me if Sept. 11, 2001, changed the character of Manhattan, but I did not find that to be so. When I first wandered around the wreck of the trade center, I feared that that the civic personality had been irreparably damaged; but within the year, it seemed to me, Manhattan's native optimism had reasserted itself, and its psyche was more or less back to normal.

Today, in 2003, I am not quite so sure. History has caught up with Gotham at last, and more insidiously than any terrorism the first intimations of hubris, it seems to me, are worrying away at my conceptual Manhattan.

I used to think of New York as a sort of international city-state, the whole world's destination, nobly detached from the rest of the U.S.A. Now it is no more cosmopolitan than many another metropolis around the world, and feels to me more and more representative of its own country. And as the great republic itself, for the moment at least, alienates itself in its omnipotence from so much of the rest of humanity, so Manhattan loses its universal empathy.

Hubris, the sad identifying abstraction of 21st-century America, is creeping into Manhattan too, if only by osmosis, and means that my last response to the place must be one of compassion. But how marvelous it has been to have watched its progress, enjoyed its friendships, wandered its streets, sailed its waterways, during half a century of its glory—the city incomparable, the city sans pareil! Nor has the magic deserted it yet.

The last time I was in Manhattan was late last winter. A minor blizzard blew in the dusk, and the people in the streets were performing particularly well in the Smile Test. I looked up through the driving snow to see the Midtown skyscrapers half-veiled in cloud, but with plumes of white steam rising like heraldic defiances into the murk; and as I sloshed on through the puddles I laughed with joy to see them there, and grinned unnervingly at everyone I passed, and felt an old tug at my heart.

For if one can't be sentimental about Manhattan, in its pride as in its pathos, what can one be soppy about?

September 7, 2003

(Rodica Prato)

9

Back to the Home Planet

My East Side, No-Name Nabe.

ROBERT LIPSYTE

MY old dry cleaner, Kevin Hwang, may have recognized the signature ink stains on my favorite shirt before he recognized me. I think his head was still down when he said, "You been on vacation?" He hadn't seen me for two years.

"I have been living on other planets," I said. "Murray Hill and Cooper Square."

Mr. Hwang smiled knowingly, and we never spoke of it again.

That was early last year and I am still refitting myself into my old neighborhood, those bracingly diverse, nay, disconnected, blocks between Gramercy Park and Union Square that have no name.

I once thought Grapus would work for a place that could embrace outer-borough high school kids by day, punk rock fans by night, welfarians, student cops, extreme delivery bikers and the members of the National Arts Club, along with a bedpan alley of hospitals, the remains of cybercool, yupster high-rises, New York University dorms, landmark brownstones and all their requisite chocolate martini watering holes. But I'm the only one who ever liked Grapus, and I'm no longer so sure about the tag. The place has changed since I've been away. So have I.

The conceit that big cities are "soft," that they shape themselves around the needs of their citizens, assumes that a big city has a central plot line, which is silly. Big cities are not novels, they are anthologies. The trick is finding the neighborhood short story in which you can be a character.

Fifteen years ago, life wrote me into a small co-op on East 16th Street, near Irving Place. The surrounding streets were restless, littered, kaleidoscopic. I had never so quickly felt so much of a place. I became the cranky character in the story who counseled and policed; I screamed at careless drivers, chased bike riders off the sidewalk, lectured careless moms and nannies, and was hardest on people who thought it amusing when their dogs growled, pooped or licked my shoes.

For six years in these pages, I described that cranky character and his everyday pals, the supers, Cindy and Sal, Greg at Mailboxes Etc., Hans upstairs, Joe the U.P.S. man. There was the dogged preservationist, Jack Taylor, who found a home for Dvorak's statue in a nearby park, and my secret sharer, Carol Roberto.

I first spied her one morning slipping among parked cars, plucking out advertising fliers from under windshields before an autumn wind could blow them onto our street. I asked her what she was doing, and her answer was typically cosmic and down-to-earth. Litter, she said, was symbolic of urban breakdown, which she wanted to forestall; but she also wanted to avoid getting a summons from the Sanitation Department. And then, pointing at the potato chip bags already in the gutter, she said she was concerned about the health of the litterers. Junk food is not good for you.

It was Carol's support that made me brave when squirrels pillaged my garden. I had called the city for advice. A succession of scraping voices warned me not to get aggressive; the city protected its squirrels as passionately as it protected its pigeons. Even shouting at squirrels could be construed as a bias crime. I whined to Carol, who never told me what to do but made it clear she expected me to do something.

I bought leather gloves and a Havahart trap, which I baited with peanut butter and chocolate. I nailed those nasty nutkins like Natty Bumppo bagging deer. I released them at night in other nabes, howling, I am Urban Trapper! Not even being elected president of my co-op board gave me a greater sense of agency. I was more than just a sidewalk monitor now or an ink-stained scribe. I was a beast master.

Such hubris must be punished. After 12 years, life wrote me out of Grapus. I first spent a year subletting a corporate condo on East 38th Street, near Park Avenue, one of the most convenient nabes I've ever lived in, and the most sterile. It had location, transportation, restaurants, an easy walk to work. But there was little sense of daily life. In the daytime, white people in suits marched by on important missions. At twilight, people who looked like them, only slumped and slower, zombied into tall, stout apartment buildings.

Maybe they intimidated me, these grown-ups with their attaché cases and BlackBerrys. Maybe I felt disfranchised as a short-term renter. I rarely yelled at the bad drivers, the sidewalk bikers, the professional walkers wrangling prides of pedigreed dogs. I was warier at night on these silent streets, no longer sure who was a mugger, who was just a cranky character.

There was the doorman issue.

I had never had a doorman before. The convenience should have been liberating. While I was away, hypothetically, people could bring me ice cream cakes, which would be magically left in my refrigerator. But the price was obligatory small talk every time I came in or out and, worse, the loss of privacy. What if I wanted to bring home, hypothetically, a transgender hooker? My children suggested I unpack that question with a mental health professional.

The second year, when I lived on East Fifth Street between Second and Third Avenues, I could have brought anybody and its mother home without notice, yet my soul was still not easy. I wasn't sure why. I enjoyed the arrhythmic vibrations of the nabe, the way it woke up in staggered waves, the rub of outlanders, predators, loonies.

I imagined my grandmother, recently off the boat from Minsk or Pinsk, living in a similar creaky walk-up tenement. I had warm childhood memories of my grandfather's printing plant nearby. I loved to sit on a high stool among his presses, watching for fires when the paper jammed.

Once, I had been a forest ranger on the Lower East Side. Now I couldn't even become the monitor I had been on 16th Street. Was it again my rental status and the intimidating denizens? The sidewalk bikers of Loisaida dare you to glare at them, and too many of the dogs are pit bulls in training for their pro season.

I felt in transit, in exile from Grapus. To make sure it still existed, I would map running routes along the East River, south from Murray Hill or north from Cooper Square, that would take me through Stuyvesant Town and then up my old block and one turn around Gramercy Park, which always made me smile. It is simply the most ludicrous real estate in the city, an underused, locked, private square block guarded by modern Victorians and under legal siege by the management of the National Arts Club, which seems to want to make it into its backyard.

I had once thought that releasing squirrels into that park would be a hilarious gesture, but then I realized how out of place they would feel among the snooty local squirrels. I was glad I had shown some restraint. Was this penitence? Would I be pardoned?

•

Last year, life wrote me back home.

Carol Roberto had died. But Sal, Cindy, Hans, Joe and Greg were still around, and Jack Taylor insisted that I celebrate my return by finally joining the Union Square Community Coalition, a 23-year-old group whose passionate advocacy has helped change the nabe for the better. It is a destination now, with many theaters, movie screens, a famous greenmarket. It even has an adequate dog run.

I have a stepdog now, the 11-year-old mixed breed rescued by Lois, my partner. Rudy is tall, dark, handsome and silent, so we are an amusing contrast. He makes us new friends while I bark at the careless drivers and sidewalk bikers who might hurt him.

One night last month, a woman walking a dog stopped us on our street. She said she had always thought I was a bad person because I hated dogs—she had clipped and distributed my cranky columns on the subject—but she was happy now to witness my conversion. One dog can do that, she said.

That was as close as I've come to a formal welcome-home party, but it wasn't the event that put me back in my place, that convinced me I had truly gone home again. Several months ago, the nice new next-door neighbor whose backyard adjoins mine complained about the squirrels pillaging her garden. Maureen and her husband had moved into my building during my exile. I told her not to worry, that I knew someone who could take care of the problem.

I dug out my old leather gloves and the metal trap. I bought two chocolate and peanut butter squares, used one for bait and ate the other as I watched the inevitable through my living room window. Those bushy-tailed rats didn't stand a chance. Urban Trapper was back in town.

September 7, 2003

10

Latte on the Hudson

New York's Original Starbucks Has Closed.
But 162 Remain, and a Day Idled Away in One
of Them Reveals That These Marvels of
Engineered Mood Have Become the City's
Ultimate Study Halls, Offices and Village Green.

PATRICIA VOLK

The Starbucks at Madison and 96th Street. (Philip Greenberg/The New York Times)

IT'S 6:05 in the morning at my local Starbucks. I'm there before the sun comes up. I'm there as the barista slides the till into the register. I'm the first customer of the day, and I want my cappuccino.

"What is this?" The barista doesn't trust my silver dollar.

She walks it to her partner (all Starbucks employees are called partners), who points to where the coin says "ONE DOLLAR." And so a new day dawns on the southwest corner of 96th Street and Madison Avenue, where Carnegie Hill cusps Spanish Harlem.

Judy Garland belts "Somewhere Over the Rainbow" on the current Starbucks playlist track. Throughout the day, strategic changes are made in the music, the personnel (women open, mostly men close), what food is available, even the lighting. Starbucks is a masterpiece of precision targeting and socially engineered mood.

This Starbucks opened in March 2001. It's three blocks south of Mount Sinai Hospital, and the highest concentration of New York independent schools falls within a 10-block radius.

It's a family neighborhood. The question is, will Starbucks last? This particular corner is the storefront of broken dreams: a shoe store, a discount clothing store, a video store all went belly up. For long stretches it stayed empty.

Since the city's first Starbucks, the one at 87th Street and Broadway, closed in August, New York is down to 162 Starbucks. Could Starbucks go the way of Bickford's? The automat? Schrafft's? Not as long as New York rents stay astronomic. Not as long as 200 square feet is called "an apartment." Starbucks is living room and dining room to the barely solvent. It's a study hall, village green, waiting room, library, clubhouse and office. It's neutral turf. It's real estate for the price of a cup of coffee. And God forbid you should have to go seven blocks without a latte. New York is Starbuckized.

I wait for my cappuccino. For $3.25, I want a cappuccino that will change my life. I want it at least as powerful as my home-brewed Chock Full o'Nuts. I know taste is particular. Just this summer, four generations of family rented a house in Maine. There were 17 of us, and in the morning we had to brew three different pots.

My niece likes decaf. My sister has to have Brown Gold or her large intestine goes into shock. I'd drink her Brown Gold, but you can't get Brown Gold in Kennebunk and her imported Florida stash got dangerously low. Eventually, my sister got up early, made her pot of Brown

Gold. I got up next and made Chock Full o'Nuts. Then the niece brewed decaf.

•

Coffee's not about the money, although money's part of it. When I buy a can of Chock Full o'Nuts for $2.79, I get 32 rounded scoops. That's 64 cups of coffee, or a week and a half supply. It's like the people who give up smoking and figure they can buy a car. Sixty-four cups of Chock Full o'Nuts for $2.79 vs. 64 Starbucks cups at $1.55 a cup. If I'm not going to Starbucks, I'm saving $96.41 a can. Hey, I owe myself a present.

Unlike the Starbucks at 102nd Street and Broadway, where my daughter's ex-boyfriend studied for his LSAT's, this one doesn't have plump upholstered furniture. It has 7 tables and 16 no-frills wooden chairs, and there's only one plug for a laptop. The walls are decorated with cute baby photos taken by a woman from the neighborhood.

The place is clean but frowzy. Plaster is chipped. Wooden joints don't mesh. But the pastry display case by the counter is gorgeous. Scones, bagels, cinnamon crisps and croissants in military alignment, like a Wayne Thiebaud painting.

At 6:18, Starbucks gets its second customer. A man ties his albino bulldog to a parking meter and orders a venti skim latte. The espresso machine hisses, the steamer gargles, and by 6:23 there's a line. A woman in a white lab coat orders a grande latte. A man in a navy suit slaps his thermo mug on the counter, and without a word it gets filled. Outside, a jogger in parachute cloth walks a leashless poodle. Sit, she motions. Stay!

"The dog will just wait there?" I ask when she comes in.

"He's my smarter one." She smiles and walks up to the counter. The dog looks both ways and bolts.

Outside, a bundle of newspapers nests beside the door. Frank Sinatra sings "One More for the Road."

At 7:50, 13 yawning people are in line and none of them look happy. Women with strollers, moms escorting boys wearing khaki shorts, blue blazers and ties, the St. David's uniform. More joggers. Mount Sinai employees. "A grande and a raspberry scone," says a woman carrying a Vuitton bag. Some customers ask for two cups. A lady files her nails. I add this to my list of Horrible Things People Now Do in Public, the worst being flossing in restaurants.

The line shuffles along the gray gum-pocked carpet. Eight minutes later, the woman who was at the end of the line reaches the front. There are three other places to buy coffee less than a block away. I wouldn't wait eight minutes for a cup of coffee, even at my favorite cafe near the Spanish Steps in Rome.

At least no one is ordering the way my friend Susan does. She likes "a decaf skim latte extra hot no whip with foam mocha grande in a venti cup." (She figures she gets more because the cup is bigger.) Maybe these people wait because Starbucks has built its franchise on the idea of customization. They'll start their day with a cup of coffee exactly the way they want it. The day may be all downhill from there. But for a moment, they have precisely what they want.

Tony Bennett croons "My Favorite Things." No dent has been made in the pastry. Most customers look as if they're on their way to work. Some spread out and read the paper. It's like Vienna. In Vienna, nobody says, "Get up; we need the table." No snarly waiter paces or glares. It's not like the old Chock Full o'Nuts, where the stools were rumored to be designed at M.I.T. to make you feel uncomfortable after 15 minutes. No. A cup of Starbucks comes with bottomless time.

•

By 10:20, the place is exploding with people. Now three baristas work the counter. They're in their early 20's and unflaggingly polite. Salads, sandwiches and yogurt have joined the pastries. Customers know one another. Starbucks feels lively, like a community.

My friend the poet Siri von Reis reads The New Yorker at the sunny table by the south window. She comes to Starbucks twice a day, at 10 and around 4. The baristas know her so well, they've named her coffee "the Siri." She has lost weight drinking her venti skim, one shot of decaf, one pump chocolate, no whip.

Starbucks is so packed, you can't hear what's on the playlist. An 8-year-old (why isn't she in school?) badgers her mother about getting another ear pierce. "Just one more here, Mom?" She points to a place above her existing pierce. "Molly has one." A man laughs into his cellphone. An anxious mother interviews a nanny over grandes.

The croissants are gone. So are the scones. The bagels haven't budged.

Three customers in low-rise jeans hang by the condiments. They look like models until they flash their braces.

A kid in a stroller is screaming. "I wannahachocolate! WAAAAAAAAAH!" He could break your heart. But hot chocolate isn't on the menu today. There's nothing listed on the board next to Children's

Special. Last winter I ordered the children-size hot chocolate for $1.45. When the barista pushed it across the counter, he said, "Two eighty-five."

"But I ordered the child's cup," I said.

"Are you a child?" he asked.

Never mind that it was the worst hot chocolate I ever had, worse than what comes out of coin machines. Nannies, children of privilege, chic moms, Starbucks midmorning feels like an Upper East Side birthday party.

At 12:26, a woman is sitting in Siri's seat eating takeout Chinese. It's lunchtime at Starbucks, even for those who buy lunch elsewhere. Three ladies in business suits chat. Gwyneth Paltrow look-alikes from Nightingale-Bamford wear gray pleated cheerleader skirts and fitted Lacostes. New Balance sneakers, no socks, complete the look. All three have cellphones. A girl with Day-Glo red hair comes in alone, wearing cargo knickers over ripped fishnets, a thermal camouflage T, a Hulk book bag and high tops covered in peace signs. She's five concurrent fads.

Suddenly a man in a red and white striped shirt bursts in from Sal Pizza across the street. He asks a barista what she's doing tonight. He follows her around while she spritzes tables. He gives up and orders three coffees. Morning pastries are replaced by afternoon goodies: cookies, Rice Krispies Squares, S'mores, a lemon Bundt cake with a glaze.

At 3:05, Starbucks rocks. Four partners pump coffee. School's out, and the Nightingale girls are back, this time with boys. They take over the north side of the store. It's standing room only. There's a lot of squealing and ponytail twitching. A young Hasidic woman waits in line. I know she's Hasidic because she's wearing seamed stockings. The stockings are opaque and the seams so straight, her legs look prosthetic. Is Starbucks kosher?

A woman at one table works on two boxes of thank-you notes. A man sips a mochaccino and studies the Journal of the American Medical Association. Three women with museum stickers on their lapels analyze the cakes. A man works on a laptop. Grandmas retrieve grandchildren from school. The kids head knowingly for the Seasonal Lollipops and Muppet Candy Sticks that surface at 3. Carrot cake and Summer Bliss Blueberry Bars replace muffins and scones. There's been a run on brownies. Marvin Gaye wails "Got to Give It Up."

•

A New York generation has come to know the Starbucks cup better than the blue Greek coffee shop Parthenon. I first saw the Starbucks logo in Seattle. It was the 80's, and people walked around carrying mugs. Coffee places were everywhere.

Customers stopped in and held out their mugs, and those mugs were filled. I especially admired the trademark of one place, Starbucks. The woman in the logo had pre-Raphaelite hair that perfectly covered her breasts the same as Ann Blyth's in "Mr. Peabody and the Mermaid," the first movie I ever saw.

Ms. Starbucks was a mermaid, too. What could be seen of her body formed, what? An hourglass? A drip coffee maker? A keyhole? She was smiling, despite needing both hands to support her bifurcated fishtail. But why the name Starbucks? Why name a coffee after Captain Ahab's first mate? Or was it Bill Starbuck, Burt Lancaster's sexy rainmaker, who convinces Katharine Hepburn that she's not an old prune?

It's starting to get dark out. At 7:08, Starbucks is in a wind-down mode. Five customers read at separate tables. Although there's no line, the counter people keep moving. Always there's something to clean or polish. A guitar solo plays in the background. Before closing, I ask for a cup of organic decaf.

"I could put a French press together in five minutes," the barista offers. The Serena Certified Organic Blend is available only by the bag, but he's willing to grind some. The Fair Trade Blend, the coffee picked by workers who get a decent salary, is by the bag, too.

I ask the partner if leftovers go on sale at the end of day, the way they do at a takeout place four blocks south.

"No," he says with concern. "We can't do that. I'm sorry."

The display case is half-filled.

"So what happens to this stuff?" I ask.

"Random Harvest comes three times a week for the cake," he says. "The sandwiches and salads don't keep, so we throw them out."

"Do homeless people wait outside?"

He stiffens. "If homeless people want food, they should go to a homeless shelter."

"And the coffee grinds? I read once that you donate them and they get rebrewed?"

"You want the grinds?" he asks. "We give them to people for their gardens."

Three customers are still reading at tables. They've been here for hours.

"Excuse me," the barista says. "We're going to be closing in 10 minutes."

They look up. They blink as if they've been in a bubble.

Two ladies in sequins come in laughing and order chocolate mocha grandes. A partner retires her broom and makes herself an iced tea. It's 9:05. Just as she's taking out the cash drawer, a woman rushes in with a coffee emergency. She needs a filter.

Starbucks coffee filters look like paper buckets. They're huge. "I'll cut it down with my Swiss Army knife," the woman pleads. "It's got a scissor."

At no time during the day have any Latinos stopped in. Spanish Harlem is right across the street. But so is the K&D deli, the Corner Bagel Market and Three Guys. Maybe it's the coffee. That could be it. Café con leche served with a little pot of steamy foamy milk is a far cry from a Starbucks latte.

What's in the future for Starbucks? This year it was iced tea lemonade and shaken iced coffee. I'd go every summer day if they had a granita di caffe con panna. I'd be there like clockwork if their hot chocolate tasted like Laduree's. I will, however, never go for my morning cup. I love brewing my own coffee. I go to sleep at night smiling at the thought of my first cup.

At 9:10, the barista says, "Good evening," and holds the door for me. Stevie Wonder and I waft out into the night.

September 21, 2003

(Ross McDonald)

74

11

Screech, Memory

The No. 2 Train Roared By Not 25 Yards From His Childhood Bedroom, Punctuating All the Rites of His Bronx Youth.

RICHARD PRICE

MY first memory of boarding the IRT was of not boarding the IRT: my mother getting on at the Simpson Street station in the East Bronx while I daydreamed on the platform. As the doors slid shut between us, she took her seat and, with what seemed an eerie calm, regarded me as I frantically slapped my palms on the outside of the windows. I was 4 years old, and when a faceless Samaritan forced the doors to reopen, I rocketed across the car into her lap, acutely aware that some of the passengers were softly laughing at my oversized relief.

"I told you," she said. "If that ever happens, you just stay put and wait for me to come back on the next train. I told you that before." Those words actually served to settle me down, since they presented me with something more subtly disturbing to think about, given the fact that she had never, ever told me anything of the sort.

There were only a few constants in the nocturnal soundtrack of my childhood: the slish and clack of mah-jongg tiles and the snap and riffle of a poker deck, both from the dinette; and from the world outside, the steel-on-steel groan of the elevated No. 2 train as it veered past my bedroom not 25 yards from my head, four or five times an hour every night for the first 18 years of my life.

From 1950 to 1968, we lived on White Plains Road in a housing project in the Williamsbridge section of the Bronx. The el tracks that cast the cobblestones of that endless strip into permanent, grid-patterned shadow also bisected the world at eye level outside our third-floor windows. Yet by dint of the unrelenting lull-roar-lull rhythms out in the street, the trains that ran along those tracks were as subliminally comforting to me as a parental heartbeat.

Lying in bed, I never thought of that train (always, in my mind, the same single train) as anything but a living and feeling creature, racing first one way and then the other in a never-ending search for something crushingly human: its mother (probably at the Simpson Street stop), a lost child, or perhaps a girl train.

In the mornings, when those trains lost their abstraction, I never gave a second thought to the hundreds of wooden, work-bound faces, motionless in their velocity, watching me eat breakfast as they blasted past the dinette window. Come the early evenings, when those faces were greenishly illuminated inside their capsules, I hardly ever looked out at them, busy as I was reading TV lips: Rod Serling's, Hoss Cartwright's, Steve Allen's. We all did, and could. No one in my family ever asked anyone else to repeat what had just been said on the tube.

This gift/affliction seemed to affect everyone whose windows faced the tracks, and it even accompanied us into the street. On sunny days or balmy nights, as the trains roared overhead, none of the parents smoking and jawing on the bench in front of the building, none of the kids playing ball or swapping insults on the sidewalk ever seemed to cup an ear or squint in concentration to stay with the flow.

There were even a few boys from the seventh floor, brothers, who were lucky enough to have the train address them directly: their father was a motorman, and whenever he piloted a train past his own apartment, he let loose with a short double blast on the horn, saying hi to the wife and kids.

And on occasion that train most definitely spoke directly to me too. For example, whenever I had to leave the projects to go to our "summer house," say, a cottage at the end of an overgrown logging road in a lonely clearing north of the city, for an endless, friendless two months of pollen asthma and bad TV reception, that Two was always there to welcome me back in September, its din and rumble penetrating the innermost recesses of our small apartment, crooning monstrously, reassuringly, "You're home, you're home."

•

As long as they existed primarily as mood music, as romantic triggers for my imagination, the trains were a benign phenomenon in my life. But in 1962, when commuting became part of my world—two stops, from

Burke Avenue past the Gun Hill Road station to East 219th Street, the stop for Olinville Junior High—the cars, stations and the tracks themselves began to smack of an amorphous dread, the intersection of freedom and free fall, of random "why me?" encounters with the heartless heart of the city, or maybe it was just the unrelentingly oppressive destination. In those years, Olinville wasn't exactly a gladiator pit, but it was a fairly knockabout place, and that vaguely hostile, stranger-filled building, combined with my lousy academic performance there, tainted whatever independence riding the Two could have afforded me.

In the mornings, starting around 7:30, the northbound Burke Avenue platform began to swell with dozens of 12- to 15-year-olds crawling up the stairs, too tired, too cold or simply too burdened by the thought of where they were headed to make for any kind of tangible drama. Still, some of those commutes had their moments: I remember the brisk fall morning when a large, wet-lipped boy in Olinville's "pre-vocational" program stood at the top of the stairs with a fistful of dollar bills, blankly handing one each to all the kids as they climbed up to the platform; girls mostly, alighting wild-eyed around him like gleeful crows, plucking bucks, flapping off back down the stairs shrieking for friends to come up and get theirs.

Then there was the bundle on the tracks. Kids freezing one wintry morning that same year, huffing out clouds of condensation as they leaned over the edge of the platform to will the northbound train into sight, until they could finally see it detach itself from Allerton, the head car ballooning as it approached Burke, but then screeching to a stop 30 yards south of the station and inches from a humped something beneath a blanket on the tracks. We began to groan with exasperation at the delay until the hump suddenly cast off its cover and started to run.

It was a neighborhood kid, a seventh grader who had been crouched on all fours beneath that ratty tent on the rails, a boy who had been mercilessly hounded and criticized all week by a teacher, a boy galumphing down the tracks as if to escape on foot to the Gun Hill Road station.

Many of us, shocked into silence, unthinkingly ran parallel to him up along the platform, keeping pace with his desperate but poky gait, until a truant officer materialized from the crowd, leapt onto the tracks and snagged the back of the kid's jacket before he could get past the far end of the station; all of us standing slack-jawed as we heard the kid plead with his captor: "C'mon, let me go. I swear I'll never do it again."

Grim as the morning ride tended to be, the return trip was even worse, primarily because the nature of the dread shifted from the existential to the corporeal, to the straight-up fear of getting smacked in the head. Mondays through Fridays, at precisely 3:15, the otherwise innocuous southbound platform of the 219th Street station became flooded with simultaneously paroled junior high schoolers, and often became something of a killing floor. All the lovingly nursed beefs of the previous seven hours, the stare-downs, hissed words and drawled insults accumulated in the halls, homerooms, shop classes and cafeteria transformed themselves at that magic moment into flurries of abrupt violence: mini-explosions of fists, flying feet, pulled hair and expletives. And then there were the "Lord of the Flies" moments, the soft-core muggings: "Hey, I like your jacket. Can I hold it?"

The afternoon on that 219th Street platform when the dread became the most manifest was also the afternoon no one so much as raised a finger: Nov. 22, 1963, the kids for once stony quiet, some wearing half-grins of shock, as a loquacious doom-prophet from the SP classes held everyone in his sway: "I'm telling you, man, now that Khrushchev's finally gotten him out of the way—anybody here, you don't have a fall-out shelter at home? You'll be dead in a week, too."

•

But not all train rides back then carried a pall. At least three stations smacked of some kind of release: Fordham Road, for an afternoon of scoping out muscle shirts and sharkskin slacks and buying 45's (records, not guns); Times Square, in all its innocent smuttiness; and West Fourth Street, where we got off to prowl the Village for the never-to-be-found beatnik chick whose image would grace the cover of my first album, "Freewheelin' Rich Price."

And there was at least one stop back then that seemed to offer both pleasure and pain: a West Bronx station, lost to me now, where we traveled twice a month to attend a community center dance at which, dressed to the nines, all we did was shout, wrestle and in general play the goon on the boys' side of the floor until the last (slow) dance of the evening, when we abruptly turned into heat-seeking missiles, desperately trying to find a girl, any girl, who would go around in blocky circles with us for three minutes.

This particular station was multilevel and had an escalator as high and steep as a Mayan pyramid. Midnights after our dance forays would invariably find us back there, howling like loons as we raced each other up the down side of these perpetual-motion stairs, leg muscles trembling to overcome the physics of stupidity.

If we made it to the top, we'd ride back down and do it again. And we'd do it over and over until our Nehru jackets were sopping, until our kneecaps were chattering, until we started seeing double, seeing triple, and had convinced ourselves that the evening (along with the rest of our proscribed lives up until that very moment) had been nothing short of a total blast.

March 28, 2004

Bungalow life. (Fred R. Conrad/The New York Times)

12

Bungalow Chic

Discovering the Romance of Rockaway, That Peninsula With an Esteem Problem.

JILL EISENSTADT

SEASIDE towns always incite nostalgia. All the sensual memories that the shore provides enhance what is essentially a yearning for summer. A summer of one's youth, most likely; if not, an imaginary summer of one's youth. Old photographs of Victorian ladies in "bathing costumes" have become cliché, and every flea market sells colorized postcards of iconic boardwalk scenes.

That Rockaway was ever such a place is news to most outsiders. A shell's throw from the ugliest part of Flatbush Avenue on one end, a wasteland à la mer on the other, the tiny peninsula that hangs off Queens has been so continually abused by city policy and neglect, fires and storms, jet roar and bad public relations since World War I that it's been a hard place for anyone but a native or a punk rocker to sentimentalize.

"Rock rock Rockaway Beach/We can hitch a ride to Rockaway Beach."

Those Queens boys the Ramones knew that Far Rockaway, long a dumping ground for the city's disenfranchised, was nothing to sing about. Joey Ramone would no doubt be relieved to learn that the street recently named in his honor is in the East Village rather than Arverne, where the city's largest vacant tract (310 acres) languished for decades.

So locals can't help looking with cautious excitement at the recent media attention given their seaside town, including three insightful books: "Old Rockaway, New York, in Early Photographs," "Between Ocean and City" and "Braving the Waves." Could it be their town would finally be encrusted with history, lit up with romance, recognized?

As "Old Rockaway, New York, in Early Photographs" proves, Rockaway did have a few aristocratic years in the mid-1800's before railroads and ferries allowed the Vanderbilt summer crowd to trade up for the Hamptons. Next, a turn-of-the-century entrepreneurial blitz brought spectacular constructions: a 1,300-foot iron pier, a 2,500-foot water flume ride, a 1,184-foot-long hotel billed as the world's largest.

The 1920's brought the summer bungalows and tent cities to which the lower and middle classes of various ethnicities fled; illustrious graduates include the Nobel Prize winner Richard Feynman, the financier Carl Icahn and Dr. Joyce Brothers. But even in these glory years, Rockaway saw too much suffering. The authors of "Between Ocean and City," Lawrence and Carol Kaplan, remind the nostalgic old-timer that an anti-Semitic radio priest, the Rev. Charles Coughlin, had a following there in the 30's and 40's. African-Americans were welcome on the peninsula's western end only as underpaid housecleaners and handymen, and their living quarters, in many cases summer shacks turned inadequately into year-round housing, were considered "some of the worst slums in the country."

Then there were the fires, repeatedly fanned out of control by ocean winds. The Marine Pavilion hotel, said to be where high society discovered ocean bathing, ignited in 1864; a fire in 1922 left 3,000 people homeless. The Wave, Rockaway's local paper and the city's oldest weekly, was named not for the Atlantic surf but for one of many devastating "Wave[s] of Fire," the first headline. Along with the homey reminiscences of spearing eels in Jamaica Bay, the paper's 110th commemorative issue features a time line listing major "Rockaway Storms" (16), "Rockaway Fires" (31) and "Shipwrecks and Maritime Disasters of the Rockaways" (more than 50).

By the time a wooden Long Island Rail Road bridge trestle burned in 1950, Rockaway's status as a resort area had already passed. The neighborhoods, which had always skewed whiter and richer the farther west you went, became ever more disconnected. Those who weren't segregated by poverty and bigotry often segregated themselves, as did the Orthodox Jews in pockets of Far Rockaway and the Irish Catholics in the gated community of Breezy Point.

As I grew up there in the 70's, my family lived in the nicest parts of town—Belle Harbor, then Neponsit. But we were still in walking distance of several S.R.O. hotels and a burned-out movie theater. Although our neighbors included Assemblywoman Gerdi Lipschutz and former

Mayor Abe Beame, we rode graffiti-covered buses choked with pot
smoke past dozens of bars and liquor stores to schools with barred windows and frequent racial strife.

•

When Rockaway's Playland closed in 1987, we mourned it like a dead
pet, but the rides had been giving us rust burns and impetigo for years,
and the "suicide drive" under the el to get there required locked doors
and windows. Medicated and disoriented mental patients wandered our
main shopping strip, Beach 116th Street. Trash blew around on the
beaches. Roads remained blocked with snow long after the rest of the
borough had been plowed.

In 1988, a magazine article I had written on local lifeguards was killed
because of a plague of high tides bearing hypodermic needles. Still, I defended my hometown to friends who made disparaging jokes about the
"red tides." Eleven miles of white sandy beach, I reminded them. Good
(for the East Coast) surfing. A six-mile boardwalk, second in length only
to Atlantic City's. Good (for the fluke) fishing. A sunset view across Jamaica Bay that included the World Trade Center, and lots of sexy lifeguards and firefighters with which to enjoy it.

The fall of 2001 changed a lot. In one season, as Kevin Boyle chronicles in his book "Braving the Waves," Belle Harbor endured not only
one of the largest Sept. 11 death tolls but the crash of American Airlines
Flight 587.

That these tragedies brought only fleeting attention to Rockaway is
hardly a surprise. Richard George's fight to preserve Rockaway's last
bungalows has recently drawn coverage in the news media, but he's been
at it, on and off, for 18 years. When Arverne by the Sea, the latest in a
long line of plans for the city's abandoned acres, was given the go-ahead,
even its contractors must have been astonished.

Living there still means you have to cross a bridge to see a movie, buy
clothing or, with few exceptions, get a good meal. Living there probably
means your basement will flood and the planes from nearby J.F.K. will
interrupt your sleep. You might get evacuated for a hurricane. You will
get stuck in beach traffic.

Hometowns incite nostalgia, seaside hometowns maybe more than
most. All the sensory memories that the shore provided—the Wednesday night fireworks, my collection of sea glass, the taste of salt on someone else's skin—enhance what must just be a yearning for summer. A

summer of my youth, most likely. An imaginary summer of my youth, perhaps.

No amount of attention can romanticize a past that is not necessarily a romantic one, but in the end, romance is personal and the present is full of potential. Today there is an explosion of construction. Real estate values are high. The water is clean. The Rockaway Music and Arts Council and the Rockaway Artists Alliance fill the cultural void. There are good waves, Dad reports. And the laughing gulls are back.

April 18, 2004

Moods and Mores

The author, up in the air. (Fred R. Conrad/The New York Times)

13

The Allure of the Ledge

Working Close to the Clouds, the Window Washer Is the Ultimate Risk Taker, the Ultimate Voyeur.

IVOR HANSON

I AM poised on a narrow ledge that angles downward to the street be-low. Drops of water fall from the mop in my left hand and form a mo-mentary trail before scattering in the breeze. My right hand grips a cold metal frame while a squeegee dangles from my waist. I am 55 stories up and set to clean a window.

At that height, wind is a factor, so I hug the building close. I look down to get my bearings; looking up can induce vertigo. Because I am on a postwar high-rise, there are no hooks to which I can secure my win-dow cleaner's belt. I can only rely on my fingertips and sense of balance. Still, I take advantage of my perch for a moment to admire the Chrysler Building a few blocks north. I feel a part of the skyline.

I trust myself with my life out on the ledge. This trust lets me know that I am in sync, combining absolute awareness with controlled fear, and allows me to do my job. It keeps my feet in place and my head clear. I know how far my body can lean out, how far I can reach with my squeegee.

Window cleaning has honed my concentration, and in close calls, this focus helps me hold on. I experience a rush, equal parts exhilaration and relief. I know the danger involved, but can also play down my derring-do. I can joke about where I would splat if I fell. I can even laugh—now —about dropping an air-conditioner out a Park Avenue apartment win-dow.

Whoever installed that air-conditioner did his best to make it appear that it would stay in place when the window was opened. It didn't. I'm lucky I didn't kill someone that morning, specifically the building porter

who had been sweeping below the window a minute before the thing fell
two stories. Rightfully, he chewed me out when my boss and I ran down
to the street and chucked the Freon-spewing unit into a nearby Dump-
ster. There was a dent in the pavement.

I'm still leery of opening that window, despite the steel bar that holds
the new air-conditioner in place. The least observed law in New York
City? Article 9, Section 27/313 of the city Building Code, which states
that an air-conditioner cannot extend more than 10 inches from a window frame when the unit is more than 10 feet from the ground, or more
than 4 inches when it is less than 10 feet. These units routinely stick out
much farther, putting a great strain on the window frame. That's why
when I walk down the sidewalk, I stick close to the curb.

Window cleaning offers an appealing mix of personal challenge—
dangerous windows—with sights I shouldn't have seen along the way.
Combining these with my squeegee's low-tech charm and an O.K. wage
helps to explain why, at the age of 36, I have kept at this dirty and demanding job for nearly nine years. It allowed me to pursue music in the
past and makes possible my writing now. As for my own windows, they
aren't as clean as you might think; I clean the three but twice a year.

I learn a lot about life as I attach myself to a window frame's belt
hook, after first testing the hook and checking for a hairpin or paper clip,
what we cleaners leave behind to mark an unsafe window. Self-reliance
comes to mind, as does knowing when to walk away from a job that's
too dangerous. Some people climb mountains simply because they are
there, and spend lots of money to do so. I climb out on a ledge simply
because some windows are dirty. And I get paid to do so.

It's funny. Many people tell me that they wouldn't do what I do for a
million dollars. And yet I do it for $10 a window ($11 if they're cut up
into smaller panes). It's not often you know the exact worth of your life.

Fortunately, a lot of what I see is priceless. Allow me a confession:
voyeurism is one of the perks of this job.

I have watched the sun rise over the East River from what was once
Irving Berlin's bedroom terrace—the Beekman Place building now
houses Luxembourg's United Nations Mission—and wished that the
diplomats there could find space for a piano.

After washing a picture window in a Harlem housing project that the
customer demanded be perfectly clean, the view did not turn out to be.
As the customer and I looked out the window, a drug deal went down in
the vacant lot across the street. Neither of us said a word.

I was with a first-time customer when she learned she had six months to live. As she broke down and cried, I sat at her side and did my best to comfort her.

"Hey, don't worry about me," she said. "You're the one hanging off the sides of buildings."

She died of cancer the next spring.

I've worn surgical booties to avoid scuffing Tom Hanks's living-room floor. I have secretly held F. Murray Abraham's Oscar. I have seen the set list of songs John Lennon wrote out for his album "Rock 'n' Roll Music." For that matter, I once came across pornographic playing cards in a drainpipe of the Dakota.

Voyeurism, after all, does have its seamier side.

I've seen people having sex from afar, interrupted couples having sex and been asked if I wanted to have sex. I've been invited to stay and have a drink. I've been asked to hang out and get high. I've come across XXX videos and books, drugs, guns, handcuffs and love letters, all left out in the open, no prying necessary.

A private investigator whose windows I used to do took a more activist approach by surreptitiously videotaping a housewife across the street who liked to clean her apartment with very little on. He played the tapes between cases when he was bored.

As I watched them, a truth emerged: people just don't think they can be seen. And the higher the window I am cleaning, the likelier it is I will see someone naked in a neighboring building. Not surprisingly, high-floor apartments usually have binoculars or telescopes at the ready, along with the owners' claim of using them only to watch boats on the Hudson.

Once, a customer in a Murray Hill high-rise readily admitted that he regularly scoped out a building two blocks away where a lot of young people lived. I chuckled because I had lived in that building a few years earlier, without curtains. Unfortunately, the client remarked, he never saw anything exciting.

I understood. I find watching a couple making love across the way often just makes sex look silly. It's not like a movie, with the lighting and the lingerie just so, the actors taut and lean. Instead, it's a bit of a let-down: two exposed and unspectacular bodies moving this way and that in silence; they're usually out of earshot.

•

While I have never considered my squeegee an aphrodisiac, Tomas, the window-cleaning character from Milan Kundera's novel "The Unbearable Lightness of Being," was quite a Don Juan. But I believe him to be the exception. After all, innocent Curious George was a window cleaner too.

As for myself, I once cleaned the windows of a lower Broadway loft for a young European woman spending her first summer in New York. There was a heat wave, and I worked up quite a sweat removing the thick dirt from the oversized windows. When I finished, she walked over to me, touched my arm and wondered if I wanted to take a shower; her boyfriend wouldn't be back for hours. I told her I was running late (I actually was). When I returned to clean the windows that fall, the boyfriend was home—it was a Saturday—but she was not. A new girlfriend had replaced her.

Another attraction: I have the privilege of working where the very privileged live. It really is a different world, one of huge rooms, perfect locations and breathtaking views. One of my favorites is an Art Deco bathroom with its own terrace overlooking Central Park, in the Century building on Central Park West. It's almost decadent, but what a space!

Not surprisingly, such surroundings can be intoxicating. I find myself making silly observations, like deciding never to live on Park Avenue: it's overrated. Most apartments don't have great views, and tenants must tolerate a lot of traffic noise.

But nonetheless, I am struck by just how far removed these people and places are from the everyday world. A prominent doctor has a few Picassos in his living room and a de Kooning in his dining room. I admire these paintings every time I visit, for beyond their beauty and genius they reveal to me why people collect art. It's not just owning masterpieces, it's having them in your home. He can view these paintings at 6 in the morning in his bathrobe, coffee in hand. They are his. How amazing that must be.

As a maid in an Upper East Side duplex once remarked to me when she had finished dusting the lady of the house's vanity, crammed with perfume bottles: All these, for one person.

Our smiles reflected both disbelief and acceptance.

Though window cleaning is a respectable profession, at times I must confront its low status. I am not, after all, a lawyer or a doctor or even a rock star. This is a job I feel I must regularly explain away.

But that's not always possible. Once when I simply wanted to kill time between jobs at my parents' apartment in the Beresford on Central Park West, the doorman made me use the back entrance. "Sorry, Ivor," Yakov said, pointing at my bucket. "You've got to go around."

The class system is alive and well in New York City. Service entrances and penthouses bracket this hierarchy, and I have to use one to get to the other. This is just a fact of life, and an unremarkable one at that, for, usually, I am quite comfortable in both worlds. Building workers, contractors, housekeepers and I all know we are in the business of taking care of the customer. We share a certain empathy, an understanding of our roles.

Upon entering the apartment, though, I am also at ease, for I have a lot in common with most of my clients. I, too, have an upper-middle-class background. I went to college and graduate school. I have the credentials to be one of them.

Unfortunately, with some customers it seems I have to let them know that I am "acceptable" before they can be at ease with me in their homes. This behavior is understandable—I am a stranger, after all—but it also irks me. None of this should matter, but it does. There was the very proper Upper East Sider who acted quite indifferent to me until I spotted a Century Club directory in his den and mentioned that my father was a member. The chap was suddenly quite chatty. I sometimes wonder if I should just wear my T-shirts from Vassar and Columbia, but I don't. Black T-shirts hide dirt better.

Most customers, however, appreciate the sacrifices artists have to make to pursue their passions. It's a different sort of empathy and understanding, one that has them wishing me good luck and giving me a tip. They are helping me out.

More often than not, I am treated warmly. When I am not, it can be quite unpleasant.

Once at the apartment of a particularly cold client, as I was going out on a ledge and pulling myself up and out of the window, this customer suddenly yelled, "Be careful!" Her outburst of humanity surprised me. Until she finished her sentence: ". . . of the drapes!" They were new; raw silk. I hadn't brought out the worst in her, just the truth.

It's not that I am treated like dirt in those moments, it's that I am merely treated like the hired help that I am. This can mean being looked down upon, or at least ignored, expected only to provide the service I am there for. Ultimately, I can't knock such attitudes too much, for the affluent make my livelihood possible. And, in the end, I am just their window cleaner.

Still, I do veer between believing myself to be better and no better than my occupation. But a day job is like that. For while it is essentially a means to an end, it is also what I spend a good amount of my time doing. And doing well. Apart from pride, I do want to keep my job. Besides, if I were lazy or sloppy, I could easily crack a window, stain a rug, or lose my life.

When I first moved to New York, I drummed in a band and needed a job. In other words, I didn't truly consider the risk of window cleaning, just the cash. Being broke does that. Now I both respect and crave risk.

Over the years, I have thought I was experiencing my death fall, realized I really did need to buy new shoes when I started slipping off a window ledge, come across the belt of a window cleaner who had plunged to his death. And yet, I can't quite shake the allure of the ledge. While the risk I encounter daily could certainly kill me, the thrill it provides makes up for the fact that I am, ultimately, just cleaning a window. It's different from a good view balancing out a long job. Because even though the spectacular sight of the Central Park Reservoir from a 21st-story apartment in the Eldorado at Central Park West and 90th Street does ease the drudgery of cleaning that building's cut-up casements—24 panes of glass per window—such a view is really just a magnificent distraction.

Risk is something else. Washing "tricky" windows (as I call them, as much out of modesty as denial) affords me both a sense of accomplishment and a surge of adrenalin. Besting a dangerous window is just more satisfying than cleaning a merely difficult one. Tricky windows, after all, involve cheating death.

•

If I am low enough to the ground, I like watching those aforementioned drops from my mop fall gracefully through the air until they suddenly splat on the sidewalk. Sometimes I go out of my way to picture myself as such a splotch. I usually do this at my first job of the day, particularly if I didn't get much sleep the night before. The image wakes me up.

It also crosses my mind when people down on the street look up at me. I clean windows in an apartment house at Madison and 75th Street, across from the Whitney Museum of American Art. Visitors outside the building invariably catch sight of me. The nice ones wave, but the idiots yell "Jump!"

But I ignore them, as I have something better to do. For once I'm hooked in, there's the moment when I let go of the belt hook and lean back, knowing that my belt will catch me.

I love that moment. I am free, defying gravity, breaking the rules. I should be splattered on the pavement below. But I'm not, so I savor the view: the Carlyle's up the street, the Whitney's just over my shoulder.

Belt windows, however, are the only windows that afford me such leisurely interludes, for I am at least attached to the hooks. Plenty of buildings don't have hooks. Instead they have windows like casements, which open out, like doors; "tilt-ins," which open downward, like a truck's tailgate; "sliders," which pop out to be cleaned, and "switchers," so called because the upper window comes down and the lower window goes up, allowing me to clean the panes by reaching over and underneath the window frames. But since all these windows are designed to be cleaned from the inside, or place me only partly outside, their risks are usually reasonable.

"Nonswitchers" are something else, since with these windows the upper frame cannot come down. So to clean the window entirely I must close it completely and stand out on a ledge that can be less than a foot wide. Nothing but my hands to save me. Simply holding on requires a certain sang-froid; I have to know exactly what I am doing. Everything must go right for nothing to go wrong. People are always telling me to take care, but this is when it really sinks in.

I make certain that whichever hand holds onto the building stays put and dig my fingers into whatever groove, bump or notch the window frame offers up. This hand I regard as a vise grip, and the rest of my body abides by it, doing whatever needs to be done to keep that hand strongly clamped down. The other holds the squeegee. One hand for the window, one hand for me.

As in a car accident, time slows down.

This is partly due to that I simply cannot clean such a window quickly. Out on the ledge, haste makes waste of my life. So I look forward to my squeegee's reaching the end of a window pane that feels impossibly wide. I am quite happy when I'm finished; I am no longer afraid.

Risk has made me quite friendly with fear. It's simple: fear keeps me aware; awareness keeps me alive. Surprisingly, the first time I experienced a close call, wry resentment flashed through me: so this is how it ends, dropping off a damn window ledge. But then pure appreciation quickly followed. I relished touching the belt hook.

There's a famous Life magazine photograph from the 40's of a woman who fell to her death from the Empire State Building. She landed on an automobile. The sedan's roof is crumpled, a mangled mess. But the woman, strangely, is not. She looks quite peaceful lying on her back, a forever sleeping beauty at 33rd and Fifth. That's how I'd like to look should a window ever best me.

January 23, 2000

14

There's No Place Like Home.
But There's . . . No Place

A Long Hunt for an Apartment Uncovers Triple
Bunk Beds, a Kitchen-Cum-Shower—and Some
Insights Into the True Meaning of Home.

TARA BAHRAMPOUR

Waiting for the movers. (Richard Perry/The New York Times)

O N an August night eight years ago, my taxi slowed on Broadway at West 79th Street. A doorman in gold buttons swept open a gate, and we rolled into the courtyard of the Apthorp, a Renaissance-style building where a childhood friend lived. It became my first home in New York.

For three weeks, I crashed in an elegant room whose walls smelled of musky perfume and whose windows were gargantuan. I bathed in a claw-foot tub in a candlelit bathroom with antique gold-leaf wallpaper. A California transplant, I was thrilled to be in the city, and it never crossed my mind, as I passed through the shady courtyard after each intoxicating day of exploring, that my living situation would never again be so sweet.

For the most part, I have had good luck with New York apartments. As a student and as a writer, I have lived in them on almost no money, mystifying my mother, who would periodically ask how it was possible. I rarely went to the theater or bought clothes, congratulating myself on doing so well on so little.

What I did not recognize was the importance of a long-term commitment. Rather than hooking into a rent-stabilized apartment or a small mortgage in the early 90's, when such things still existed, I got lucky on long-term sublets.

For four years I paid $650 for a large East Village one-bedroom and kept an eye on the landlord. "I know that Jasmin doesn't live here!" he would yell as he hammered on the door, referring to the actual tenant. He'd tell me he had hired a private eye and was preparing an eviction notice. But then he'd go away.

Many of my friends lived like this; it was temporary, we thought, part of being young. One day we'd get real jobs and move into real apartments with leases and airtight windows and nothing that crumbled when we touched it.

For now, though, we could take a little discomfort. Our standards hadn't been high to begin with. We'd come of age in the 80's, saddled with the prophecy that we would be the first American generation to earn less than our parents.

The dot-com gold rush disproved that. But recently I prepared for my seventh move in eight years. And I realized yet again what the prophets forgot to tell us: our generation would pay more money to live in smaller, shabbier apartments than any generation of educated, employed, middle-class Americans ever had.

A couple of weeks ago I was talking to a self-described 60's activist. "Don't take this wrong," she said, "but I don't understand your generation. Why aren't you all in the streets fighting for the environment?"

It is because we are fighting for real estate, I replied. Among people my age, from wealthy lawyers to struggling musicians, I never attend a party where the subject doesn't come up. The head-shaking. The low clucks of the tongue. The "Oh, it's so horrible," and "If I didn't have my place, I'd have to leave the city." I slink away from these conversations and wonder how the demographic makeup of the city might be different in a softer market. What have we lost in the couples who move away to have children, in the artists who buy cheap farmhouses upstate, in the countless people who leave each day because they didn't have enough money to live here?

I imagine older people in sprawling rent-controlled digs, whose parties are free from this obsession. Unless they're going through divorce, they tend to be settled. They might have slummed in their youth, but they had room to grow out of it.

What does home mean when you don't have a steady one? For a while, nothing. When I moved here at age 25 I would have liked a nice apartment, but I did not need one. I knew that my peers in other cities owned houses, but still, I gasped when I visited a high school friend's Victorian home in New Orleans. It felt obscene, for someone so young.

But even then I felt stirrings of desire. I'd long been primed for it. My father, an architect, had spent much of my childhood designing and building our dream home in a suburb of Tehran. That three-story yellow brick house, which we visited excitedly every week, was almost ready when the Islamic revolution struck. We flew to America and became migrants in a series of houses that my parents fixed up and sold. These houses were never quite finished, and they were never really ours.

•

In my latest searches for an apartment in New York, it felt increasingly wrong that all my time living here had not bought me something. Shouldn't I have built up some equity, a squatter's right to these streets and buildings that feel so familiar? Not having secured shelter made me feel flawed, embarrassed in front of myself.

I asked Laura Gold, an Upper West Side psychologist, how the housing market affects her patients. Before answering, she regaled me with her own apartment nightmare; then she spoke of how house-hunting, a happy experience in most of the country, can turn everything rancid here. "What does it mean," she said, "to have a great job or be in a fulfilling relationship when week after week, month after month, even year after year, one obsesses over finding a place that might finally become a home?"

Our collective love affair with New York is commonly invoked as a justification for living in a closet. Dr. Gold took that further: with so little domestic square footage, she said, New Yorkers embrace the city itself as their true home. "They know the city's back streets and alleys," she said, "the way house-owners know the nooks and crannies of their basements and attics."

But when you don't have a stable place to live, big or little, even the back streets and alleys are not yours. As a journalist, I write often about people fighting to protect their neighborhoods—from developers, from environmental threats, from social homogeneity, from rent deregulation. Sitting one night at a meeting about gentrification in Park Slope that pitted renters against owners and old-time homesteaders against new arrivals, I felt like the intruder at a family feast. As I watched residents greet each other and testify in passionate voices about their homes, I realized that I was also missing community. That call to outrage, that loyalty to the sidewalks and the neighbors, was as important as actual rooms.

A sublettor must always be on the lookout for her own apartment. In my on-again, off-again searches over the years, there have been close contenders. There was the $750-a-month, rent-stabilized two-bedroom in Williamsburg with views of two horizons. It was the first place I looked at in Brooklyn three years ago, and I decided to look a little more. There was the two-bedroom floor-through in Park Slope with inlaid floors, a wood-paneled dining room and stained-glass windows. The tenant had moved out and the landlord had died. I left a few messages for the landlord's son but then dropped it; he sold it a few months later for $70,000.

I still gaze up at these places. At low moments they have haunted me: whatever was wrong in my life would surely be mitigated if only I had taken that apartment. And I am not alone. "Each apartment you see you build a life around it, the life you could have had in there," says my perpetually nomadic friend Jeff. "I've found myself showing people the apartment I didn't get."

•

My last illegal sublet, a one-bedroom on East Ninth Street, ended two years ago when the landlord finally offered the actual tenant $3,000 to tear up her $563-per-month lease. (I did not tell her the guys next door had held out for $25,000.) My boyfriend lived on Astor Place in a two-bedroom duplex with a skylight, a terrace and a roommate who lived abroad. I moved in.

Most of my neighbors there were kids in designer boots and leather pants who stayed out all night. Riding the elevator, I knew I was an interloper. For a few months I worried about the doormen, wondering if they would still smile so sweetly if they knew the truth about me.

Over two years I did not unpack my boxes. I wasn't really living there; I was looking for my own place. But if looking for a one-bedroom apartment for under $1,000 is demoralizing, looking for one while enjoying a dishwasher, a laundry down the hall and an attentive cavalry of doormen was near-paralyzing. So were the looks of amused disbelief when I told people I couldn't afford to leave Manhattan for Brooklyn.

Still, I had sporadic periods of searching. A Greenpoint apartment was spacious but opened onto the exhaust vent of a Dunkin' Donuts. A place in Red Hook was cheap and charming but more than 20 minutes from the subway. One apartment had a picture-window view of the Gowanus Expressway. "Ah, listen," the realtor said as the cars zoomed toward the living room. "To me, the sound of a freeway is like the sound of the ocean. In fact, I like it better."

A Williamsburg apartment had no bathroom. "But the toilet down the hall is exclusively yours," said the realtor. Where would I shower? A portable plastic shower unit in the kitchen wobbled when I pushed on it. I could make pancakes while I washed my hair. I could rinse off large sides of beef.

People I knew were buying houses in New Jersey, in upstate New York, in Vermont. Why did I have to be in the city? Or why couldn't I pick less expensive neighborhoods? What did it say about me that I stayed within the bourgeois bohemian belt of Park Slope, Carroll Gardens, Brooklyn Heights and Williamsburg instead of finding a great deal in Ridgewood or Mott Haven?

First, I wanted to feel safe walking home alone at night. Second, as someone not yet married, not yet ensconced with my own mini-tribe, I wanted to live near others who share my interests. It sounds unadventurous, but I wanted to be where my friends were. And I craved the satisfaction of finally finding the elusive good deal, of having held my own against the market's terrible odds.

So I called realtors. I offered finders' fees. I wondered what I would be like if I were not always thinking about houses. What thoughts would run through my mind when I walked down the street if I weren't peering into parlor windows at other people's arches and molding? How sick is it, really, to stroll past brownstones thinking idly of neutron bombs that would take out the people but spare the buildings?

•

Last month, during yet another round of house-hunting, I was sitting at work when the phone rang. It was my friend Marta. "Tara!" she gasped. "Apartment . . . $900 . . . couldn't find your work number . . . ran home to call you!"

Walking in Williamsburg, Marta had seen an agent post a flier for a one-bedroom apartment. As Marta talked to him, another woman hurried up. He showed them the place; it was small but bright. The other woman ran off to get her checkbook, and Marta raced home to call me.

"I can run over right now and give him a check," she panted. "Just say the word."

"Can I go see it?"

"No. That girl is probably already back there. You have to decide now."

When I called, the agent said another women had given him a check. I could come look, but I shouldn't hold out hope.

The tenement sat a block from the Williamsburg Bridge, beside a lot full of rusting cars. The apartment was tiny. Its lights were fluorescent. Its floorboards were partly rotted. On the living room wall was a giant pasted-on paper sunset, half torn off. There was a bathroom, but no sink in it. There was a claw-foot tub, but it had only one foot. There were no closets. I stood in the living room and thought: I am 33 years old, and this is what it's come down to.

"It'll be completely renovated," said the agent, a young hipster who lived in the building. "The landlord did mine beautifully. Want to see it?" We inspected his gleaming kitchen tiles, granite counter tops and new wooden cabinets, then trooped back to the first apartment, where a black plastic rosary was draped over the kitchen sink.

I wrote a check to hold my spot. An hour later, the broker called: "I have very good news. The girl who gave us the check, she has bad credit, so she doesn't get the apartment." I had passed the credit test. I was to bring in six months of bank statements. I was to bring in my last year's tax forms. I was to pay three months' rent, plus 15 percent on the year, totaling $4,320.

My stomach pitched. My first impulse was to ask for more time. But how many times had I delayed and lost something? Cash the check, I told him.

That night I dreamed the bedroom was large and had closets. The living room had wood-framed windows on three sides, looking out onto English gardens. In another dream the street outside my new apartment was narrow and tree-lined, with sun-baked steps. I would put geraniums along them.

"Can you dance in it?" my mother asked.

I'm just wondering if I can do sit-ups in it.

I laid down a tape measure. Living room: 12 x 10. Bedroom: 7 x 12. Kitchen: 17 x 5. A total of 289 square feet. But fully renovated.

A dream: The renovations were done. But floorboards were missing. Underneath were dark caverns and rats but also an undiscovered closet containing the missing bathroom sink, plus a pole on which to hang my clothes. A friend tells me his grandmother, who lived in a tiny Bronx apartment, "dreamed often of opening her linen closet and stepping into a paradise of clean, well-lighted space." Asking around, I find this dream is a recurring one for most women I know. Only we had thought that by the time we were grandmothers, or mothers, we would have our paradises.

A call from the broker: the renovations are done, the place is ready.

An e-mail from my editors: "We are all having a little trouble wrapping our minds around the concept of a 289-sq-foot apt w/ a separate bedroom AND an eat-in kitchen."

I am exotic. People are awed by me, although they would never want to be me. I am a soldier on crutches in wartime.

•

The night before I moved, I said goodbye to the doorman. He was shocked. Why would you leave, he asked. You always pay your rent. Then, in a low voice, he said only a third of the building's tenants actually paid theirs: "Every month the marshal comes. I'm here, I see it. People owe $15,000, $18,000, $30,000. They move in, they move out. Only the millionaires can afford $4,500 a month."

In one one-bedroom, he told me, six girls sleep in triple bunk beds. Some people move every six months from one luxury building to the next, never paying a cent. "Every night they come in drunk, they go out dancing," he said. "But these people, they don't pay for three, four months. Then they get evicted."

The next morning the movers loaded me up and drove me across the bridge. The broker, whose office was on the ground floor of my new building, handed me keys and said, "Enjoy."

I skipped upstairs, unlocked the door, and froze.

There were no kitchen counters, no wooden cabinets, no tiled floor. There were gaping holes in the walls. The stained linoleum floor curled up at the edges. A cockroach lay smashed on the stove. The movers stacked my boxes along the walls and waved goodbye; they didn't notice my silent, desperate pleas to take me with them.

Downstairs, the broker shook his head and clicked his tongue. "The agent had no right to promise you those things," he said. "The reason the landlord fixed up his apartment like that was because it was a disaster." But the landlord is a reasonable man, he assured me. "He'll be right over."

The landlord arrived. I listed everything I was promised. He began to bargain. "If I put down new linoleum, will you pay $100 more a month? If I give you a cabinet, will you pay $50 more?"

"What about the holes in the wall?" He looked at the two-foot gap behind the toilet. "My men can't reach that," he said.

"Rats could come through there," I said. "And cockroaches."

"No cockroaches. I have exterminators."

"There's a roach in the bathtub."

He stooped over, suddenly squinting like an old man. "Where? I don't see anything."

A workman appeared at the door and handed him a cigarette. He straightened up and lighted it.

"I want my money back," I said.

"When will you leave?"

"In the next two days," I replied firmly, although, my boyfriend having moved to California and my having given up my space on Astor Place, I had no idea where I'd go.

He shrugged and flicked his ash into my sink. I walked to a friend's house and fell into her arms, crying.

•

In the following days, as I returned to the apartment to retrieve clothes and argue with the brokers about getting my money back, I saw other shocked tenants complaining about unfulfilled promises. I stood silently as they showed my apartment to unsuspecting clients, fearing that if I said anything they could accuse me of scaring people off and keep my money. My friend Nika generously cleared out a room for my things; her roommate left for a month and gave me her bed. I was lucky; still, it took a week to recover and another week to start thinking about my next step.

Then I got a call. A friend had seen someone post a flier for a $1,000 apartment in Williamsburg. I walked dutifully over in the rain. The current tenant, a woman in paint-splattered pants, led me into an industrial building and opened the door to a loft more vast than any room from my dreams.

"There are problems," she was saying. 'That's a concrete factory outside. Every morning from 7 a.m. to 2 p.m. there's this loud rumbling. The windows don't open, and you'll have to buy your own stove."

As if in a dream, I wrote out the checks. She told me to come by the next day to sign the lease. She did not ask about my income or my savings. The next day she handed me the lease, the keys and a note from the landlord that said, "Welcome to the studio."

But no New York housing story ends smoothly. Two days later, the radio woke me. "Thousands of tenants in trendy sections of Brooklyn could be evicted from their lofts after a Fire Department report identified illegal conversions in Williamsburg, Dumbo and other areas." Some tenants had already been evicted, carrying their television sets out into the night rain.

My loft was on one of the city's lists, a fact I took in with the equanimity of one who has already seen it all. Then came the news that most of the listed places would not be evacuated. I took that in calmly, too, and decided to move in on Jan. 1 no matter what.

For the first time since I moved to New York, I don't envy anyone's apartment. It's a strange feeling. Friends tell me I deserve it, that the fates owed this to me after all I went through. But I know that's not so. Real estate in New York has nothing to do with what you deserve. It is a rolling sea. People are dropped in, and some find what they want right away. Others never do. The rest of us bob around on the surface, pushed up and pulled under at intervals, always keeping our faith in that lucky wave that will come along and carry us to the next port.

December 31, 2000

A writer in the city. (Carin and David Riley/The New York Times)

15

The Town That Gags Its Writers

The Buzz and Banter of New York, a Novelist Argues, Can Make It Hard to Hear Your Own Voice. Try Gainesville.

DAVID LEAVITT

RECENTLY one of my students at the University of Florida wrote a story about a young writer who lives at 895 NE 107th Street in New York City. It goes without saying that this student had never been to New York. In her story, the hero, an aspiring novelist, rents a charmingly rundown flat in Manhattan, has an interesting if low-paying job and spends much of his time sitting in coffeehouses with his friends, talking about literature and philosophy.

After I read the story, I asked my student to come and see me. I wanted to set her straight on a number of points, not the least of them how New York addresses work, but I also wanted to offer her a dose of reality—if possible, without injuring any fragile illusions on which her education might depend. After all, I had once nurtured fantasies not unlike her own. In 1983 I moved to New York to be a writer in New York, found myself an overpriced and uncharmingly run-down flat, and got a job as a slush reader for a publisher. And New York, in a matter of weeks, managed to destroy entirely the idealism that had brought me there.

Herewith another version of the story, the one I told my student.

In this version, as in the original, the fictional hero is a fledgling novelist. I shall call him Paul, after the novelist played by George Peppard in the movie "Breakfast at Tiffany's," and also after the glamour-besotted hero of Willa Cather's story "Paul's Case."

Paul, my Paul, moves to Manhattan straight out of college to hone his craft. To make a living, he takes a job in publishing. Many of the people with whom he works turn out to be writers as well, so almost instantly he finds himself living, as he had hoped he would, in a community of fellow aspirants. They eat many meals together.

On weekends they sit in coffeehouses, sipping lattes and tea, and sometimes talking about literature. Yet more often, because they work in publishing, they talk about publishing. They talk about money. They talk about X, 23 and fresh out of the Columbia M.F.A. program, who has just gotten a six-figure advance for her first novel. Is it true that X's agent included a Marion Ettlinger head shot with her manuscript when he sent it out? Is it true . . . ? Is it true . . . ?

One evening a friend of Paul's, also a writer (but published), takes him to a book party. There he is introduced to numerous agents and editors, including X's, most of whom look over his shoulder while they talk to him, their eyes on the door through which someone more important might be about to enter. By and large the editors are smooth-talking and urbane, yet more than a few are wallflowers, lacking, it seems, in even the most basic social skills.

As for the agents, one gives him her card and suggests that he call her. He does. Her assistant tells him that she is in a meeting. He calls again a week later, and she is still in a meeting. She is in a meeting for the next six months. Another agent tells him that if he hasn't made it by this point, he never will. A third insists that he must cement his reputation with a collection of short stories before he can even hope to publish a novel. A fourth tells him that short stories don't sell, and that he shouldn't even bother writing them.

Paul shares a chunk of his manuscript with an editor at the house where he works. She expresses guarded enthusiasm and asks to see more. Before he has a chance to show her anything, however, she takes another job. Her replacement, finding his pages in a file drawer, and not yet having learned his name, sends him a form rejection letter. Paul is too shy to explain that the pages were his.

•

He buys a season ticket to the reading series at the 92nd Street Y, and never goes once. He subscribes to The New Yorker, The New York Review of Books and Publisher's Weekly, the last of which he reads more avidly than either of the others, especially the advance reviews and the rights column, from which he learns that X has now sold the foreign rights to her book in 15 countries, that Redbook has bought first serial rights, and that two studios are vying to option one of her short stories. X is now rich; he sees her at another party, surrounded by admirers, wearing a Hermès scarf.

In the evenings, when he is not eating with his friends, Paul attends panels on publishing issues sponsored by the Authors Guild or PEN. After a panel called "Asian Writers: New Voices," he worries that because he is white, he will never find a publisher. After a panel called "Women Writers: New Voices," he worries that because he is male, he will never find a publisher. After a panel called "Gay Writers: New Voices," he worries that because he is heterosexual, he will never find a publisher.

A friend of his (who is also my friend, Mark Mitchell) has told him: "In New York, I worry about other people's work. Away from New York, I worry about mine." On strolls through bookstores, Paul memorizes the logos of the most famous publishers—dogs, dolphins, ships— and learns by heart whose books they grace and whose they do not.

X's novel comes out. It is a flop. On the other hand, the buzz about another first novel, this one by Y, could not be more enthusiastic. Although Y was not paid a six-figure advance, The New Yorker is bringing out his first chapter. Elizabeth Hardwick, Renata Adler and Susan Sontag have all given him blurbs. When Y's novel appears, it is featured on the front page of The New York Times Book Review.

Having read the review, Paul looks in despair at the manuscript of his own unfinished novel, which could not differ more, either in tone or content, from Y's. Has he made a dreadful mistake? Should he start again? On the other hand, when he actually sits down to read Y's novel, the reading of it takes him so far from the chatter surrounding its publication that upon finishing, he has trouble coming to. For Y, despite everything, is the real thing, a writer.

Still, a consciousness of the industry (and all that word implies) ferments just on the other side of the glossy jacket. Paul knows from friends with inside information that Y's novel will have its debut at No. 7 on the New York Times best-seller list, that Y is to be the subject of a profile in New York, that someone is thinking of composing an opera based on his book.

So it goes. All around Paul, the media make noise, in many ways louder than that of the traffic outside his window. Among other things, it tells him that he must learn to sell himself, a labor that takes him every day further from his computer, and deeper into the churning chaos of the market.

•

In her wonderfully satirical story "Levitation," Cynthia Ozick gives us a couple, both novelists, called Feingold and Lucy. Feingold, in addition to writing, works as an editor. The one principle on which he and his wife agree is "the importance of never writing about writers," which they call "The Forbidden Thing." Eventually "The Forbidden Thing" is transformed into "The Forbidden City, because not only were they (but Lucy especially) tempted to write—solipsistically, narcissistically, tediously, and without common appeal—about writers, but more narrowly yet, about writers in New York."

As Paul, like Feingold and Lucy, is a fictional character, let us introduce him to them at a Sunday afternoon brunch whose host is Feingold's agent. Seeing something of themselves in Paul, themselves in youth, they take him under their common wing. They introduce him around. They offer him detailed editorial advice. Theirs is a city, in Ozick's words, full of people who live on "pity, and therefore on gossip . . . who had lost three successive jobs, who was in danger of being fired, which agent's prestige had fallen, who could not get her second novel published, who was persona non grata at this or that magazine . . . who was being snubbed, who counted or did not count."

The Feingolds joke that they are "secondary-level people."

"Feingold had a secondary-level job with a secondary-level house. Lucy's own publisher was secondary-level; even the address was on Second Avenue." Theirs may even be the "secondary city" of which George Steiner writes in "Real Presences," when he calls for the sweeping away of the very ephemera, the "high gossip" with its "tenor of busy vacancy" that the Feingolds personify. At night, Paul begins to dream about bombs dropping on publishing parties, wiping out every source of his anxiety.

Sometimes he wonders if he should leave. Should he leave? The truth is, after only a few months, he finds it hard to imagine living anywhere else besides Manhattan. Once he could have. But since then the island seems to have ruined him for life elsewhere. For six months, he realizes, he has not crossed either river even once. He recalls Woody Allen in "Annie Hall," driving in a daze through Beverly Hills at Christmas. To the rest of the world, even to his hometown and the town where he went to college, he has become allergic.

On weekends, when he wakes up in the morning, the first thing he does is pick up the phone to call one of his friends. "Any news?" he asks. If the refrain sounds familiar, it is because it is one of the catch phrases from E. F. Benson's Mapp and Lucia novels: New York City has become, for Paul, as hermetic, as provincial, as Benson's Tilling-by-the-Sea.

•

Paul loses his apartment, which he is subletting illegally. The landlord finds him out, and the woman from whom he is renting, in a panic, evicts him. He has to find another apartment quickly, and as he refuses categorically to move to Brooklyn or Queens, he ends up on the Lower East Side, in a sixth-floor walk-up, paying close to $1,000 a month for one room. He must ask for help from his parents to make his rent.

He becomes acutely conscious of real estate. In one of the design magazines to which he turns when he wants to relax, he sees a spread of X's new loft in SoHo. Y, he hears, has just bought a floor-through in a converted church in Greenwich Village. The parties he goes to seem always to take place in palatial Upper East Side duplexes full of high ceilings and views.

In an effort to make himself feel better, he tries to remember that in living as he does he is following in a long tradition. After all, from "La Bohème" onward, literature and opera and cinema have exalted the idea of the young writer starving in a garret.

And yet in the old days being poor in New York was easier, because New York was cheap. It's hard to lose yourself in the fog of art when you can't afford an air-conditioner, and the erratic thrum of a jackhammer rises up from the street. Through the thin walls comes the sound of techno played too loudly. Babies and sirens cry.

At a party Paul meets a novelist he has long admired. "When I'm working," she tells him, "I can disappear into my study and not come out . . . for days." As it happens, this novelist is married to a stockbroker, and lives on Central Park West. How enviously Paul envisions her study, its walls upholstered in some quieting damask fabric, its capacious oak desk overlooking the park.

•

Where does this story end? What will happen to Paul? His fate, I'm sorry to say, is uncertain. Perhaps he will publish a novel and have a great New York success, be voted into the American Academy, and win the Pulitzer

Prize. Or perhaps he will get a promotion and become a powerful editor who snubs young supplicants at parties. Or perhaps he will lose his job and be forced, by economic necessity, to leave New York.

This last outcome, in my view, would be the most salutary. For once he gets out of New York (and in Paul's case he would have to be dragged kicking and screaming), he may discover, in the sudden quiet, that he can hear his own voice. No matter what the Feingolds of the world may say, writing itself is the thing that really counts.

Let's move him to Gainesville, Fla., where I write now. Let's put him in a decent apartment that rents for $500 a month. Is he happier? There aren't nearly so many movies to choose among, nor is the local independent bookstore as well stocked as the Strand. Yet the street on which he lives is tranquil and tree-lined, and if he drives a few miles, he can swim in a lake.

My purpose in telling this story is not to discourage young writers from developing the business acumen, or the instinct for fashion, or even the shell of self-protective irony that writers need in order to survive and that they have needed since the age of Dickens. These muscles matter, yet something about New York teaches us to tone them, to flex them at the expense of others that matter more: imagination and craft.

In New York we live surrounded by monoliths, institutions both vast and self-sustaining that must convince us of our dependency on them in order to survive. Thus the myth persists in the publishing industry that publishers create writers, and not the other way around, that dog or dolphin on the spine of a book will make what he writes literature. Yet the truth is that only writers can make literature. The whole massive enterprise rests on the scrawny shoulders of novices like Paul.

If he is to learn this lesson, though—which is really the lesson of his own power—he will first have to get out of New York.

February 18, 2001

16

Rockaway Idyll

Eight in a Bungalow, $250 Each, for a Summer of Stars and Waves.

FIELD MALONEY

The author, seated in doorway, with friends. (Fred R. Conrad/The New York Times)

▎RIDE the A train out from Manhattan to my summer bungalow in
the Rockaways. Crossing Jamaica Bay, I get a little lightheaded. The
subway car, which has been chugging along over the bay, plunges downward with a jerk, as if it's headed straight for the bottom. Then abruptly,
almost at the waterline, the car seems to skim right across the top of the
waves. It's as if a gust of wind could swirl up and tip it over. Hitting open
water in a crowded New York City subway car is one of the strangest
satisfactions of metropolitan life.

This summer, with four men and three women, I rented a summer
share in Rockaway Beach, Queens. We work together at a magazine in
the city, and don't make a lot of money. We had found our own beach
house for only $250 apiece for the whole summer, and we felt wildly
lucky. All I knew about the Rockaways was that it was at the far end of
a subway line, on the ocean, and that there was a punk song that went:

> The sun is out and I want some
> It's not hard, not far to reach
> Rock rock Rockaway Beach
> Rock rock Rockaway Beach.

At dusk the night before Memorial Day, I packed up my surfboard in
its shiny silver case, ducked down into the subway and headed out with
two housemates to the Rockaways for the first time. My companions: a
tough-nerved editorial assistant and a fact checker who claims to have
body-surfed 6,758 waves.

Our bungalow sat off Beach 101st Street, in an alley where two rows
of cabins were squeezed together like roosting hens. It was two blocks
from the ocean, three blocks from a sewage treatment plant, and not
much bigger than some people's tool sheds. At the turn of the century,
this land was part of a giant open-air colony where for $300 a family
could rent a tent for the summer. The bungalows were built right before
World War I in Gravesend, Brooklyn, to house Army officers, and then
hauled to the Rockaways by barge.

Since the 1940's, more than 100 of the bungalows were used as private residences in a community called the Marcellus Colony. In 1985, 17
of them united as the Seashell Gardens Association. Ours was chipped,
tattered, flaked and windbeaten, but otherwise much the same as when it
was built.

In the front was a narrow, screened-in porch carpeted with AstroTurf. Inside was a daybed covered by a madras bedspread, a kitchen table with a brown plastic tablecloth, and, in back, two bedrooms, separated from each other by paper-thin, head-high wood partitions. Strings dangled from bare light bulbs that had been fastened to the pine rafters. Synthetic Irish lace curtains hung primly in the windows.

The bathroom was the size of a phone booth. On the wall was a sign. In faded 50's typescript, it listed the rules of the house and concluded: "Remember This Is Your Home for the Summer. Be Proud of It."

The bungalow, which had been meant for a small family, felt crowded with just the three of us. A plane taking off from Kennedy Airport roared past, so low that the house shook. A lanky 13-year-old strolled by the porch like a pasha, a brown python draped around his neck, a twittering pack of younger boys in his wake. Soon we heard barks and shrieks. The boys had decided it would be fun for the snake to meet the neighborhood pit bull. We sank into mattresses that sagged on broken springs; our beds felt as if they might swallow us whole.

"It's pretty small," the fact checker said. "Yes," came the reply from across the partition. "Small."

•

The Rockaways are a sandy strip of barrier beach at the southern shore of Brooklyn and Queens. In the 19th century, Rockaway boomed as a summer resort, with many hotels, both the fancy and the flophouse variety, along with bathhouses, saloons, amusement parks and brothels. New Yorkers came in droves until World War II, after which Rockaway began a long, slow decline from which it still hasn't emerged.

The number of summer renters shrunk drastically. These days most Rockawayans, even the bungalow dwellers, live there year round. The famed Boardwalk that stretches along six miles of shoreline and has the middling honor of being the world's second-longest, behind Atlantic City, now runs past drab high-rise apartment complexes, housing projects, acres of overgrown vacant lots and faded pastel buildings: hourly hotels, halfway houses and nursing homes (80 percent of Queens nursing homes are in Rockaway).

There are still some shiny, affluent neighborhoods on Rockaway's West End, but much of the peninsula has a wistful, bleached-out quality —gritty and definitely urban—that has the desolate beauty of an early Bruce Springsteen song.

When I mention my "summer share in the Rockaways" to Manhattanites, I get several types of responses: the scrutinizing, eyebrow-raised glance that means, "You're joking, right?"; blank incomprehension: "Where? There's an ocean there?"; and the knowing reminiscence that usually begins with something like, "Back in high school" and continues to, "Ah, Rosalita in the two-piece at the disco beach with that snake tattoo you know where" and takes another 20 minutes to finish. A man who'd spent his youth in Rockaway said, "You'd better not turn it into another Williamsburg."

When I mentioned my bungalow at an Upper East Side dinner party, the hostess instructed me not to refer to my summer plans too loudly in good company. I did not tell her the cream of New York society used to go out to Rockaway. In the mid-19th century, Vanderbilts, Astors, even Henry Wadsworth Longfellow stayed at the Marine Pavilion, Rockaway's first grand oceanfront hotel.

Back then, elaborately dressed women clambered into beachside cabins to change; at a signal, pack horses towed the cabins out into the water so the women could discreetly float out into the surf. After the Civil War, large numbers of Irish immigrants came out to escape hot tenements, and when some of them got rich, they took over the old WASP summer strongholds. Far Rockaway became known as the Irish Riviera.

I began going to Rockaway alone, on some weeknights when the house was empty. I had grown up on a farm in rural Massachusetts where the rhythm of summer days was marked by alternations of physical work and breaks to swim in the cold river down the road, and in Rockaway, I returned to that. I'd drop my bag at the cabin, put on my trunks and go to the water, waving to the boys in the alley. (They'd found a new pastime, climbing onto the roof of a shed at a nearby sweater factory and hurling themselves into thick piles of garbage bags filled with yarn.)

Usually it was dark or nearly dark when I swam, and the onrushing surf would lapse in and out of focus. I couldn't see the lines of waves so well, and all of a sudden I'd be surprised by a big one right in front of me. I'd float in the surf on my back, looking toward the shore. The street lights that lined the Boardwalk ribboned across the shoreline like the dotted yellow lines on a highway. Afterward I'd sit, sopping wet, in the empty lifeguard chair and eat my dinner.

The bungalow had no phone, so on the way home I sometimes stopped at the phone booth on the corner to call my girlfriend, who had begun to accuse me of loving Rockaway more than I loved her. The phone booth was near the New Irish Circle, a popular Irish bar, and as I held the receiver, still sopping wet in my flip-flops and a towel, streams of girls dressed for a night out would pass by, leaving a summer trail of hair spray, laughter and perfume.

•

We decided to have a big Fourth of July party in Rockaway. It rained. We sat on a concrete wall in the Beach Channel High School parking lot and looked across Jamaica Bay toward Manhattan, waiting for the Macy's fireworks. All we could see was fog and darkness and the outline of the Marine Parkway Bridge. There were one or two small flashes of light across the bay.

"There they are!" someone said.

"No, that's Brooklyn," a middle-aged couple corrected him.

Finally, we watched a guy wave a sparkler around for awhile. Don Henley's "Boys of Summer" blared from an open Trans-Am parked behind us. A police car came and told us all to leave.

We didn't end up having to do the car-with-30-clowns trick very often; rarely did more than four people sleep in the bungalow at once. One housemate, a rocker girl who commuted to work from her parents' house in New Jersey, made it out to the bungalow only twice. Another housemate, a Lower East Sider with a domesticizing touch, on her first visit neatly set out a pair of tiny rainbow flip-flops; hung up in the closet an 80's concert T-shirt and a pair of plaid flannel pj's; and put on the shelf in the bathroom a small bottle of shampoo and a toothbrush. She never came back, and everything is still where she put it.

But a bunch of us came out at least once every weekend. The fact checker became enamored of the pretty girls at the New Irish Circle and was always searching for excuses to head out there, especially on Thursday nights: D.J. Hip Hop Healy's Top 40 dance party.

Another housemate, a born and bred Manhattanite, was reunited on the Rockaway Boardwalk with a long-lost childhood love, Whalcamena, the giant gray and aquamarine stucco whale that he used to clamber over as a boy in the Central Park Zoo and that has beached on Beach 95th Street and is now in better shape than it was back then. (Animal activists note that the Central Park seal statue is also alive and well, up the Board-walk from Whaleamena.) The Rockaways, which might complain about being a dumping ground for public housing, bad Robert Moses projects and methadone clinics, also seem to be a dumping ground for silly Man-hattan sculpture. Even a painted cow from the recent Cow Parade stands on Beach 110th Street, its head half severed from its neck.

You would think that with young tenants, hot summer nights and moonlit waves, our bungalow would have been a hotbed of romance. But the walls were so thin that any coupling would have been public coupling.

●

At first glance, Rockaway Beach seems to be like any other public beach, just one long strip of sand with people on it. But the natural segregations of city life seem to follow New Yorkers when they get off the A train or the No. 53 bus from Queens.

On the beach, I asked a few of Rockaway's Sunday sociologists to ex-plain. Public beaches here are tribal, they said. In the 1980's, Beach 116th and 117th was the heavy metal beach. (Tattooed guys, bikers, Ozzy Osbourne T-shirts.) Now it's the Brazilian section. (Are those things really bikinis?) Beach 108th, the Italian section, was called Disco Beach because of the "Italian boogie freaks."

Beach 98th Street belongs mostly to Puerto Ricans, who hold all-day picnics in the slatted shade under the Boardwalk. Ninetieth is the surfer territory. Surfers cluster out in the waves, their bare heads and black wet suits poking out of the water, making them look like packs of seals. Fur-ther down are the Russians.

It's all pretty simple, a Rockaway man with a silvered walrus mus-tache told me: "If you see little kids in underpants, it's a Puerto Rican beach. If you see grown men in their underpants, it's the Russian beach."

If the Rockaway Beach is a series of ethnic fiefs, the lifeguards are still the lords. They sit on their wooden towers and survey their domains in bright orange body suits (or if it's really hot, just a bathing suit). One day, I saw a woman carried out to sea by a riptide. The beach was packed and had that lazily anarchic quality found when hundreds of barely clothed men, women and children are all trying to be leisurely at once.

Everything froze as four guards dashed across the sand carrying life preservers. A heavyset woman with long black hair was far out in the break, waving her hands. It was amazing to see the jaded lassitude that the lifeguards maintain so well on their towers snap so suddenly into pure focus. One after another, they dove into the surf and took hard knife strokes through the waves. In a second, they had formed a ring around the woman and hauled her to shore.

"I just grabbed her," a lifeguard with freckles and a crew cut told me. (The lassitude had quickly returned.) "The bad thing is when you go in and break your shades. Put that in the paper."

Further down the beach that day, I saw a man in a blue zebra-print Speedo chase after a large seagull. He tackled the squawking bird, wrested it to the ground and pried open its beak. Out popped a yellow parakeet. The man, whose name was Robert, was from Howard Beach, and the bird was his pet, Peggy Sue. He has two others.

"Hey, they get warmed up like you and me," he said. "That's why we go to the beach. They like to go frolic in the water. I teach them to swim in the bathtub."

•

I woke up one morning in Manhattan to find the Rockaways plastered across the front page of all the newspapers. Three teenage girls had drowned in the surf off Far Rockaway, a few miles down the shore from our bungalow. An hour before the lifeguards came on duty, they had been sucked out to sea by a nasty riptide.

The night after the drowning, I got out of work late and went out to the Rockaways with two housemates. It was one of those desperately humid August nights that ushered in the heat wave—and we went swimming. The moon was almost full, and it lit up the beach like a giant street lamp.

There were no lifeguards, of course, and swimming was prohibited. I had expected the beach to be empty. But two men swam right next to us and then sat on the sand staring out at the ocean. People were having picnics, salsa blared out of boomboxes. I passed by the dark silhouette of a couple making love in a lifeguard tower. I never again saw the beach so busy at night. At 2 o'clock, it still hadn't emptied out.

A few weekends ago we had a big party. Streams of people moved between the beach, the porch and the kitchen table. We played football on the sand at midnight. We swam, even though it was the weekend of squid eggs—translucent, gelatinous things that littered the surf—and it was like swimming in wet tapioca pudding.

That night we slept seven: two to each single bed, one in the daybed and one on the floor. I put a sheet on my silver surfboard cover, set it on the porch AstroTurf and slept very well.

And another thing. We're not leaving on Labor Day. We've extended our lease for another month and will stay in our bungalow through September. Maybe even longer. October and November are hurricane season, and the waves get really big.

September 2, 2001

17

Waiting to Exhale

In a Town of Towers and Tight Spaces, Claustrophobics Yearn to Breathe Free.

KATHERINE MARSH

The crowds at Macy's. (Nancy Siesel/The New York Times)

L AST winter I moved into a new apartment on the sixth floor of an elevator building in Brooklyn Heights. Everything was perfect except for one problem. The first time I stepped inside the small, musty, wood-paneled elevator, I instantly felt like a character from an Edgar Allan Poe story, buried alive. My fingers grew clammy, my chest began to tighten, and I started to flush. Suddenly even my clothes felt constrictive, and with shaky hands, I ripped off my sweater. As the door started to slide shut, I lunged out of the elevator, to the hallway and to freedom.

New York is a horrible place for a claustrophobe. It's a city of ambition, of verticality, of literal as well as symbolic height, and to make it to the top, you must first squeeze yourself into a series of small spaces: studio apartments, rush-hour subway trains, elevators, office cubicles. I've been living in this city and working my way up as a reporter for three years now, and in order to cope, I end up climbing a lot of stairs. When traveling, I leave myself extra time to get off one subway train and wait for a less crowded one. I bow out of all social engagements that involve being packed en masse into an elevator and sent skyward.

Some months ago, I finally decided to do something about my claustrophobia. Perhaps it was those six flights of stairs I climbed every day to my apartment. Or the sense of shame I felt when I concocted excuses about why I needed to get off the No. 4 train several stops early ("I need the exercise"). Or perhaps it was just the paradox of absolutely loving New York but hating the congestion that made it New York. It felt like a doomed love affair, like hopelessly falling for someone charming and larger than life who also makes you unhappy.

It was time to undergo a New York rite of passage and, for the first time in my life, to see a shrink. A friend referred me to Harvey Baker, a professor of psychology at Queens College who had successfully treated New Yorkers with fears of water bugs, rats and even math. I would be his first claustrophobe.

He treated his phobics with something called the Emotional Freedom Technique, a combination of acupressure, affirmations and behavioral therapy. Among his greatest accomplishments was curing a man who had a fear of having his neck touched.

"He wouldn't even let his wife touch his neck," Dr. Baker remarked during our initial consultation. "Though remarkably they did produce two children."

I wasn't really sure what the guy's neck had to do with that, but after Dr. Baker described the miraculous effects of the Emotional Freedom Technique, I decided to give it a try. With his corona of white hair, ample waist and LensCrafters case peeking out of the pocket of his Oxford shirt, Dr. Baker had a soothing, grandfatherly presence. There, in his comforting academic lair, we worked on conquering my claustrophobia.

•

No one knows what causes claustrophobia, though there is some evidence that it is genetic. (This holds up in my case, since my father and grandfather are slightly claustrophobic as well.) According to Dr. Michael Liebowitz, director of the Anxiety Disorders Clinic at the New York State Psychiatric Institute in Upper Manhattan, most claustrophobes suffer from panic disorder. Although between 1.5 percent and 2 percent of the adult population is afflicted with panic disorder, there are no hard numbers on how many also exhibit claustrophobia.

In many ways, claustrophobia is a disease of New York, or at least of the modern city. The term, which comes from the Greek "claustrum," meaning fence or barrier, first appeared in medical literature in 1870's Paris, when Dr. Benjamin Ball described two patients who couldn't remain in their apartments when the doors were closed.

According to Anthony Vidler, a U.C.L.A. professor of art history and architecture and the author of "Warped Space: Art, Architecture and Anxiety in Modern Culture," Parisians and later residents of other urban centers started attributing their nervous ailments to their environment, because the mid- to late 19th century was a time of rapid and unsettling change.

"Between 1853 and 1867, Paris underwent a vast transformation," Professor Vidler said. "Big boulevards were added. The new living quarters of the new middle class were in multistory buildings with lots of doors. There were a lot of physical changes for people to pin their fears to. By 1914, when Freud came along, there were over 200 phobias listed in the psychoanalytic dictionary."

After making its debut in Europe, claustrophobia immigrated to the New World at the turn of the 20th century, first appearing in the medical literature in Boston in 1898 and showing up in a case study in New York in 1915. Like Paris, New York had been undergoing jarring physical changes. In 1857, the first passenger elevator was introduced at the Haughwout Building on lower Broadway. In the 1870's and 1880's, as demand for central locations increased, so did the value of Manhattan real estate.

In response, architects took advantage of new technologies, first internal metal supports and later steel-cage construction, to build increasingly tall structures. By the 1890's, New York was shooting up into a gangly city of skyscrapers and boom-time ambition.

New Yorkers were also tunneling down. In October 1904, the first subway opened, attracting huge crowds, and, inadvertently, the first subway claustrophobe. Described by The New York Times in an account of the subway's opening day as a "gray-haired gentleman who, in the rush for tickets, was carried along in the current," he was overheard telling a policeman: "I didn't mean to come down here. The crowd brought me with them. I want to get out. I'm timid."

By 1900, there were almost 1,000 people per acre living in some sections of the Lower East Side, and by 1910, Manhattan reached its peak population of 2.3 million, compared with 1.5 million now. In 1930, the subway carried almost twice the number of riders that it does now.

"The cars had only incandescent lighting," said Peter Derrick, an archivist at the Bronx Historical Society and the author of "Tunneling to the Future: The Story of the Great Subway Expansion That Saved New York." "There was also no air-conditioning till the mid-70's, a big factor in terms of claustrophobia."

As New Yorkers built the subway, they explored the subterranean corners not only of the city but also of the psyche. In March 1912, a 27-year-old Irish-American subway engineer went to see Dr. C. P. Oberndorf, an Upper West Side neurologist, complaining of claustrophobia so severe that he had quit his job because he could no longer enter the subway shaft. He had suffered his first attack of claustrophobia three years earlier while watching vaudeville at the American Theater.

The patient, New York's first official claustrophobe, lived at home with his family, trying to avoid commitment with his girlfriend (one Miss B.) and questioning his sexuality. He spent most of his days sleeping late and wondering what to do with his life.

In his 1915 case study, Dr. Oberndorf, a devout Freudian, thoroughly analyzed the young engineer's childhood sexual exploits, finally attributing his claustrophobia to his fears of impotence and commitment. After being told this, the patient decided to embrace chastity, and apparently felt much better. "Since his discharge as cured in March 1913," Dr.

Oberndorf concluded proudly, "he has been working steadily and contentedly far underground in the subway shaft."

•

Not quite ready to go the chastity route myself, I instead took the F train to Queens and had sessions with Dr. Baker, preferably at midday to avoid the rush-hour crowds. After discussing my elevator or subway experiences of the previous week, he would ask me to envision a claustrophobic situation and rate my anxiety level from 1 to 10. Then we would launch into the Emotional Freedom Technique, a therapy not of talk but of tap. (Behavioral therapy is orthodox treatment for phobias, but acupressure is not, though he is not the only therapist who uses it.)

As I repeated a Stuart Smiley–like affirmation of claustrophobic self-acceptance, I would mimic Dr. Baker as he tapped himself on various acupuncture points from head to hands. At first it seemed pretty silly, but by the third round, I usually could lower my score on the anxiety scale.

However, it was one thing to tap and shout affirmations in Dr. Baker's office, and another to do this in the subway. I was particularly concerned about one part of the Emotional Freedom Technique that called for a "Me Tarzan, you Jane" type of chest-beating motion. "No one will notice," Dr. Baker replied when I worried aloud about how fellow straphangers would respond to my attempts to assert emotional freedom.

Fear of embarrassment is a big part of the anxiety of claustrophobia. One of my own embarrassing moments occurred when, riding an elevator with a source for an article I was writing, I felt compelled to get out several floors short of the lobby because it got too crowded. In an attempt to save face, I mumbled something about having once been stuck in an elevator.

"Many people feel a sense of personal defeat," said Dr. Carol Lindemann, an Upper East Side psychologist, "and are embarrassed that they are less than perfect."

This is particularly true in an environment like New York. The city is full of self-conscious high achievers who strive to appear as confident and fearless as New York itself. Claustrophobia, which involves both the fear of being unable to escape the crowd and the feeling of being painfully self-aware and isolated by one's own limitations, has become the predominant metaphor of postwar art.

From Walker Evans's series of photographs of subway riders, "Many Are Called," to Reginald Marsh's haunted urban landscapes to the neurotic antiheroes played by Woody Allen, artists have tried to capture the claustrophobe in all of us.

Mr. Allen, who has described himself as a "world-renowned claustrophobe," is the avatar of the postwar New York claustrophobe, someone who loves the city and yet who finds, and creatively needs to find, that what he loves is constricting. In one of the funnier scenes in his 1993 film "Manhattan Murder Mystery," the director's alter ego, Larry, has a panic attack in a jammed elevator and tries to mentally escape to the countryside: "I'm running over a field! I see open meadows! I see a stallion! I am a stallion!"

In the latter part of the last century, New Yorkers actually began to welcome congestion. "In the 1960's, people began to say crowds are a good thing; they make the streets safe and vibrant," said Kenneth Jackson, a historian at Columbia University and president of the New-York Historical Society. Although New Yorkers, living on a small island, will always have a fetish for space, Professor Jackson notes that there is now more residential square footage per person than ever before.

"People find New York City exciting because of the crowds," he said. "I'm claustrophobic; if a subway comes and it's really crowded, I wait for the next one. But as someone who is terrified of being limited, I love the freedom of New York, of having a hundred galleries in a mile, of being able to walk to Lincoln Center in your pajamas."

William Shawn, the legendary editor of The New Yorker, also loved this city, even though it challenged him as a claustrophobe. According to his colleague Lillian Ross, author of a memoir about their life together, Mr. Shawn had a special arrangement so that he could take the elevator up to his New Yorker office alone.

"He didn't like being confined with strangers," she remembered, adding that he also avoided subways, never flew and would get out of a cab in the middle of Central Park rather then feel trapped in traffic. "But," Ms. Ross added, "I don't want to paint a picture of him as this trembly, nervous, sweaty figure."

Still, there are plenty of trembly, nervous, sweaty figures among us. Carol Lindemann, the Upper East Side psychologist, says that she has treated hundreds, including one patient who was forced to abandon his business because he felt claustrophobic driving over a bridge to Manhattan in heavy traffic. Barbara Milrod, another Manhattan psychologist, says she has treated patients who would rather walk up 25 flights of stairs than set foot in an elevator. One of Dr. Michael Liebowitz's patients walked from West 79th Street to Washington Heights rather than get on the subway.

Most claustrophobes follow their own individualized set of rules for what situations they can tolerate and which they must avoid. Part of the shame of being claustrophobic in New York is the feeling that in this most hard-headed and sophisticated of cities, you alone are following a ritualized and not quite rational code of behavior.

"Muggers, no problem; an Otis elevator, forget about it," said one New Yorker who works in law enforcement and has kept her claustrophobia hidden from friends and co-workers for a decade. "I have to take elevators for work, and each time, it's like jumping in a pool and holding my breath. One doctor I went to said, 'Maybe you should switch jobs.' But to me that's a cop-out."

•

Claustrophobes who live here are adept at finding ways to accommodate and even manage their claustrophobia. Typical is Mike Garofalo, a computer repair expert in Midtown, whom I met when we were both unhappily riding down on the small elevator in his office building.

"Can you believe this thing can actually fit 11 people?" he said, pointing to the sign that claustrophobes always check declaring the elevator's maximum capacity. Mr. Garofalo leaves his home in Bensonhurst, Brooklyn, at 6:30 a.m. to beat the claustrophobic morning rush on the subway, and gets off the elevator if more than three other people enter.

Andrew Skidmore of Chelsea worked on a submarine but would rather walk 40 blocks than take the New York subway. "The submarine was tight and constricting," he said, "but at least your head wasn't in someone else's armpit."

Robert Slagle, a creative director at a weekly newspaper magazine, travels the city with a flashlight, a hand-held fan, a Powerbar and a bottle of water in case he runs into a claustrophobic situation. "For me, it really is an urban jungle out there," said Mr. Slagle, who says he has felt claustrophobic on subways, trains, buses, elevators and even, on some nights, on the island of Manhattan, where he lives.

The Emotional Freedom Technique was making my own expeditions through the urban jungle a little less stressful, but after several sessions, I still didn't feel comfortable enough to take the elevator in my building. On my fourth session, I confessed my disappointment to Dr. Baker.

"If a man takes little baby steps all the way to Manhattan, he'll go slow but he'll make it," he replied. I tried hard to look encouraged.

Then later that session, I had a breakthrough. Dr. Baker and I had been talking about my job, one that involves travel and is thus particularly demanding on a claustrophobe. "Why did you choose this job and this city, knowing that you have this fear?" Dr. Baker asked.

It was a logical question, one that I often asked myself. But this time, I knew the answer. It was the feeling of excitement I felt each time I managed to take an elevator or a crowded subway, each time I went on assignment in the urban jungle.

Often, things didn't work out exactly as I'd hoped—I'd take the stairs, or the longer, harder route—but I liked the feeling that the city wasn't going to make it easy for me. The fight made me feel alive, even free.

Dr. Baker listened carefully and then said, "Perhaps you don't want to give up this fear?"

Perhaps, I thought, I didn't.

A part of me still wanted to be cured, to be normal, to be in love with New York in a less complicated way. But as I took the F train back to my apartment in Brooklyn and to the six flights of stairs I knew I would climb, I had one of those New York moments—even claustrophobes have them—when your own little corner of the city opens up.

January 27, 2002

18

A "Law and Order" Addict Tells All

The TV Series Is a Hit Around the Country.
But Its Heart Beats to a New York Rhythm,
for Us and Us Alone.

MOLLY HASKELL

Filming "Law and Order" on West 17th Street. (Nicole Bengiveno/The New York Times)

WALKING up Madison Avenue through the usual thicket of cell-phones, I heard my first interesting snatch of conversation since that accursed invention forced an avalanche of inanities on our ears. A woman was saying: "He's a bastard. Justified homicide." She didn't have to mention the quality of the food on Rikers Island for me to know she was one of us, the not-so-secret addicts of "Law and Order," Dick Wolf's long-running, ubiquitously syndicated, hydra-headed NBC series about New York cops and district attorneys. I know it's a hit of major proportions around the country, too. Its ratings are phenomenal. Like Woody Allen, it travels better than you'd think.

But its heart beats to a New York rhythm, its in-jokes and phony addresses and familiar locations are for us and us alone. These days, with its spinoffs and reruns, the show has become something of a joke itself, risking critical contumely and self-parody by spreading like an oil slick into every unoccupied slot on television. But the miracle is that it hasn't worn out its welcome, and the spinoffs have developed distinct and different virtues of their own. If anything, like an old friend, like New York itself, "Law and Order" has grown more precious since Sept. 11.

Familiar stories (the Mayflower Madam, Lisa Steinberg); locations from Chinatown and the Battery to the quadrangle of a certain well-known uptown university (bordered by the Low Memorial Library and Butler Library); working-class cops and D.A.'s with their own baggage and biases; a story with a beginning, middle and end: all have become, since the terrorist tragedy, as much consolation as diversion.

The standard and often justified criticism of long-running shows is that they begin to try too hard, recycle material, make disastrous cast changes. Of those cast changes "Law and Order" can certainly be accused: How could they kill Claire? How could they get rid of Jamie for the fashion-plate Angie? I still miss George Dzundza, and some of the new D.A. babes look as if they spent more time on their hair than their law books. But I'm amazed at the health of the basic organism, how it survives and adapts not only to weaker cast members but also to the changing times and moods of the city itself. It seems to me the number of convictions on the show rose during the Giuliani years, for example, as exasperation with judges throwing out evidence and perps getting off on technicalities reached critical mass.

On the other hand, the show remains marvelously evenhanded. The sheer quantity, the multiplicity of shows, allows for a roughly equal distribution of venality over time. Good and bad apples are to be found among whites and blacks, Asians and Hispanics, cops and robbers, thus avoiding the deadening hand of political correctness.

In its 12-year history, and as it roams with egalitarian fervor into every area of the city, showing how intertwined different ethnic groups and neighborhoods are, "Law and Order" has rubbed up against a remarkably complex range of social issues: from capital punishment (a harrowing show in which Sam Waterston's D.A. is forced to watch the execution of a criminal his office had prosecuted) and biotechnology (is a dead man's widow entitled to his ex-wife's frozen embryos as part of the estate?) to constant badgering and second-guessing from the media, and ever-present issues of class and race. (Should blacks be accorded more lenient treatment after years of inequity, or is that a more pernicious form of racism, damaging to both blacks and the law?) And there's the vexing question of how we temper the either-or edicts of criminal law with a more nuanced appreciation of the enormous (but incalculable) influence of environment and genes.

•

All of these thorny matters, plus the often questionable tactics of the law enforcers themselves (deals and lies and subterfuges for the greater good), constitute pressures that bend and sway the law so that its determinations are never completely clean or bias-free. Yet for all the question marks it leaves, and however queasy the aftertaste, its conclusions are never open-ended. There is a thin line between outright corruption and necessary compromises, but there is a line, and it is faithfully maintained. And there's a consolation in watching our city, its institutions and protectors survive, battered but intact, week after week.

Especially welcome after the real-life cataclysm that robbed us of many of our finest and bravest, "Law and Order" remains a testimonial to the teamwork and no-nonsense valor of the cop on the beat. Long before 9/11 shifted our perceptions in that direction, the show had been chipping away at the stereotype of the bad cop, humanizing the men and women in blue.

Central to that process and to the proletarian soul of the show has been Jerry Orbach's divorced detective with a hard-drinking past, Lennie Briscoe, the 27th Precinct's maestro of the reality-check wisecrack that zaps the pretensions and fads of the upper-crust celebrity-plutocracy of New York. Managing the complex tone of black humor in the face of horror, he surveys bodies lying in an East Village boutique and when told it's a "vintage" clothing shop, says, "Oh, yeah, I think I recognized my old bowling shirt." When told a perp smokes high-end cigars, he remarks, "They're hard to find since Demi Moore and the beautiful people started smoking them."

The show is a time capsule, reminding us of a time when the worst things that happened were individual crimes with (mostly) single vics: a Park Avenue philanderer found in a pool of blood, or a black dope pusher wrongfully arrested for murder, or an S-and-M artiste hanging by his leather belt, or a ranting homicidal psychopath, suddenly back on his meds, turning into a slick legal mind who can mount his own defense.

Even the show's more lurid siblings—"Special Victims Unit" (which deals with sex crimes) and "Criminal Intent" (in which a Columbo-like Vincent D'Onofrio uses guile and brainpower to seduce a villain into self-exposure)—are not so harrowing that they keep you up at night. The original classic is, for some people I know, the cup of Ovaltine that, with reassuring predictability, tucks them in at night. One couple falls asleep, like clockwork, just before Sam Waterston or Steven Hill (the pre–Dianne Wiest D.A.) has closed the office door with yet another rueful aperçu. They're on the late-night rerun track, whereas my husband and I are on the early-bird cocktail-hour shift, on A&E at 7, or at least we were until recently, when the 7 p.m. reruns moved to 6, and we followed.

•

For those of us who are hopelessly hooked, the symbiosis with "Law and Order" begins with its physical presence on this corner or that, turning iconic and less well-known quarters of the city into a New York set. As it reaches into all areas of the city, from the barrio to the boardroom, from prisons to institutes of higher learning, the show restores New York's rightful place as capital of glamour and grit at a time Hollywood has abandoned us for Toronto, that cheaper, cleaner but ersatz "New York."

The New York of "Law and Order" may be as much a myth as the skylines and dance floors and Park Avenue apartments that starred in an earlier, more rhapsodic vision of the city. But its myth is modern, multi-ethnic, capacious in its reach, and startlingly close, something you can reach out and touch. Many's the time I've stumbled onto a shooting and felt as if I were living inside it, like "The Truman Show."

Likewise when watching an episode with particular geographical resonance. Like the scene in "Criminal Intent" in which the art dealer perp is
standing in front of the Church of the Heavenly Rest (where my husband
and I were married) with the Guggenheim Museum (right around the corner from our apartment) in the background, complaining about the vacu-
ity of the museum's motorcycle show. Or the "Law and Order" episode
in which the highbrow suspect (a New York variant of the Unabomber,
Ted Kaczynski) provides his alibi: at the time in question, he was, he
says, at the Metropolitan Museum, listening to the free chamber music
on Friday night, "one of the few civilized things left in this city."

Then at a more advanced level of addiction, the show is a member of
the family. It is a ritual woven into our lives as "their stories" become
ours, a mirror that not only reflects matters of civic concern, that packs a
wallop as a crime show and is wittier than most (streetwise suspects with
"priors" know the angles and how to deal better than any law student),
but also serves as a template in which we vicariously act out and perhaps
exorcise little conflicts of our own.

When in a group the subject comes up, we shriek with delight at dis-
covering fellow hard-core fans. The first question is, When did you first
turn on? The conversation becomes more sheepishly confessional. Which
show(s) and how often? Time(s) of day? Do you have a limit on repeats
of any particular episode? How long until you recognize it?

We compare notes on how the show insinuates itself into our lives,
creating a whole set of games and guilty rituals that vary from person to
person, couple to couple. My husband and I have established ground
rules: only one a day. Watch no episode more than three times. One of
the few benefits of growing old and dim, I remind my friends, is that
we'll all be able to watch "Law and Order" over and over again without
remembering if we've seen it.

For us, the evening begins with the Dragnet-like opening: "There are
two separate and equal . . . These are their stories." Then the teaser precredit sequence: cops in a patrol car stopping at a deli for coffee, their
kvetching rudely interrupted by a gunshot. Two black women walk into
a pawn shop to find its owner dead on the floor. A husband and wife
arguing—in a car, on the sidewalk, in the garage— when suddenly they
stumble over a corpse. In the precredit sequence, husbands and wives are
always arguing, presaging the connubial carnage to come.

I remember the sequence vividly, but not what follows, since the opening is a deliberate feint, setting you up for one kind of tragedy before zigzagging in a whole other direction. My husband, who has total recall for movies, has none for the opening scenes of each episode of "Law and Order" and will insist that we've never seen a particular show. I counter that not only have we seen it, but we've seen it more than the allowed three times. A dispute ensues, as difficult to adjudicate as some of the conflicts on "Law and Order." Will we watch it again until his memory clicks in (by which time we're already into the courtroom, too late to start another) or will we go ahead and put on one of the "Law and Order" tapes we keep in reserve?

We love the episodes in which husbands or wives kill each other. They allow us to express all sorts of murderous feelings vicariously and playfully. We pretend (heh, heh) to pick up tips and ideas, using the jargon of the show. The efficiency of various weapons and methods, alibis, and so on, we've got it all figured out, even how we'll play it when arrested.

Bail, for instance. My husband, though perhaps not an upstanding member of the community (his fondness for the prone position works against that), is such a known homebody, so averse to travel of any kind, that the idea that he might pose a "flight risk" would have the judge falling off the bench. On the other hand, that same clinging to the hearth will limit the freedom of movement and location that provides plausible alibis. An "accident" in a car or private plane, indeed one that involves extensive locomotion of any kind, is out of the question. But my husband does teach at Columbia. Does the student employment office offer hit men as well as bartenders?

Bonding with the show means that you feel its sorrows as your own. The departure of a beloved cast member can be traumatic. The stories themselves can break your hearts: parents, of both the victims and the perpetrators, who lose their children, to death, to drugs, to crime, to lovelessness and missed communication.

Even more wrenching are the rare eruptions of grief from the regulars. Who can forget the scene in which Lennie sits in wordless companionship with an old friend, a cop recently exposed for corruption, on the small patio of the friend's house in Queens? Or when Mike Logan visits his wounded partner, at the hospital, and offers desperate words of cheer, trying to reassure him—and himself—that he'll be back on the street in no time. I could be dead. I could be wounded. I could be crooked. I could have gone down in a river of booze. But here I am. So goes the unsung threnody, the there-but-for-the-grace-of-God lament, that runs through the show, imbuing it with a magisterial tone of dignity.

Over and over it is brought home to us, at the end of each episode, that whatever small triumph has been achieved, it's just a drop in the bucket. We're holding fast for now, but tomorrow's another day when we might prove less resistant to temptation, might finally slip across that thin line between the urge to kill or steal or betray or take a little on the side and actually enjoy doing it.

April 7, 2002

Rush hour at Times Square. (Nancy Siesel/The New York Times)

19

Look Away

The Unwritten Law of Survival in the Teeming City.

SIRI HUSTVEDT

N rural Minnesota, where I grew up, it was the custom to greet every-one you met on the road, whether you knew the person or not, with a "hi." A muttered, uninflected "hi" was entirely acceptable, but the word had to be spoken. Passing someone in silence wasn't only rude, it could also lead to accusations of snobbery, the worst possible sin in my small corner of the egalitarian state.

When I moved to New York in 1978, I discovered what it meant to live among hordes of strangers and how impractical and unsound it would be to greet all of them. Within days, I absorbed the unwritten code of survival in this town, a convention communicated silently but forcefully. This simple law, one nearly every New Yorker subscribes to whenever possible, is: pretend it isn't happening.

This widely applied coping technique is what separates New Yorkers from tourists, and seasoned citizens from those who have just come here. An Iranian friend told me that about a week after he arrived in the city, he was traveling on the Second Avenue bus. At 24th Street, the door opened for a woman who was wearing nothing but a flimsy bathrobe over her naked body. When she reached the top step, she started feeling her pockets for something, and then, with a shocked look on her face, exclaimed: "My token! My token! Oh, my God, I must have left it in the other bathrobe!"

The driver sighed and waved her onto the bus. My friend had been staring at the woman, but was a little ashamed when he realized that no-body else had given the woman a first glance, much less a second.

In October of last year, I was on the F train when I noticed a wild-eyed man enter the car. He boomed out a few verses from Revelations,

135

and then, in an equally loud voice, began his sermon, informing us that Sept. 11 had been God's just punishment for our sins. I could feel the cold, stiff resistance to his words among the passengers, but not a single one of us turned to look at him.

A couple of weeks ago, after seeing a play at the Brooklyn Academy of Music, my husband and I walked down the stairs at the Atlantic Avenue Station to wait for the No. 2 train. I wanted to sit and noticed a single bench with several empty seats. At the end of that bench sat a man with five or six plastic bags, and although he was perhaps 20 yards away, I did sense that he might be someone to avoid because even at that distance he gave off an aura of silent hostility.

Nevertheless, fortified by the presence of my husband, I led the way to the bench. We seated ourselves at its far end, leaving four empty seats between us and the man. After a minute, he gathered up his bags, shuffled past us and spit in our direction. His aim wasn't good, but when I looked down, I saw a gleaming microdot of saliva on the knee of my pants. We let it go.

These three stories—the bathrobe lady, the fanatical preacher and the spitter—show a range of increasingly outrageous behavior that may be dealt with through the pretend-it-isn't-happening law. And yet, as my husband pointed out, in the case of the spitter, had there been more saliva on me, he would have felt forced to act. And acting, as everyone in the city knows, can be dangerous. It is usually better to treat the unpredictable among us as ghosts, wandering phantoms who play out their lonely narratives for an audience that appears to be deaf, dumb and blind.

Taking action may be viewed as courageous or merely stupid, depending on your point of view. A number of years ago, my husband witnessed a memorable exchange on a subway going to Pennsylvania Station. A very tall black man entered the car with a woman dressed in short shorts and high vinyl boots. The woman found a place to sit and immediately nodded off. The man, who was weaving a bit on his feet, took out a cigarette and lighted it. Within seconds of that infraction, a little white guy with blond hair, probably in his late 20's, wearing a beige trench coat buttoned up to his neck, politely demurred. "Excuse me, sir, for bothering you," he said, in a voice obviously formed somewhere in the Midwest, "but I want to point out that it's against the law to smoke on the subway." The tall man looked down at his interlocutor, sized him up, paused, and then, in deep mellifluous tones, uttered: "Do you wanna die?"

Most New York stories would have ended there, but not this one. No, the short fellow admitted, he did not want to die, but neither had he finished what he had to say. He persisted, calmly defending the law and its demonstrable rightness. The big man continued puffing on his cigarette as he eyed his opponent with growing amusement. The train stopped. It was time for the smoker to leave, but before he made his exit, he turned to the indefatigable little Midwesterner, nodded, and said, "Have a good Dale Carnegie."

•

That story ended well and with wit, but it carries no moral insight into when to act and when not to act. There are moments, however, when a smile or a well-timed comment may change the course of what might otherwise be a sorry event.

For the last year and a half, my 15-year-old daughter has been refining the blank expression that accompanies the Pretend Law, because she spends a couple of hours each day on the subway going to and from school. With her Walkman securely over her ears, she feigns deafness when the inevitable stray character comes along and attempts a pickup.

She told me that one day, she found herself sitting across from "a white guy in his 30's" who stared at her so shamelessly that she felt uncomfortable and was relieved when the man finally left the car. But before the train pulled out of the station, the ogler threw himself against the window and began to pound on the glass. "I love you!" he yelled. "I love you! You're the most beautiful girl I've ever seen in my life."

Deeply embarrassed, Sophie didn't move. Her fellow passengers treated the man as if he were an invisible mute. But as the train began to rumble forward, leaving the histrionic troubadour behind, the man sitting next to her looked up from his newspaper and said in a deadpan voice, "It looks like you have an admirer."

By breaking the code, the man acknowledged himself as a witness to what, despite the pretense, had been a very public outburst. His understatement not only defined the comedy inherent in the scene, but it also lifted my daughter out of the solitary misery that comes from being the object of unwanted attention among strangers who collectively participate in a game of erasure. With those few words, and at no cost to himself, he gave her what she needed—a feeling of ordinary human solidarity.

The truth is that whatever we might pretend not to see or hear or sometimes smell, most of us actually see, hear and smell a lot. Behind the mask of oblivion lies alertness (or exhaustion from having to be so alert). Daydreaming on a country road is one thing. Daydreaming on Fifth Avenue with hundreds of other people striding down the same sidewalk is quite another. But because we are so crowded here, active recognition of other people has become mostly a matter of choice. Even so, compliments, insults, banter, smiles and genuine conversations among strangers are part of the city's noise, its stimulus, its charm. To live in strict accordance to the Pretend Law all the time would be unbearably dull.

For us urbanites, there is a delight that comes from thinking on our feet, from sizing up situations and making the decision to act or not to act. Most of the time, we insulate ourselves out of necessity, but once in a while we break through to one another and discover unexpected depths of intelligence or heart or just plain sweetness. Whenever that happens, I am reminded of a truth: everyone has an inner life that is as large and complex and rich as my own.

Sometimes a brief exchange with a stranger marks you forever, not because it is profound, but because it is uncommonly vivid. More than 20 years ago, I saw a man sprawled on the sidewalk at Broadway and 105th Street. Unshaven, filthy and ragged, he lay on his side in an apparent stupor, clutching a bottle in a torn and wrinkled paper bag. As I walked past, he suddenly propped himself up, and called out: "Hey, beautiful! Want to have dinner with me?"

His question was so loud, so direct, that I stopped. Looking down at the man at my feet, I said, "Thank you so much for the invitation, but I'm busy tonight."

Without a moment's hesitation, he grinned up at me, lifted the bottle in a mock toast and said, "Lunch?"

December 8, 2002

20

On the Run

New York, Fast Paced and Deeply Social,
Taught Him to Love to Smoke. Now the City
Has Changed Its Mind and Demands
That He Do the Same.

D E N N Y   L E E

The author, lighting up. (Joyce Dopkeen/The New York Times)

POETS have compared the cigarette to a lover. They say it fires up the senses and unleashes a forbidden pleasure, like an alluring but dangerous mistress.

I tend to think of a cigarette more as a trusty friend. It is the first thing that touches my lips in the morning and, very often, the last thing at night. In between, smoking keeps me jolted throughout the day, and enables me to indulge in moments of reflection. My cigarettes are always there, next to the computer and phone, whether I'm distracted or focused like a laser.

But cigarettes are best enjoyed with others, like marshmallows around a campfire. To offer someone a smoke is to invite him into your circle. To light a cigarette is to signal the start of an intimate chat. To extinguish a cigarette is to reach a fork in the conversation, an occasion to continue or turn back.

Every smoker knows that cigarettes are not healthy, but then again, neither, often, is drinking. And when the two meet, it is an exhilarating mixture that underscores why so many smoke only after a drink or two. The ritual of lighting up, like the act of toasting, is a time-honored garnish for civilized cocktails. They go together like gin and tonic.

A cigarette is a drinking buddy who never leaves your side, even when you're standing by yourself. That is why, on the eve of Mayor Bloomberg's smoking ban, it felt as if a close friend were leaving forever. It was March 29, it was raining, and it was a Saturday night, when taxis are normally scarce and the bar crowds grow thick with working stiffs and suburban visitors. I just wanted to stay home and curl up with my ashtrays.

But social obligations beckoned. I found myself at Sea, a cavernous Thai restaurant and bar in Williamsburg, Brooklyn, that features a reflecting pool and a plywood D.J. booth. We finished dinner at 11 p.m., an hour before the ban would propel law-abiding smokers like myself onto the cold and rainy sidewalk. It would be a historic moment. I imagined someone snatching away Dorothy Parker's gin at the dawn of Prohibition.

Still, I could not stay at Sea. The city that had nurtured my habit, that had taught me the thrills of smoking, was about to be transformed into something like Cleveland or, worse, Los Angeles. I hopped into a taxi and went home to the West Village.

A friend from Los Angeles, who smokes only when I visit, had sent me an e-mail. "I sincerely hope you're out there, taking your last drags," she wrote. "Or will this compel you to quit?"

Unlike many smokers, I have never tried to quit, despite the new ban and despite the cigarette tax imposed last July that pushed the price of a pack to nearly $8. My only nod to not smoking is a half-empty box of Nicorette gum in my medicine cabinet, which I bought expressly for trans-Atlantic flights.

I replied to my friend's e-mail: "I'm determined to flout the law at every possible opportunity."

For the first two weeks of the ban, that was what I set out to do. On average, I find myself at bars two or three times a week. I'm lucky to squeeze four around my dinner table, so, as for many New Yorkers, bars are an extension of my apartment.

But despite my plan for defiance, and without realizing it, I avoided the bars like ex-lovers. Sure, I was curious how the ban was playing out. Would bar owners find creative ways to bypass it? Would smokers ignore it? I suppose it was denial. Instead of heading to the neighborhood bar, I went to my corner liquor store and invited friends over for cocktails—and cigarettes. Confronting the new ban was not my idea of fun. "I heard a lot of people say that," said a friend, Jack, who owns a couple of East Village bars. "They just didn't want to deal."

•

The cold wind blew on my virgin outing into the smokeless city. It was the middle of the week and I was meeting friends at Passerby, a stylish bar attached to the Gavin Brown Enterprise gallery in Chelsea. Of the four of us, three were smokers.

It was like walking into a gay bar for the first time: a familiar scene that is slightly, disconcertingly different. About 10 patrons were seated along a hard bench. A D.J. was spinning a mix of garage and techno beats. A bartender stood behind the wooden bar. Then finally, I noticed the new blue-on-white sign behind him. "This is a smoke-free environment," it read. It reminded me of one of those generic airline safety cards.

Still, I held out hope. The city had announced a month-long grace period before bars were fined over the ban. But as I looked around, there was nary an ashtray or cigarette in sight. My heart sank. I felt as if I were back at the high school dance, under the watchful eye of chaperones.

I approached the bar warily. I am friendly with the bartender, but now he stood before me like the enemy, the first line of defense in the city's war against my smoking enjoyment.

The antagonism was probably mutual. The no-smoking signs mention the city's 311 complaint line and the Web site of the city's Department of Health, so that patrons can report sightings of secondhand smoke. Every customer, including myself, was now a potential snitch.

I ordered vodka on the rocks and slumped in the corner. The atmosphere in here was never too smoky, but tonight there wasn't a trace of cigarettes. The air seemed so clean, so featureless, so thoroughly unlike a bar. If I didn't want a cigarette before, I wanted one now.

We left after one drink and smoked en route to our next stop: a nearby restaurant and lounge with a European outlook, which is to say, a smoker-friendly reputation. The 50's Modernist dining room was empty at 10 p.m., save for one table occupied by a handful of people, including the actor Danny Aiello.

We settled into a corner booth and lighted our cigarettes. Within minutes, the maître d', a fellow dressed head to toe in black, rushed over with an ashtray and ordered us to extinguish. But there was no one here except for Mr. Aiello, we pleaded, and he did not seem to mind. The maître d' was unmoved.

We muttered Bloomberg's name under our breath and carried on. Then, like a gift from the heavens, an ashtray magically appeared with our third round of drinks. The manager, I suspect, had assumed that the nicotine police would be in bed by 11 p.m.

For a moment, we sat and puffed away in silence. I can't remember the last time a smoke tasted so good. A fresh cigarette has hints of sweet plum and walnut, mixed with a bit of spice. The first drag scorches the throat, like a shot of strong Italian espresso; later ones mellow into a nutty, milky plume.

To my dismay, that restaurant was the exception, aside from a few "smoke-easies" that quietly cropped up around town. During an ambling tour of two dozen bars in Downtown Manhattan and Williamsburg during the grace period, most were in compliance. "No smoking" signs were taped to the wall. Ashtrays were removed. Bartenders watched vigilantly.

I had predicted the opposite, that most bars would test the limits of the ban, at least until the grace period ended. The odds were certainly in smokers' favor: a dozen city inspectors versus several thousand establishments. It would be like finding a butt in a haystack. But most bar owners I chatted with said they did not want to be flagged for repeat visits.

Meanwhile, the ban had put smokers on the defensive. Although the city had said that smokers themselves would not be punished (despite legislation that allows for $100 fines), few wanted to antagonize their favorite watering holes, or risk the wrath of sanctimonious nonsmokers. By the time the fines kicked in on May 1, New York night life was firmly under the control of nonsmokers.

It would be one thing if bar owners were given the right to forbid smoking on their premises. But the ban prohibits smoking in every bar, leaving no room for choice.

As a native New Yorker, I feel a certain ownership of the city. But the gritty city I grew up in, where dark pockets beckoned and boundaries were constantly pushed, is feeling more and more suburban in temperament.

•

My life as a smoker began during my junior year at Stuyvesant High School, when it was located in a dilapidated building on East 15th Street. It was the mid-80's, and bars and dance clubs back then never carded us at the door, even though we were clearly under age. If we were caught in the streets drinking a beer, the police would tell us to pour it out and send us on our merry way.

Not only could we smoke in movie theaters, alongside the sultry stars on screen, but we smoked in school, behind the thick auditorium curtains. The teacher who oversaw the stage productions could not have missed the butts strewn on the floor, but he must have figured we were old enough to make our own decisions.

I thought about this a few weeks ago at Lava Gina, a dimly lit salsa bar on Avenue C. I was trying to do my part for the city by going outside for a smoke. But a young woman in a tank top stopped me at the door with her arm, held out like a security checkpoint.

She might have been a bartender or bouncer, but tonight her job was to patrol for troublemakers like me who might wander outside with a cocktail in hand. Before I could explain that it was an oversight, my drink disappeared. I wrote in my notepad, "You can't smoke inside, you can't drink outside."

I found myself on the sidewalk, staring at five other people sucking on cigarettes. Smoking was no longer relaxing, but a source of stress. I was

not savoring my cigarette like a glass of wine that complements a pleas-
ant conversation. I was smoking because I needed one, like a drug. I took
a long drag and wondered if I was missing out on a better party, perhaps
in another city.

Another thought occurred to me. If Mayor Bloomberg was indeed
running City Hall like a private corporation, then the entire city was
turning into one giant cubicled office, where every inch is designed to be
bland and inoffensive and smokers have to take sidewalk breaks.

For smokers, there is a distinct feeling that the walls are closing in.
First, there was the cigarette tax, which make our packs among the
world's most expensive, up there with Norway's. Next, the new ban required us to smoke these costly butts on the street corner, like prosti-
tutes. Now, even sidewalk smoking seems to be under attack. There are
the pedestrians who would be happy to see the city turn into a gated
community for nonsmokers, and a new bill introduced by the mayor that
would increase penalties for outdoor drinking. The fines, currently at
$25, would be raised to a maximum of $150.

Smokers are not going gently into this new city. For the last year, for
example, most smokers I know have been dodging the new tax by buying their cigarettes online—the more resourceful from countries like
Switzerland, where a pack costs about $1.60, including shipping. (By the
way, thanks to the new taxes, I now smoke more because it's cheaper
and there is always a carton lying around the apartment.)

•

Then there are the smoke-easies. Smokers were cautious when the ban
was new, unsure how this unfamiliar law would play out. But now these
places—known mostly to their regulars and determined to keep out
what one bartender called the "nonsmoking riffraff"—seem to be increasing.

One bar, on the Lower East Side, does not display its name on the
door and requires a reservation for a table. With its antique tin ceiling
and unrushed service, it evokes an era when men wore hats and smoking
was a symbol of women's liberation. I happened to be there on a recent
night when a city health inspector was making a routine visit, burdened
with a knapsack full of paperwork. As soon as he walked out, the waiter
brought over an ashtray.

Another place, a restaurant and bar in the West Village, draws its curtains after a certain hour and passes out ashtrays disguised as saucers

along with the drinks. Most of the patrons seem to know the owner, and the place has the feel of a homespun private club.

On Avenue C, a bar that is marked by a blue light over its entrance has turned what looks like a sunroom into a smoke room. On the weekend I visited, there was hardly space to stand. Smokers were camped out on the floor, like junkies in a heroin den. Smoke-easies are also sprouting in Brooklyn and other parts of the city. Some Korean bars in Midtown seem to have given no thought to the ban.

These secret havens are a favorite topic among smokers exiled to the sidewalks from city bars. "Have you been to that spot on Ludlow Street?" "I heard there was a place downtown where police officers go." On the Internet, word of other places is starting to filter out on blogs.

Some smokers are creating their own smoke-easies. On a recent Thursday night, I was at a nightclub near the Holland Tunnel for the opening-night party for a documentary film. A lone smoker lighted up the underground lounge with the strike of a single match. A group of strangers seated across from him broke into applause, soon followed by the flicker of lighters and the orange glow of burning cigarettes. By the end of the evening, the place was lit up like Christmas in May.

June 8, 2003

(John Hendrix)

21

Marriage of Inconvenience?

She Was Living Young and Carefree in the East Village. Then Came the Robbery.

SUKI KIM

THE first time I realized that I must get married, I was standing at J&R, down near City Hall, surrounded by men who were all trying to sell me something. I was looking for a new stereo, a computer, a TV set, a phone. I had been in the store before and had been dutifully confused by the sheer number of choices. But this time, I wanted a way out.

I had been living in the East Village for several years. I was in my mid-20's and not yet afraid of being alone. I imagined myself as a modern-day Holly Golightly, she of "Breakfast at Tiffany's" fame, the sort of girl whom you saw at a party in a pink boa, pinstriped bellbottoms, Mary Jane slippers. I aspired to be the adorable anemic over whom men from Park Avenue to Park Slope swooned. I would have adopted a cat and called it "Cat," had I not been allergic to small furry animals. Then one night, I came home and found my apartment ransacked.

Earlier, I had been having trouble with a novel I was working on. I gulped down my third Diet Coke and stared at the blank computer screen. I even opened the window wide for fresh air, never guessing that a couple of strangers would climb through that very window only a few hours later. Finally I called a friend.

"I need an enthralling conversation," I told him. "You need a drink," he said. We met at a local dive, not for conversation but for pints of the Australian beer Cooper, which had double the alcohol count of regular beer. The night loomed peculiarly silent.

I don't read tarot cards or follow stars over the rainbow. I don't get struck by freak dreams. I don't even like yoga. Yet when we left the bar around 3 a.m., I noticed that we were the only ones on the street.

147

"Strange, no one's out tonight," I said. My friend smiled. "I guess that's enthralling for the East Village." When we stood in front of my sixth-floor walkup, I handed him my key. I wonder why I did that.

"You're really spacey tonight," he said, turning the doorknob. "You didn't even lock the door." I shrugged, although I was sure I had locked it. Then he announced, "You even forgot to close the window."

I had not forgotten; someone else had, the people who had broken in while I was out and stolen virtually everything that wasn't nailed down, from my computer to my jewelry to my Filofax.

The police showed up soon afterward, took notes, and left within five minutes. Their blank faces told me that it would be a miracle if I ever saw my things again.

I stumbled over to my friend's house and collapsed in his bed, like Holly Golightly falling asleep in Fred's arms after escaping from the evil men and sneaking into his bedroom. Except it was the robbers on my fire escape who had snuck into mine; except I did not get away but they did; except I was not falling in love, just getting sadder and poorer.

I spent the next few days ordering window-guard locks, plastic blinds and a door chain. I had no choice but to hire my lecherous super to in-stall each piece. But I needed either a boyfriend or an assistant to help me with the overwhelming number of electronic items I had to replace at once. The friend with whom I had gone drinking on the night of the rob-bery proved useless, since he was the sort of person I saw only at night. He stopped calling me anyway, as did other men whose names had filled my Filofax. I didn't blame them. I wasn't much fun anymore. I wanted someone to look over a warranty or tell me the right number of B.T.U.'s for an air conditioner. I needed someone to accompany me to J&R. More important, I now longed for someone who would not suddenly disappear the way everything else had.

For the first time, I felt alone as a single girl in the big city. The dark truth is that you need a man every time a mouse gets caught in a trap, or a ridiculously tight lid on a jar of tomato sauce won't budge, or the com-puter freezes, or the light bulb on the ceiling needs changing, or a fuse blows. You never admit to it, because as a member of the post-feminist generation, you know you should either manage those chores yourself or at least not rely on the opposite sex for rescue. Especially in a city like New York, women are supposed to be tough and never needy. Besides, who says men are better at getting rid of dead mice than cats are? But I had suddenly been struck by a household crisis, and all I could think of was that I no longer welcomed the role of the sole caretaker.

•

Women marry for all sorts of reasons besides love and respect. Some women won't even date a guy unless he has a college degree and a house in the Hamptons. Some have racial preferences, a height requirement, a scale of good looks. I've known a few women who said yes to some silly guy simply because they panicked when they hit 30. The society pages are full of their stories.

So why not marry for protection? Why not a husband in place of renters' insurance? What is a girl to do when living alone in the city no longer feels fun or safe?

One good thing did come out of all this. My next-door neighbor no longer hated me. Sharon, the 40-something-ex-hippie whose hair is always a shade redder than it was the last time, kept knocking on my door to make sure that I was O.K. Perhaps she felt sorry for me. Perhaps she felt relieved that I wouldn't be bringing home a stream of men or blasting Lauryn Hill until dawn for a while.

I kept trying to restart the chapter of the novel that was stolen. But it didn't flow. The rhythm fell loose. The words lacked spark. I was not used to the silence in my apartment. I missed the blue beam of my old PowerBook. Finally, one night, I chucked the notes, threw on my green velvet jacket and reached in the drawer for my red lipstick. I found nothing; it had been stolen too. Under the Golightly rule, a girl simply cannot do without lipstick. With my face bare more like Eliza Doolittle than Holly Golightly I charged out the door and headed to the corner of Seventh Street and Second Avenue, where boosters crawl out at night with their stolen jewels.

I strolled back and forth as though this were my Tiffany's, looking for that red leather Filofax, that silk box of pearls and diamonds, that last remnant of my past radiance. I could almost hear the tinkling of "Moon River."

June 22, 2003

Puddle jumping in the Bronx. (James Estrin/The New York Times)

22

Rain, Rain, Come Again

When It Pours in the City, There's a Sense of Limited Possibilities. That's Not So Bad.

MEG WOLITZER

THE heat wave this past week made all the recent rain seem as quaint and distant as the Carter administration; but while it was raining, everyone around me was miserable. Call me madcap, but I actually liked all the rain. (Hey, I liked Jimmy Carter, too.) I realize that I'm a member of a freakish minority, and so I've learned to hide my views, just the way people who don't like "The Sopranos" have learned a few catch phrases to get them through chance conversations: "Yeah, Tony really should go back to Dr. Melfi" or "I still can't get over that he whacked Ralphie."

Just the other morning, walking through the vestibule of my apartment building, I ran into a neighbor who was heading out. "Can you believe it?" she asked, shaking her head.

At first, I had no idea of what she was talking about. Had those elusive weapons of mass destruction been found? Had the elevator been fixed? Then I caught sight of my reflection in the mirror, saw my spattering umbrella and my flat but frizzy hair, and I suddenly realized what we'd been talking about: Oh, yeah, right. The rain. That thing that's supposedly ruining all our lives, turning June in New York into any month on the all-water planet of Precipitor.

"I know," I said after a beat, shaking my own head. "It's incredible."

But in truth, I don't think the rain in New York is particularly incredible or unbelievable or, as some people seem to feel, tragic. Above and beyond my lack of incredulity about this marathon of rain lies my actual pleasure in the phenomenon. New York in the rain is an extraordinary place.

Maybe the Korean grocery analogy will help explain why I feel this way: Picture how fresh and beautiful the rows of fruits and vegetables look when they're continuously spritzed from a hose all day. Those

151

wildly overpriced nectarines with dew beads of water clinging to them seem delectable, far more so than the cheaper, nonwet ones in the fluorescence of the Gristede's around the corner.

New York in the rain follows a similar principle. The falling water serves to give the entire landscape a certain allure that it doesn't have when the pavement is dry and the umbrellas are rolled tight in closets. Flowers planted on the meridians of Park Avenue open up and drink, their colors ratcheted up to new brightness. Central Park starts to look pastoral, and the water flooding along the gutters on Fifth Avenue creates a Joycean "rivverrun past Eve and Adam" effect, or, at the very least, a pleasing gurgling noise. The rain is like a cleansing sorbet between courses, those courses being spring and summer.

What I also like about New York in the rain, I'm embarrassed to admit, is not only the aesthetics of it, but the sense of limited possibilities. New York is largely about limitlessness, and that's why we live here, but it can also be exhausting.

When the weather in the city is good, you're expected to partake of all the urban delights available, from picnics in Morningside Park to fusion jazz concerts on a tugboat. Bicycles are meant to be brought out of storage, spontaneous trips taken to the Cloisters. Edible-herb walking tours of Central Park become an option. These are all well and good, and I have actually enjoyed some of these activities in my years as a New Yorker.

However, when the weather is bad and it's not possible to go on that bicycle jaunt or walk across that bridge, you are left within the confines of a sub-city, a smaller, wetter version of New York.

This is a place I know well, and which I love. In the rain, movies become a priority (especially movies in theaters, with popcorn and coming attractions) no matter how bad they may be, or how tired you are of Renee Zellweger. In fair weather, anyone who has ever been a child can still hear their mother shouting: "How can you stay inside today? It's gorgeous out!"

You can also, of course, simply stay home in the rain with no particular plans in mind and no videos in your VCR, except if you have children, and in that case all bets are off. A friend likes to remind me that every time I leave my apartment to go to the post office, I will have spent a vast and unrecoverable fortune in wasted rent money. Essentially, New Yorkers pay so much for their apartments that it is foolish not to be in them all the time. Rain takes care of this problem.

I understand that my arguments may seem unconvincing to those people who feel as though they've been owed more than this spate of spitting weather. June in New York is supposed to be the weather version of a Christmas bonus: after working long hours for such a long time, after slogging through hardships, month after month, you finally catch a break, get sent a reward.

For New Yorkers, that reward comes in the form of sunny, breezy, perfect days, during which the entire city takes on a Mardi Gras atmosphere, minus the vomiting and jambalaya. Various scooters start to appear on the streets, and the Great Lawn starts to look like a love-in from days of yore. Everyone eats lunch outside on a wall.

New York, in sunshine, comes together like one of those cities that sponsors a book club for its citizens, giving them something wonderful and cheerful to talk about: "Bridget Jones's Diary" vs., say, the inclement weather choice, "The Red and the Black."

•

New York in fair weather is indeed a beatific place, ready-made for its close-up, ablaze in painterly light and flowers and helmets and kneepads and loaded picnic baskets from Williams-Sonoma. But New York in the rain can be a more interesting place, whether it's the vision of blurry taxi lights up and down Lexington Avenue at rush hour, the solidarity of being one of many ducking under an awning in a sudden storm with a newspaper over your head, the view of lightning flaring up over Midtown at night, or even the kind of manageable drizzle that isn't quite umbrella-worthy, but also can't quite be ignored.

New Yorkers live through their weather together, as all people in cities must, and circumstances in recent years have given us a greater desire to talk to one another. The rain highlights our frustrations and pleasures, and it sets the details of the city into relief.

When I was a kid, my mother, during a brief and puzzling Joan Baez phase, taught me a song called "What Have They Done to the Rain?" The opening lines went like this: "Just a little rain, falling all around/the grass lifts its head to the heavenly sound/just a little rain, just a little rain/what have they done to the rain?" I loved this song, and would sing it while looking out over our suburban backyard at the rain. It seemed so beautiful, so peaceful. Of course, the song was actually about nuclear fallout, but that's beside the point.

If this weather returns, I may have to come clean. Next time my neighbor stops me, grimly eyeing my frizzy-haired, sopping self and my inside-out new $2 umbrella, and says, "Can you believe it?" I might just say, "Yeah, I know, it's pretty great." Or then again, maybe I'll change the subject to how much I like "The Sopranos."

June 29, 2003

23

The Agony of Victory

The Yankees Have Won 26 World Series Titles and 38 Pennants. The Giants, Knicks, Jets, Rangers—Even the Mets—Win Once in a While, Too. So Why Do New York Fans Whine So Much?

JOE QUEENAN

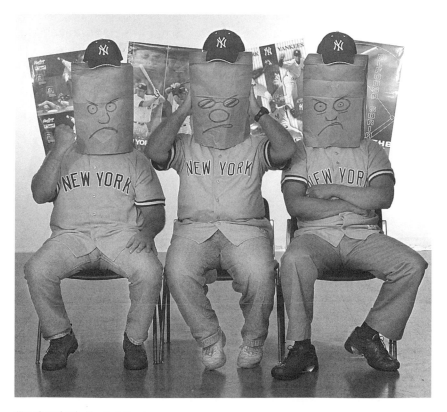

(Tony Cenicola/The New York Times)

L AST fall, I accidentally discovered that New York Yankees fans are
not actually happy. I derived little glee in unearthing this awful
truth, for if Yankees fans are not happy, what hope is there for the rest of
us? Reared in blighted cow towns like Chicago, Boston and Philadelphia,
the average fan drags out his pathetic "three score and ten" dreaming of
a life in a parallel universe where his baseball club wins championships
by the fistful, never having to endure a drought of more than a few seasons.

Longingly, he casts his eyes toward the Bronx and imagines what it
would be like to support a team that has won 26 World Series and 38
league pennants in the past 82 years. And the answer, judging from the
way Yankees fans comport themselves is: Awful.

Like lab rats that will stimulate themselves to death on the pleasure
bar, Yankee fans are so addicted to the thrill of winning that they derive
no joy from the glory of our national pastime. Incapable of understanding that capturing 30 percent of the total championships available is a
statistical anomaly stemming largely, though not entirely, from access to
an enormous hoard of cash, they view any defeat as an unmitigated horror, as a blight on mankind, as an unparalleled tragedy that is simply not
fair.

Worse, the Yankees' absurd success ratio makes it difficult for their
fans to enjoy the exploits of the other New York teams, which win at a
more statistically plausible pace. The football Giants, never dynastic,
occasionally win; the Knicks have not won in recent memory; the Jets
never win (well, once); and the Rangers only win every 54 years, which
seems longer than never. For obvious reasons, not the least of which is
the bafflingly chipper franchise mascot, Mr. Met, the Mets, despite winning the 1969 and 1986 World Series, have become a hopelessly down-
scale franchise that does not fit into this, or any other, discussion.

Emotionally handicapped by supporting a team that almost never
loses, but then turning around and rooting for teams that almost
never win, the average New York sports fan finds himself marooned
in a microcosm that nobody else in the country understands or even
cares about, because nobody else has ever been in that position. New
York fans whining about their sporting disappointments to the vast
American public—poor Don Mattingly never got to play in a World
Series (boo-hoo)—is like Romans whining to the Gauls just because
they once lost a battle to Hannibal. No, it's like Julia Roberts complain-

ing that her teeth are too big. No, it's like a billionaire complaining about his eczema; sorry about the scales, Mr. Big Stuff, but you've still got all that money.

•

I first realized that there was something emotionally impoverished about Yankees fans during last year's World Series when the San Francisco Giants squared off against the traditionally pitiful Anaheim Angels. The West Coast Giants had never won the Fall Classic (their last victory was in 1954 in the Polo Grounds), and the Angels had never even appeared in a World Series.

The last time the Angels got close to the Series, an otherwise stellar relief pitcher named Donnie Moore threw a home run pitch that allowed the Red Sox to erase a three-run deficit and win the 1986 American League pennant. Three years later, Moore killed himself. The '86 Angels were managed by the doomed Gene Mauch, the Captain Ahab whose 1964 Phillies team blew a six-and-a-half-game lead with 12 games to play, breaking the City of Brotherly Love's heart forever. Mine with it. Thus, all the mythological configurations were in place for a truly magical World Series.

It was a rip-roaring set-to, filled with thrills and spills, including a truly Homeric moment when the Giants' skipper, Dusty Baker, spitting in the eye of the Furies, handed pitcher Russ Ortiz the ball as a memento when he left the mound with a 5-0 lead in the seventh inning of Game 6. Alas, the plucky Angels came back to win that game, and obliterated the Giants in Game 7, putting the accursed souvenir in the same category as the ball that squirted through Bosox first sacker Bill Buckner's legs in 1986. It was the kind of series that pitted titans (Barry Bonds, Jeff Kent) against mere mortals (the Angels), the kind of series you could tell your grandchildren about. But you had to watch it to tell them about it.

Sadly, many Yankees fans I know decided to sit this one out, not even deigning to turn on the television. Miffed that their team would not have a chance to win its fifth World Series in seven seasons, devastated that an epochal span of 23 months had gone by without a ticker-tape parade, these malingerers went off and pouted.

This confirmed what I had long suspected: these sorest of losers loved only the Yankees, not the sport. Yet it is the sport itself that unites us as a people: the harking back to our sandlot youth, our first hot dog in the cheap seats, the awesome majesty of the late-afternoon shadows as they steal across the facades of our green cathedrals. I know all this to be true, because I saw the Ken Burns series.

For most Americans, being a sports fan is a matter of processing, analyzing, rationalizing and coping with defeat. It is a question of repeatedly getting slammed to the canvas, but getting back up in the hope that you might land a lucky punch and actually win something. It is the nature of the ordinary sports fan to groan and moan and complain that his team never gets a break.

Though technically Americans, albeit distant cousins emotionally, New Yorkers like to do the same thing, ceaselessly complaining that life is not fair. But the statistical evidence makes their whining seem ignoble.

•

Since I moved from Philadelphia to New York in 1976, the Phillies and 76ers have each won a lone championship, the Flyers and Eagles none. During that period, the 76ers lost four N.B.A. finals, the Phillies two World Series, the Flyers five Stanley Cup finals and the Eagles the only Super Bowl they ever appeared in. Of the last 80 championships in the four major professional sports, teams from Philadelphia do not own a single one. New Yorkers cannot even imagine such misfortune; it's like trying to explain leprosy to a particularly naïve snow fairy.

Other cities have fared even worse. The San Diego Padres have never won a championship, and the Chargers' last championship came when the team still played in the old American Football League. Cleveland has not had a winner since the Browns beat the Colts for the N.F.L. title in 1964, and even that was an upset. Portland has not had a winner since the Trail Blazers beat the 76ers in 1977. There have been no championships in Seattle since the Sonics beat the Bullets in the 1979 N.B.A. finals.

Since 1976, the Yankees have won six World Series and nine pennants, the Mets a World Series and two pennants, the Giants two Super Bowls, and the Rangers a Stanley Cup. If you throw in the three Devils Stanley Cups and the four Islanders championships, 8 of the last 24 Cups have been won by New York teams. True, Rangers fans despise the Islanders and the Devils, refusing to recognize them as authentic New York teams. This is little comfort to fans in Chicago (last Cup, 1961), Toronto (1967) and Boston (1972). Not only do New Yorkers get to win 8 of the last 24 Stanley Cups, but they get to moan about it because seven of them weren't won by the pitiful Rangers.

They do not seem to understand that to the rest of the country, the Devils and Islanders are New York teams, as are the Nets, who appeared in the last two N.B.A. finals. This is because the Nets and Devils, reviled by locals as bogus suburban carpetbaggers, play in an arena (in the Meadowlands) that is actually physically closer to New York than Giants Stadium (also in the Meadowlands), whose gridiron tenants are revered as authentic exponents of the true metropolitan spirit. You can see how the rest of the country could get a bit confused about all this.

Sports fans are united by a sense of a shared common fate. Fans from Philadelphia, Kansas City, Milwaukee, Seattle, San Diego, Buffalo, Minneapolis and even Chicago and Boston all belong, to some extent, to a club of lost souls. The Vikings and Bills have lost all eight Super Bowls they appeared in. St. Louis Cardinals fans never saw their football team appear in a single playoff game. The Lions haven't won an N.F.L. championship since 1957. Yet their fans never give up.

By contrast, Yankees fans sob into their handkerchiefs if the Yanks win fewer than five World Series a decade. There was even talk this spring of axing manager Joe Torre because of the team's slow start. And then they have the nerve to call themselves die-hard fans. This question goes to Mr. Billy Crystal: When's the last time a Yankees fan ever had to die?

It is true that not all New Yorkers are Yankees fans. It is also true that if you grew up rooting for the Mets, Knicks, Rangers and Jets, you might as well have been born in Milwaukee, though the night life isn't as good. But nobody told those fans to make these choices. They could just as easily have rooted for the Yankees, the Devils and the Giants. No one forced them to drink the hemlock.

Sadly, the local news media encourage fans in their delusions. A few months ago a local sportswriter groaned that the five-game, first-round American League Championship Series was unfair to the Yankees because it gave inferior teams with two good starting pitchers a chance to win a short series. O tempora! O mores! Other teams actually had a chance to beat the Yankees once a millennium! Call out the dragoons! Notify the Supreme Court! Get Commissioner Selig on Line 1!

After Yankees fans, nobody in human history whines more than Knicks fans. If Michael Jordan weren't around all those years, they hypothesize, surely the hapless, charm-free Patrick Ewing Knickerbockers would have won at least a few championships. Yes, just like Elgin Baylor, Wilt Chamberlain and Rick Barry would have a ring for every finger

if Bill Russell had never existed, and the Sacramento Kings would be
world champions if Shaquille O'Neal had gone to work for Vanity Fair.

Anyway, what difference does it make if Pat Riley's arrogant, unpleasant Knicks never won a championship? They always acted as if they had.
In the skewed reality of the New York sports world, fans have deluded
themselves into thinking that the scrappy, workmanlike Knicks of the
1970's were mythical titans like the Lakers and Celtics and Sixers of old.
History gets rewritten so quickly in Gotham that a spare part like Bill
Bradley gets his number hoisted to the rafters. Bradley, a star in college
but a mediocrity in the pros, is the worst N.B.A. player to ever have his
number retired.

You can look it up.

•

In the best of all possible worlds, a city spoiled by success would carry
itself with a bit of taste and class. Not this one. I have lost track of the
number of senior citizens I have met who admit that they never once
visited Ebbets Field because as Yankees fans they didn't think it was
worth the trip to watch the Brooklyn Dodgers.

Unlike the millions of true baseball fans who make pilgrimages to
Wrigley Field and Fenway Park to honor those mythical franchises and
the fans who live and die with them, Yankees fans are content to sit in
their Bronx rat trap congratulating themselves on what splendid fellows
they are. Growing up in New York without visiting Ebbets Field is like
growing up in Rome without once visiting the Vatican. Presbyterian or
not.

Last month when the Yankees visited Wrigley for the first time since
1938, the Windy City and most particularly the hotel I was trapped in
were filled with belligerent, juiced-up Yankee fans who had come to see
the Bronx Bombers pound the Cubs into submission. Oh, the gnashing
of teeth and rending of sackcloth when the normally passive Cubbies actually took two out of three from the visitors, and had the temerity to
temporarily deprive Roger Clemens of his 300th career victory! How
cruel! How unfair! Would Zeus not stem this rising tide of injustice? We
came all the way to Illinois and got nothing for our efforts?

Guys, guys, I tried to explain to a couple of mashers in the hotel
lobby, every once in a while the other team has to win a game or two.
Just to make it look good. Honest, it's part of the commissioner's master
plan.

I was coming home from Manhattan in early July the day the Red Sox lost the getaway game of their recent four-game series with the Yankees when I spotted a young Yankees fan standing on the subway platform at 125th Street. A fresh recruit from Front-Runner Central, he was wearing one of those newly minted caps like the one sported by Hillary Rodham Clinton, a woman who spat on the festering corpse of the Democratic Party by rooting for the Republican Yankees. In his hand were two signs: one reading "1918" and the other "Bucky Dent."

The Red Sox had traded away Babe Ruth, they had not won the World Series since 1918, they had been victimized by the most ignominious play in the history of the sport and their greatest player (Ted Williams) had recently died. Twenty-six World Series championships, 38 pennants, and eight decades of domination of the Bosox had not taught this bozo a smidgen of class.

Grizzled football coaches like to tell their players, "When you get to the end zone, act like you've been there before." Yankees fans have been to the end zone 26 times, but they still don't know how to behave. Some people simply can't take "yes" for an answer.

July 20, 2003

Suzanne Vega on West 101st Street. (Joyce Dopkeen/The New York Times)

24

Street Legal, Finally

Married. Divorced. In Your 40's. Life Has Its Stops and Starts. Getting Your Driver's License Is One of Them.

SUZANNE VEGA

EVERYBODY says: "Don't learn to drive in the city. It's crazy." But as the song says, if you can make it here, and so forth.

And I really wanted a driver's license. I was 43, had my learner's permit and had failed the test once already—but that was in Riverhead, on Long Island. I'm an urban girl. This time, I would learn how to drive in the city. My city.

But my quest, like driving in New York (and like life), was full of stops and starts, unexpected dead ends and mysterious spirals (like the streets of Greenwich Village). In the end, my pursuit of the elusive New York State driver's license became about much more than a divorced woman learning to drive for the first time.

I recently moved back to my old neighborhood, near 102nd Street and Broadway, where I lived from 1967 to 1979, and I decided I would learn to drive there. It was strange, rolling down the very roads where I had taken my first small steps away from home. We moved to 102nd Street when I was 7, and I remember crossing Broadway for the first time. It was as big as an ocean. I remember learning to navigate the neighborhood in concentric circles—you can go around the corner to the grocery store to get Daddy's cigarettes, but you can't go across any streets. O.K., you can cross four streets to get to your friend's house, but you can't go down to 96th Street. Eventually, I could walk to school on 97th Street, several blocks from my house.

How weird it was to drive streets I knew so well! What a different perspective! I could rumble down streets I would have been too afraid to walk on, especially as a kid. Now I zipped past everyone, and everyone was a pedestrian. There were lots of them. Big ones, too. I didn't hit any, even the slow ones who took their time strolling through the intersection when I had to turn right.

My first lesson last fall was given by Mr. R., an elderly, gentle Puerto Rican man. I got in the car, an old beat-up Toyota, and started it up. He smiled encouragingly.

"Let's just go forward," he said. "Are you nervous? Don't be nervous. Make a left here."

As I drove, he hummed or sang old Spanish ballads under his breath. From time to time, he talked on his cellphone. I figured I was doing well, since he didn't seem very concerned. At the end of the first lesson, he said: "You are a smart, careful driver. How many lessons did you buy? Ten? At the end you will drive better than me. And you look like a driver!"

I didn't know what to say, but I thanked him.

I liked Mr. R. He never yelled. Here was his method: "What color do you think that light was back there?" he would muse.

"Um, green?" I said hopefully as my mind raced: What light? I saw a stop sign, so I turned left. I didn't see any light.

"It was red," he murmured. "Try not to do that again."

Once, as we zipped along 125th Street right above Columbia University and Barnard College, where I went to school 20 years ago, he said, "You are going to have to merge here."

How did he know this? Did he just feel it in his bones? I asked him. He just smiled.

"Let's do that again," he said. The third time through, I saw the merge sign. "Oh, there's the sign," I said. We did it a fourth time, to make sure I kept seeing the sign.

One day, instead of getting Mr. R., I got Nelson, a short, square-shouldered young man. Hmm, I thought. There had been a Nelson in my first-grade class in East Harlem. That Nelson's name had been Badillo and his birthday was in July, like mine, and his coat hook was next to mine. We were delighted by these discoveries; they seemed significant to us. I remember him saying, "Maybe we'll get married."

Wouldn't it be amazing if it were the same guy?

"How old are you?" I asked the current Nelson.

"Twenty-four," he said.

I am 19 years older than he is. I could be his mother. But the coincidence of his name makes me feel as though I am traveling a spiral, around the same streets but in a different time. Those were the 60's and 70's, when Manhattan looked the way it did in "Shaft" and "Serpico" and "The French Connection." Now it's cleaner, mostly, and there are "Safe Haven" stickers in the stores on Broadway. My daughter, who is 9, has never stood on the sidewalk unattended or crossed a street by herself.

Nelson is different from Mr. R. He is casual, funny, streetwise. He chats with me about Howard Stern, about 9/11, about how much coffee he drinks, the merits of Starbucks over Bustelo. Every time we start a lesson, he wants to be reminded of what problems we are working on.

Parallel parking and observing.

"Oh, yeah."

I learn fast as we sail around all my old neighborhoods. Here is where P.S. 179 used to be, where I was the only one who could read in the second grade. Here is 110th Street, where we had a family friend whose cat's name was Bonnie and Clyde. Here is the Cathedral Church of St. John the Divine, where I once had a midnight picnic. Each street is saturated with emotion, with memory.

One day I get stuck behind a stalled bus. I have to do a real three-point turn into oncoming traffic, fast. Amazingly, I do. I make eye contact with the driver on the opposite side and motion for him to stop. He does! I do my three points and dart up the other side, thrilled.

Another time I have to begin the lesson by backing down the street the whole length of the block, turning backward onto Broadway. Wow.

I learn about the different times of day and the obstacles they bring. At 10 a.m. there's U.P.S. trucks and FedEx trucks, double parkers, women with strollers. And 3 p.m. brings the masses of yelling schoolchildren.

We work on parallel parking. For days that's all we do: me, Nelson, the car and the curb. There is a formula, a parallel parking geometry, if you will:

Pull up to the car you want to park behind. Indicate right. Line up the wheel of your car with the front tire of the car next to you. Try to be parallel and not sticking out. Rotate the steering wheel one full revolution to the right. Put the car in reverse. Look behind you and try not to depend on your mirrors while the car is in motion. When your right mirror has lined up with the left rear taillight of the car in front of you, cut the wheel the other way, turn it left as far as it will go. Slide into the space without hitting the curb, or the car in front of you, or the car in back of you, or the garbage on the sidewalk.

Nelson doesn't even open the door. He is cracking himself up laughing. "Well, you paralleled, but you didn't park."

The formula has failed, or I have failed the formula. I am indeed parallel, but nowhere near the curb. I am about three feet away. For an hour I try. And fail.

Then Nelson says: "You just touched that man's BMW. Let's get the hell out of here."

Finally, I get the date for my actual driving test. I do so much want to be a good driver, but I just don't get how. It is so frustrating. I ask my neighbor if I can go driving with her. She has a great big van with exquisitely responsive brakes. I try to show her where Nelson and I usually go—the lovely drive down Morningside overlooking a little park that nobody knows about, that winds so beautifully you don't even know you're in Manhattan.

Somehow we end up on the other side, but at least there are parking spaces. She watches me.

"What are you doing?" she asks. "Why are you throwing the wheel to one side, and then the other? Here, watch me."

She gets in and expertly handles the big machine, adjusting first one way, then the next, keeping the distance between the car and the curb in her mind at all times.

I decide that I have been following an abstract principle instead of living in the real world. This is a good lesson. Don't follow the formula. Just look at the curb as it really exists, and adjust to it. This works!

On that day I feel enlightened. I have learned a basic principle I should apply to my entire life.

But this joy is blotted out when I become distracted as we approach the parking garage. For one moment, as we are talking about something, I get the brake and the gas pedal confused, and accelerate hard toward a brick wall. I finally brake, but my friend has her head in her hands, whispering in horror. She thinks we are going to die. I look out the window. Everyone is staring.

The garage attendant and all the passers-by are staring at me as I get out of the van.

"Hello!" I wave cheerfully. "Sorry!"

But I go back to Nelson with my new, hard-won knowledge. This time I get half the parking right, a huge improvement. I would be really happy about it, but one of Nelson's relatives is in jail, and he's not happy about that, so I am not happy either. He talks on the cellphone.

He tells me: "My cousin's girlfriend is pregnant, and when he gets in trouble, she calls me up. Do I look like the president?"

I assure him that he doesn't. I have had relatives in jail, too, and wonder if I should tell him I know how it can be. I start to, but he is not listening. So I drive here and there, parking randomly in all our usual spots as he sighs into the cellphone.

Next time, the incident is gone from Nelson's mind. But he starts to tease me about my powers of observation. On the way to the lesson, I notice the tarot reader on the same street, past the sign for the driving school. This begins a chain of thought, and I sail right past a bewildered Nelson, standing in the doorway.

"Where are you going?" he shouts at me. "How can you work on your observation when you don't even observe the teacher!"

We go up to Harlem. "Oh, here is Convent Avenue!" I say. "My sister just got married up here! Look at the great old Gothic buildings!"

We head toward Broadway and students from City College clog the intersection. I slow down.

"Why you slowing down?" Nelson says to me.

"Mr. R. told me not to hit the pedestrians."

"These guys are wiseguys. They see your student sign, and they are giving you a hard time. Don't slow down." He reaches across me and honks the horn. The students scatter, laughing.

Another time we are on Riverside, about to turn right. I notice two old ladies in the car to my left. They cut me off, still chatting away, while I seethe. I think to myself, as Mr. R. said, if someone wants the right of way, give it to them, it's not worth getting into a fight over. So I let them go and turn right myself without stopping, but in hot pursuit of the two old ladies.

"You know what you did back there?" he said.

"What?" I say, jolted back to reality.

"You went through a stop sign. Didn't you see it?"

I explained to him that I wasn't going to let those two ladies get ahead of me. Nelson throws his head back and laughs.

"You're competitive," he says. "I like that."

The morning of the test arrives, bright, clear. I wonder if I will pass this time? I show up for my warm-up lesson. Nelson confides that the job is getting to him. He puts his life at risk every day, and he's only getting $10 an hour. His dream is to be a truck driver. A truck driver? He has never been outside New York except to go to Puerto Rico and back. I imagine him on a highway, droning through the Midwest somewhere, and wonder what he would think of the huge flatlands, all that open space.

"What's horrible is how you're driving today," he says.

Oh.

"Your problem is you got to observate, and that's not something I can teach you. If you keep your head on your head, you should do O.K. But I can't teach you to observate."

With that endorsement ringing in my ears, I'm ready for Yonkers, ready to face the test again.

The tester gets into the car, looks at my permit. "What a nice smile," he says.

It flashes through my mind that the photograph is from the day my husband and I separated, but I figure there is no need to go into that.

"Thanks," I say.

As we drive, he corrects a couple of things without writing them down: slow down, you nicked the yellow line here, you have to look both ways on the three-point turn.

We parallel park. I seize the moment. I adjust. I look at the curb. I do not touch it, and I am close, though, three inches to be exact. I turn the wheel so the tires face forward, pull the car up and ease it into park. I try not to act surprised. Imagine if I fainted? He looks at me.

"What do you think?" he says.

"I think it's pretty good." I say.

"I do, too." he says. "I am impressed."

I feel victory in my bones. I pass the test! I can't believe it! I want to throw my arms around this man's neck and kiss him. But I don't. I'm relieved that I won't have to take any more lessons, although I had gotten used to Nelson and his moods, his humor. I suddenly realize that I will probably never see him again.

Even though I got my license, I still feel cautious about driving, and I haven't driven in the city since I passed. I am still an urban girl, but right now I feel most comfortable driving in Orange County, Calif., when I visit family, because the roads are nice and wide, and the signs are really big.

And, from time to time, I wonder about Nelson, wonder whether he'll ever end up on that highway, driving a truck through the Midwest.

August 24, 2003

(John Hendrix)

25

Time Out

Loving the Sport. Hating the Scene.
Confessions of a Reluctant Soccer Dad.

ANDRÉ ACIMAN

IT'S an early, overcast weekend morning. The house is quiet. Our block is quiet. It's still dark outside, and perhaps there are hours of sleep left before anyone gets up. As I'm about to shut my eyes again, I try to guess what the weather is like behind the blinds. But the silence—no patter of rain, no splash of car tires along the streets—already tells me what I don't want to know. It's not raining outside. At best, just drizzling.

They said it would rain all day today, and I had gone to bed relishing the picture of late autumnal showers all over Manhattan and on the empty fields of Wards Island and Central Park and Riverside Park and Dyckman Field—on every inch of land claimed by the West Side Soccer League. I even went to bed expecting a wake-up call breaking the catastrophic news in clipped, take-it-like-a-man syllables—"Soccer canceled!"—to which I had already rehearsed the strained, doleful response I'd affect before hanging up and shouting a triumphant "Yessss!!"

Now, there's to be soccer all day long. And it's cold outside. And, let's face it; it's not dawn any longer. And, to make things worse, it's my turn to bring snacks for my twins' team. And since brilliant me never buys anything ahead of time, I'll have to rush to the supermarket and shop for odd snacks and hope none of the other parents complain, especially those health-freak, do-gooder couples who gently manage to persuade the other parents that we should all really try bringing oranges, preferably cut in four, and plenty of juice, of course, preferably rich in vitamin C.

On a morning like this, junk food will do just fine. I like to watch how these caring parents, holding Starbucks grandes with both hands, sidle up to me and ever so discreetly throw sidelong glances into my bag only to find two dozen Krispy Kreme doughnuts staring at them. In their face!

171

No one in my family is a soccer fanatic. We joined because everyone else joined. Because everyone said that children in Manhattan need to let off steam and have fun for a change. Plus don't they look cute running around in their little uniforms? And the game teaches them teamwork and self-discipline, and at the end of the eight or so weeks, there's even an awards ceremony in a jam-packed public school auditorium where every child gets a trophy, a handshake and a slice of pizza.

Nobody tells you that many of the coaches do nothing but shout and care nothing about the game except winning. Nor do they tell you about the referees who strut about the fields in their regulation-black uniforms like implacable mothers superior whose mission in life is to blow their whistles when your child's foot—or, worse yet, your own—strays on the wrong side of the line. And no one will say anything about all the parents who brave the coldest weather, lug the heaviest snacks and find the dampest spot to sit on, confident that therein lies the essence of good parenting and good sportsmanship.

I've grown to hate the soccer scene.

And yet, of all the sports I have played in my life, this is the one I loved the most. Not a day went by in my childhood when I didn't play. Soccer is in my blood—literally—for I've hurt myself and bled for soccer as a child more than for anything else.

But the game has changed. It used to last hours back then, not a measly four 15-minute segments. Manhattan cannot be host to pickup soccer games. Ours were improvised games that started with seven or so players, one goal and one goalie for both teams, and then inevitably swelled to 20 and more by the end, with people constantly changing sides.

Parents never came. We didn't have referees, and if we did, they almost never mattered, because far better to keep the ball rolling than stop the action. "Outs" were easily overlooked, hand balls more often than not forgiven. There were fights, but no one stopped the clock. There was no clock. There was no whistle. All that mattered was speed, cunning and endless passion for the game.

•

Of course you wouldn't guess I'd ever kicked a soccer ball before. Once I bring my twins to the park, the last thing I want is for people to suspect I know anything about the game: how to dribble, how to kick, how to fake kicks, and above all, the one thing no one even dreams of teaching you, even though it is the heart and soul of soccer: how to pass. I don't want to be asked to practice shots with the children, and I certainly don't want to be asked to be a linesman. I arrive with a wad of paper on a clipboard affecting the totally distracted air of a writer who is very much on deadline.

I stay away from everyone. I watch the boys huddle—no one ever huddled in soccer—and I watch them listen to meaningless bromides like "watch the ball" (a baseball obsession) and "focus, focus, focus" (an attention-deficit mantra imported from the classroom onto the playing field).

This morning, before leaving our home, we'll probably have another crisis regarding a missing shin guard. Then there'll be the shoelace that is so gnarled up in generations of old knots that the only way to undo it is to use the tine of a fork and all the patience and concentration of a master safecracker. In between these mini-crises come the larger ones. A red gelatinous glob sits on one of my sons' regulation-yellow shirts. He has pilfered one of the jelly doughnuts and in his haste to gulp it down has managed to splatter the jelly on his shirt. He is now spreading it all over with his finger in a last-ditch effort to hide the evidence.

On our way out, I'm already making a list of possible brushfires: the coach who knows so little about soccer, ditto the referee, the East Side mother who's taking her son to a Met matinee after the game and needs to tell everyone about it, the doting father who has videotaped every game of the season and can't believe you haven't.

And yet there is a moment, and it hardly lasts 10 seconds, as I watch the boys play and am sitting by myself in the perfect stillness of an early Saturday morning, when it all comes back to me. This game that is like no other, that never stops once it starts, that is forever linked to the presence of grass: grass you fall on, grass stains on your clothes, grass whose smell stays on your skin all day. Grass you lie sprawled on as you rest a moment and become one with the earth, the sky, and the voice of your teammates weaving in and out of earshot, reaching you as though from light years away.

And then suddenly the game comes to life, when you'd run as fast as you could, dribbled as deftly and as cunningly as your legs allowed, and then that crowning moment, when from some unknown brilliant impulse you did something as selfless as pass a ball to someone and then, from the corner of your eye, you saw him pass it back to you, and you knew, you simply knew, before even kicking the ball again, that you'd score a goal, and that what had happened on the field just now between one teammate and another was the closest soccer would ever come to love.

I think back to these days and wonder whether the Met mother or energy-bar-crunching dad would ever understand why I sit away from them. They probably suspect I'll just never get the game.

November 9, 2003

26

Wild Masonry, Murderous Metal and Mr. Blonde

An Electrical Mistake, an Accidental Death. New Yorkers Learn That Even Their Powerful City Must Kneel Before the Random Hand of Fate.

JEROME CHARYN

Manhole cover on East 11th Street. (Frances Roberts/The New York Times)

175

I WASN'T in Manhattan when Jodie S. Lane was electrocuted two weeks ago while walking her two dogs. I couldn't participate in the anger and bewilderment of most New Yorkers. I'd just returned to Paris. I was locked in a classroom with a bunch of movie mavens, talking about Mr. Blonde (Michael Madsen), the psychopathic killer in Quentin Tarantino's 1992 film, "Reservoir Dogs," a devil who dances around the cop he's just captured, cuts off his ear and douses him with gasoline.

There was something so malevolent about Mr. Blonde and his little dance that it felt like a random act outside the dynamic of cinema itself. The cop is played by an actor who seems part of some elemental universe where nothing and no one has a name—the gods are against this poor policeman, whose fate it was to bump against Mr. Blonde.

There was no Mr. Blonde in Ms. Lane's mysterious death on Jan. 16, but there might have been. "Reservoir Dogs" is a tale of L.A., where nobody walks, where sidewalks are hard to find. Ms. Lane would probably have gotten a traffic ticket before she ever crossed a street. But New York is a nation of walkers. And before she was electrocuted outside Veniero's pastry shop in the East Village (with the best marzipan on the planet), she chatted with another dog owner about their dogs.

She and her dogs had wandered near a metal plate covering an underground utility box; improper insulation, according to Consolidated Edison, had turned that metal cover into a weird kind of electric chair. One of the dogs stepped on the cover, went berserk, bit the nose of the other dog. Ms. Lane tried to calm them, but she touched the wrong dog, and an electrical current went through the dog like a murderous conductor and into her.

"It's just unacceptable that somebody can walk down the street and get electrocuted," Mayor Bloomberg said soon after the accident. But how can anyone patrol 90,000 miles of cable, with 250,000 manholes and utility boxes? In 1999 a carriage horse was electrocuted when it stepped on a Con Ed cover near Park Avenue. Who can say how many other horses fell, or how many children were electrocuted for burrowing in the wrong hole, or being in the wrong place?

`And it isn't only bad wiring. In 1979 a Barnard student, Grace Gold, was killed by a piece of masonry that dropped like a bomb from an eighth-story window on West 115th Street. "This is like a 10-million-to-1 possibility—no, more than that," said a detective on the scene, as if 10 million to 1 were improbable odds for New Yorkers, who have to dodge 10 million possibilities every day.

We can't do much about the labyrinth that lives under the ground— not just wires but pipes, subway tunnels and gas lines. It is a subterranean country that seems to mock each of our moves, mimic our own complexity, as if we were expendable, not the wires. There are abandoned subway stations that belong to another era, stations that would bother our dreams if we ever decided to examine them. It's better that they're lost in their own stop-time.

But Ms. Lane belonged to us. She wasn't some wild creature that rose up from the ground. She was a 30-year-old doctoral student at Columbia University Teachers College, and she was writing a book about children with obsessive compulsive disorder.

A graduate of Sarah Lawrence, she'd lived in New York for the last 10 years. She was of the city, as much as any single one of us. But we seem to have more vivid information about the dogs than about Ms. Lane herself. One of them lost a couple of nails on its back paws. The dogs were brought to nearby St. Marks Veterinary Hospital.

"They were mostly shaken up," said the veterinarian who administered to them. "They just saw what happened to their mother and were terrified."

That word "mother" startled me, as if we lived in a veterinarian's world, where dogs could adopt us as part of their kingdom. Ms. Lane had touched a nerve in New York. We're still raw after 9/11. Her crazy disappearance reminds us how fragile we all are in a town that was attacked by a diabolic killer-poet, Osama bin Laden, a Mr. Blonde who hides behind a holy war. We're a city that can't quite recover from a carnage that makes no sense.

We are the most welcoming, various people in the world. Over half of us are foreign-born. I grew up during one colossal wave of immigrants, when Italians from Sicily, Jews from Eastern Europe, and their children strode through our public schools and learned New York's powerful song: none of us was alone; we would give back to each new generation what had been given to us. Rather than a melting pot, we were pieces of a mosaic. That was our strength. Unlike bin Laden, who would narrow us down to some rigid formula where foreigners couldn't find a place, we are all foreigners who look one another in the eye.

I remember as a small boy in the Bronx watching Joe DiMaggio, the son of Italian immigrants, striding along the Grand Concourse in his

Yankee uniform, absorbed in himself but still curious enough to smile at us and tip his hat. No one would have interfered with this Yankee Clipper who'd been lent to the Bronx for a little while. "Clipper's coming," we would whisper, and it gave us an edge over Manhattan. Manhattan had the Chrysler Building, but we had the Clipper. . . .

And now, after 9/11, our own history seems in danger. The mosaic may not hold. I doubt that another DiMaggio will ever walk the Concourse in his cleats. And who knows what mad bomber might rip away the witch's silver cap that sits on top of Chrysler? We remain a city in mourning, no matter what memorial we fasten onto the site of the twin towers.

I'm privileged enough to have an apartment in Greenwich Village; Tony Soprano (aka James Gandolfini) is my neighbor. I see him wander in his bomber jacket, clutching a baby carriage.

Why does Soprano comfort me? Is he a good Mr. Blonde, a devil who has his own harried family, who kisses as often as he kills? In my corner of Manhattan he's not a Mafia don, just a papa who haunts West 12th Street.

I miss New York when I'm away. Paris is a city of monuments and streets with buildings that are so symmetrical, they look like stranded ocean liners. But I cannot find that great, brooding mix of faces, that sense of a constant carnival.

Ms. Lane was part of this carnival, a young woman who wrote about disturbed children, walked her dogs near Veniero's, and encountered the wrong electrical grid. Any one of us might have stood under a piece of wild masonry that dropped from the sky, or a crane that happened to fall, or bumped into a taxicab that caromed out of control—a kind of random malevolence, as if the metropolis were populated with a world of Mr. Blondes, cruel puppeteers who picked on us, at the odds of 10 million to 1. And each of us, as New Yorkers, might remember Ms. Lane, even mourn for her, while we dance out of the devil's way.

February 1, 2004

Part III

New Yorkers

Celia Maguire in the New York Botanical Garden. (Richard Perry/The New York Times)

27

Love's Labors

She and Her Husband Roamed the World in Search of Exotic Plants. Now, Alone in a Bronx Office, Celia Maguire Tends to His Legacy.

LAURA SHAINE CUNNINGHAM

IT was so feverish-hot, so sticky and infested, that Celia Maguire would have risked anything to dive into the river. Her husband, the famed botanist Bassett Maguire, would test the water first, poking the bottom to scare up any stingrays. All manner of poisonous creatures lurked below the murk in that uncharted waterway in Guyana.

"But I was so desperate to get in the water, I almost didn't care what was down there," Ms. Maguire remembered. "I was being eaten by the 24-hour ants."

She recalled the discomfort, the prickly heat, the rashes and bites. The pain of such trips was almost unbearable, but so was the pleasure.

"Oh, it was wonderful! We sailed around the world on tankers. We went everywhere. I was often the only woman on board." On one ship, the Italian captain said: "Here are two staterooms. One for you, one for your wife."

"I said, 'We want only one.' I insisted on my rights." She smiled. "I wanted to be with Bassett."

Far from Guyana, in the LuEsther Mertz Library of the New York Botanical Garden in the Bronx, another sort of journey is taking place. For the last 11 years, ever since Mr. Maguire died in 1991 at 86, his widow has been organizing the archive of his 50 years as curator of the garden, explorer-botanist, and discoverer of six new genera of plants and a mountain range in Venezuela. Celia Maguire, just turned 83 last month, overcomes the frailty of her years and health to document the half-century of their romance, with flora and with one another.

The task is daunting. Mr. Maguire collected more than 67,000 specimens, wrote copious notes, shot film. It would seem to require a staff of dozens of botanists to do what this one tiny woman has accomplished. But when one accompanies Ms. Maguire on her mission, the reasons for her commitment become clear. They were physically divergent—he was 15 years older and a foot taller—but they had a singular union.

Ms. Maguire is time-traveling with him now, back to the 1940's, 50's, 60's, 70's and 80's. She takes her listener on their botanic safaris, under lush green canopies, accompanied by the music of rushing waterfalls and the cries of songbirds. Recounting almost half a century of fieldwork, she described the thrills of sleeping in a tent, under a cascade of flowers.

"A jaguar passed under my mosquito net, and Bassett didn't wake me," she remembered of one trip. "The morning after, Bassett told me, 'Oh, that jaguar was just moving through the camp on his way.'" On another trip, a snake, a fer-de-lance, was neither so benign nor so lucky. The snake had to be chopped and his head was shown to Ms. Maguire by the natives. "I never saw a snake head so large; his fangs were like my fingers." She gestured with her small hands as if holding a snake's head as large as a cantaloupe.

There were the long climbs to the mountain in Venezuela they named Cerro de la Neblina, Hill of the Mist, a discovery for which Mr. Maguire was awarded the David Livingstone Centenary Medal in 1965. On that mountain, the couple discovered unknown plant life, an abundance of exotic leaves and blooms. The next peak in that mysterious mountain range was named for them: Pico Maguire.

•

As she speaks in her low, clipped voice, Ms. Maguire conjures a verdant world that could not be more alien from the fluorescent basement storage area where she now sits. Here, the record of that green, pulsing jungle life is boxed and stacked in plain gray cartons, arranged in towers that reach the ceiling. She sits at a plain desk, unadorned save for small cameo photographs of her husband. "His passport pictures," she said with a smile that also conveyed her longing.

How apt, that Bassett Maguire, handsome, bespectacled, jaw set, is represented by passport pictures. His was a life led in transit, from one exotic forest to another, from mountain to coral reef and beyond. In the opinion of Brian M. Boom, the garden's longtime vice president for botanical science, Mr. Maguire explored and identified the natural world more than any other botanist.

"He was my hero," Dr. Boom said. "No one discovered more in the field. He went where it was very dangerous to go." Dr. Boom recalled Mr. Maguire as "strong willed," adding: "He would raise his voice. He knew a lot, and he wanted things done his way. He fired me once, then rehired me. I accepted it because of who he was and the enormity of what he accomplished. He and Celia were closer to each other than any couple."

Ms. Maguire and the archives have come to rest in this windowless and sometimes almost airless storeroom in the basement of the garden's library. Archival work is, in its way, as dirty as fieldwork. For 11 years, she has breathed the residue of her and her husband's shared past. She coughs, clears her throat and goes on.

In this arid, urban indoor setting, Ms. Maguire relives the wild journeys, like the time they fled Nigeria during the 1967 uprising. "The message came while we were in the field: 'Get out of the country.' We were on the last plane out of Lagos."

They drove past fires and heard shots. "But we made it out, with the seeds of the great Gmelina arborea, an enormous, powerful tree. When we boarded the plane, the steward held out two large frosted vodka tonics. We got out and the seeds did, too."

As Ms. Maguire tells it, their life together sounds like an extended, annotated botanical version of "Out of Africa" (also out of South America, British Guiana, Central America, the Dominican Republic and Surinam). The couple slept in jungles, in tents and on mountain tops. They were threatened by disease, insects, natives with machetes.

"And I had never left New York before Bassett took me with him," Ms. Maguire recalls. "I had never even worn flats."

The first thing Ms. Maguire did, after it was agreed she would accompany him, was to buy field clothes. "We went to Macy's, and I got my first pair of jeans." Because she was so petite, she wore children's sizes; she stepped through the jungle in size 4 kiddie sneakers.

Sometimes she slipped, which brings her to the story of that dip in the jungle river.

"Bassett wanted me to go farther in, away from the still water, to where it was moving," she recalled. "He said, 'Step on the stones.' I was used to wearing high heels. Of course, I slipped. He was so cross. I fell into the rushing water and he saved the soap first. You know why? Because we couldn't get more."

•

Now, the tendriled greenery they collected on this and so many other trips is dried and saved between newspapers in the Cold Room, where plant material is stored to keep it from decaying. Tens of thousands of documents and notes, along with reels of old film and photographs, remain boxed in the library basement.

To visit Ms. Maguire at her work, one enters a long rectangular storeroom of which she occupies a front section, walled by her husband's files. The floor is a checkerboard of two-tone brown linoleum squares. The "old" files are still present but dwindling. Their olive drab boxes and cabinets with yellowing cards stand in contrast to the higher stacks of the clean, pale "new" boxes that contain the massive amount of sorted material.

In this drab area, Ms. Maguire appears not only determined but also decorative. Her azure-blue eye shadow is the single highlight of color; her jewelry the only ornamentation. While this room is dedicated to the study of the natural world, it appears unnatural. A petrified cross-section of a tree, which used to be in the museum building, is there.

In this latest chapter of her life, Ms. Maguire has been commuting between the storage area and an apartment in nearby Co-op City, where the couple lived for decades. They lived in Co-op City because of its proximity to the garden, in a two-bedroom, 24th-floor apartment with a view of Long Island Sound.

The Maguires created the apartment very much as a world of their own. They decorated it with photographs and mementoes of their travels, bits of Central America, Africa. One imagines their apartment as a time capsule, a museum of memory.

Ms. Maguire also commutes between the present and the past. Organizing film, notes, cards, documents, she relives their history. Although it would be easy to give in to the ennui of lifting towers of papers and deciphering endless Latin scribbles, she will not surrender. She travels through time at odd hours, rising three mornings a week at 4 to arrive at the garden by 6:30.

At first sight, she appears a fragile soldier in this war against loss. With her upswept crown of hair, penciled brows and the azure eye shadow, she is the human equivalent of the exotic birds that inhabit those jungles of her past exploits. Perhaps a hummingbird. She stands 4 feet 11 inches in her size 4 1/2 Ferragamos. She almost always wears high heels—"I like standing on heels, the sense of control"—and she is semi-formally attired in a neat black dress that buttons down the front.

When she demonstrates how she was bitten by the 24-hour ants in Guyana, she displays a stockinged leg as pretty as a dancer's. It is easy to see how her husband must have fallen in love with her when she walked into his office at the garden almost 60 years ago. In a sense, she has always worked for him. She began in 1944, by taking dictation, and in a profound sense, she is still doing so. Her husband's voice is heard through hers, and she often uses the marital "we" to describe her life today.

•

She was connected to the New York Botanical Garden even before she met Mr. Maguire. Her family moved to the Bronx when she was only 5. "We were a tragic family," she says. "Very sad." Her brother had died as a child, and his death left her parents in the shadow of near-permanent mourning. The shadow became literal: the shade in the Botanical Garden. "I first knew this place through my mother's grief," she recalls. "We walked here, in circles. I think of her sitting here, weeping. I hated it in a way."

Then fate decreed that Celia Kramer, just out of Hunter College, be interviewed for a job as an assistant to the garden's botanists. "Oh, no, not here!" she thought.

She worked for many of the botanists, too many. She was tired and wanted to leave. When she was offered a job on what she described as "one of those old homes and gardens magazines," she told Mr. Maguire, then a curator, that she intended to quit.

She claims that she did not feel the "spark" when she first met him, although today she recalls him as "electric—you knew when he entered the room."

Tall, handsome, accomplished, he was also married. He was a Southerner, born in Alabama. She was the child of immigrant Jews who came to America to escape the pogroms.

Perhaps Mr. Maguire was already in love, for the day she mentioned quitting he reacted with unanticipated vehemence. "No," he protested. "Tell me why." When she cited the overwork and confusion of assisting so many botanists, he declared that she would work only for him: "As of yesterday, I shall tell the office, you work for me." Her superior, whose name she still hisses, fought the decision, but Mr. Maguire insisted.

"As of yesterday, Celia Kramer works only for me."

The yesterdays stretched into thousands of tomorrows. The Maguires toured the world. At their first destination, in Central America, "I showed my ignorance," she admitted. "I wore a white dress from B. Altman's. I wore it in the back of a truck. It was ruined. I had to throw it out." She conceded that at first she knew nothing. "I ironed our field clothes. That's how little prepared I was."

Although the couple began traveling together in the 1940's, they did not marry until 1951. "After all," she admitted, a sparkle in her eye, "he was married."

She is beyond censoring herself. "I was the reason he divorced." Of course.

"I was the reason, and it was a mess," she adds. "He had children. It was very, very difficult. We got married at a justice's office in New Rochelle. As soon as he had his documents." There was no wedding party. And, oddly, no flowers.

In fact, in the couple's long history of working with botanicals, they did not take the interest home, at least not in its living form. "Never had a houseplant either," she says. "Not one." If she bought flowers, they were cut. She has no special favorite.

"But now," she added, "I do bring Bassett roses. He is in a mausoleum in Woodlawn Cemetery, very near here, and every Saturday, I bring him roses. Usually dark red ones, but now I let the florist choose. I say, 'Anthony, what do you have for us today?' And he has given me some quite extraordinary colors."

The couple never had children, but that, she says, was her choice: "He said he felt guilty, that he had deprived me, but I said, no, I never wanted any. They would have intruded between us."

As her husband's death drew near, after a long illness, Ms. Maguire summoned his son, Bassett Jr., to the bedside. The son, who had long ago been bitter at the remarriage and angry toward the woman who had replaced his mother, "saw how Bassett still reached for me, how our touch always connected, and he said, 'I think your marriage is grand.'"

Today, she lives alone in what had been the apartment they shared, not engaging much with her neighbors. "We like to be alone," she said. "That's important. I don't want anything to encroach."

Her work at the garden is almost done. "A couple of months," she says. The boxes are stacked. Only a few more cabinets wait. The chaos has turned to cartons, mountains to files, flowers to cardboard mounts and slides. Everything has a Latin label. When completed, the archive will be both a record of a singular achievement and an invaluable tool for future research.

One can't help imagining her return home to her apartment, where she goes to bed at 7 and rises again at 4. The dawn will illuminate the artifacts that are kept as a shrine to her husband, like the golden nugget pendant in the shape of Venezuela, with a diamond placed exactly upon the mountain he discovered: Cerro de la Neblina, Hill of the Mist.

The light will then glance off the diamond and refract across the glass-covered photograph of Mr. Maguire's long, serious face. His widow will move into her morning, resuming her commute between her past and present, carrying her husband's legacy forward into the new century.

Many hours before, the sunlight that shines in the Bronx filtered through the palms and shimmered upon the river where, so long ago, Celia and Bassett Maguire entered the water to bathe away the sting and scorch of the jungles. There, they bathed in darkness, and swam together.

Is there anything she still looks for? Her eyes lower, along with her whisper, "Only Bassett." Perhaps it's the way she breathes his name, but it is easy to hear his voice through hers. "As of yesterday," he said, "Celia works for me. As of yesterday."

July 21, 2002

Larry Ritter in his Upper West Side apartment. (Fred R. Conrad/The New York Times)

28

Ballpark of Memory

Decades Ago, Lawrence Ritter Journeyed From
the West Side to Roam the Country in Search of
Baseball's Past. He Came Back With Perhaps
the Best Book Ever Written on the Sport.

DAVID MARGOLICK

EVERY month they gather on the Upper West Side, and no matter what the season, the subject is always the same: baseball.

It may be the game last night, or the 1941 All-Star Game, or Game 6 of the 1947 World Series. Bouncing as naturally as a friendly hop to short between John J. McGraw and George Steinbrenner, from Casey Stengel to Jerry Lumpe to Derek Jeter, they spout statistics, exchange yarns and disgorge oddities, always in the peculiar Esperanto of the sport, sprinkled with odd abbreviations and obscure names and defunct teams. All speak this language fluently, some from memory, others from lifetimes spent mainlining The Baseball Encyclopedia and the backs of baseball cards.

There's nothing like an agenda, but the topics are usually historic; the Yankees' recent demise would surely warrant some comment, but no one would dwell on it. Thus at one recent gathering the topics discussed included how The New York Herald Tribune helped expose the racism on the 1947 St. Louis Cardinals, how much Babe Ruth's bat weighed, and how, while everyone remembers Bill Mazeroski's famous home run that day, few realize that no one struck out in the seventh game of the 1960 World Series. On a loftier level, they pondered the classic conundrum of the true New York baseball fan: What would you do if you had Hitler, Stalin and Walter O'Malley (for the uninitiated, the man who moved the Brooklyn Dodgers to Los Angeles) standing before you, and had only two bullets in your gun? Actually, it's not all that difficult. You save them both for O'Malley.

Ernie's, at Broadway and 75th Street, is an empty aircraft hangar of a restaurant, at least during a weekday lunchtime when most gainfully employed neighborhood residents are toiling a few subway stops south. But crowded around one table toward the back not long ago were such consummate New York baseball chroniclers as the biographers of Babe Ruth (Robert Creamer) and Lou Gehrig (Ray Robinson). Even in this illustrious company, though, Lawrence S. Ritter stands apart.

Mr. Ritter doesn't hold the career record for triples, as does Wahoo Sam Crawford, who played from 1899 to 1917. Nor did he win 34 games in a season, like Smoky Joe Wood in 1912. He did not drop a fly ball in the World Series that year, like Fred Snodgrass, nor turn an unassisted triple play in the 1920 World Series, like Bill Wambsganss. Nor is he in the Hall of Fame, like Crawford or Goose Goslin or Rube Marquard.

But if historians of the sport were eligible for Cooperstown, Mr. Ritter would be elected unanimously the first time out. More than 40 years ago, determined to do for baseball what John and Alan Lomax did for vernacular American music, he began interviewing ballplayers who'd been active in the early years of the 20th century, including Crawford, Wood, Snodgrass, Wambsganss and 29 others. (Chief Meyers, who played for both the Giants and Dodgers, told him, "I started playing ball when Dewey took Manila," and it was actually true.)

Five years, 75,000 miles and two hernias later—the ancient Tandberg reel-to-reel tape recorder he lugged around weighed 27 pounds—Mr. Ritter turned the interviews into "The Glory of Their Times: The Story of the Early Days of Baseball Told by the Men Who Played It," published in 1966.

The Brooklyn Dodgers and the Yankees' announcer Red Barber called it the greatest baseball book ever written. The novelist Nelson Algren predicted the book would "be around as long as baseball," and so far, he's right. If you doubt its continued popularity and the astonishing impact it still has on people, just check the reader comments about it on Amazon.com. What makes Mr. Ritter's achievement all the more remarkable is that he was not a sportswriter at all, but a professor of economics and finance at the New York University School of Business, where he taught from 1961 to 1991.

"I didn't think this whole thing would amount to anything," Mr. Ritter, who turned 80 a few months ago, recalled recently in his apartment on West End Avenue. Initially, that was true: every publisher that saw the book spurned it. Macmillan eventually bought it for $3,000, and since then it has sold some 375,000 copies. True, another of Mr. Ritter's 10 books—"Principles of Money, Banking and Financial Markets"—has sold more. But for some reason, people never embraced it in quite the same way.

Many people love attributing their success to their New Yorkness, which, they believe, gives them half a step on everyone else. And Mr. Ritter is very much the New Yorker. He grew up in Hollis, Queens, graduated from Boys High School in Brooklyn, and made all of the usual pilgrimages to Yankee Stadium and Ebbets Field and the Polo Grounds. He attended his first ballgame with his father, a principal of Public School 139 in Rego Park, Queens, in 1931. The Yankees were playing the Philadelphia Athletics. (Mr. Ritter still swears that Ruth, Gehrig and Jimmie Foxx hit home runs that day, though years later, when he searched the box scores, he could find no such game.)

But he knows that New Yorkers can just as surely put people off, and believes that his ballplayers talked so candidly because his years away from the city—wartime service in the Navy, plus long spells studying and teaching in places like Bloomington, Ind., and Madison, Wis.—had obscured his New York origins. "If it had come up, in a number of cases, there would have been a lot less warmth," he recalled. "I was a Midwesterner. They liked that. I wasn't a New York Jewish person, so it was a whole different ballgame."

His obvious love of the sport also helped, as did his uncanny ability to listen. "These people for 30 years had never talked about this stuff," he said. "Their grandchildren ran away when they saw them coming, because they were afraid of being bombarded by more bull about old-time baseball." In several cases, what began as interviews turned into lifelong friendships.

•

Reading "The Glory of Their Times"—a phrase from Ecclesiastes—is a rite of passage for serious baseball fans. Many, like the broadcaster Bob Costas, who, like other broadcasting celebrities—Ralph Kiner, Ernie Harwell—stops by Ernie's periodically for the baseball lunch, first read it as teenagers, and never forgot it.

For Mr. Costas, a St. Louis native whose torrent of anecdotes at one recent lunch helped turn what is generally a two-hour affair into a 15-inning marathon, the book colorized a world that, until then, had existed for him solely in fuzzy, sunless black and white. "It made these guys come to life," he said of the early ballplayers. "It was like hearing baseball's Mount Rushmore, with more than four heads talking. It humanized them and gave them texture, which made them—from my perspective as a kid—all the more heroic."

Mr. Creamer, a veteran Sports Illustrated reporter and the author of books on Ruth, Stengel and Mickey Mantle, agreed. "All these fabulous names that I heard about all my life became people," he said.

When, two years ago, several hours of Mr. Ritter's original audiotapes, now housed at the Hall of Fame, were released on tape cassettes and compact discs, the book took on new life, and power, and charm. Its stories are even more winning when heard aloud, spun by weathered voices with archaic accents ("Cincinna-tah," "Eye-o-way"), with cars backfiring, chairs creaking, matches igniting, wives scoffing and pop bottles popping in the background.

Men who died decades ago—the last of Mr. Ritter's subjects, Smoky Joe Wood, passed on in 1985—suddenly leap back to life. Few things can summon the dead more quickly than hearing them laugh—and, discussing the game and their youth, these old men laughed a lot. The charmless, plutocratic superstars of today only enhance the old-timers' appeal. (But if it's any consolation to them, Mr. Ritter's interviewees regarded the ballplayers of the 1960's as pampered crybabies, too.)

In Mr. Ritter's materials, legends like Walter Johnson, Ty Cobb, Christy Mathewson and Cy Young are no longer figures off bronze basreliefs and eBay collectibles, but teammates, adversaries, human beings. Mitts and salaries shrink to nothing. Dead balls and emery balls and shine balls and coffee balls and paraffin balls and mud balls fly around once again.

So, too, do spikes, though gashes are treated with chewing tobacco rather than the unguents of roly-poly, obsequious trainers. There is only one umpire on the field, the American League is still an outlaw enterprise, the Yankees are still the Highlanders. And the World Series is still the best of nine.

It is a rite of reportage: young people interview old people, frantically rescuing their recollections from oblivion, and, if they're lucky, or talented, or durable enough, someone someday will interview them, too. Mr. Ritter is now the age of the ballplayers he interviewed. He speaks with difficulty, a result of a stroke last year. The words are all still in him, but they can be slow to emerge; phrases as hard-wired into his soul as

"Pittsburgh Pirates" and "Wahoo Sam Crawford" sometimes take a while to percolate up. But Mr. Ritter's personality, simultaneously astringent and sweet, has survived. While his tongue may no longer be so nimble, it is still tart. "I always said that when I turn 80, I wanted to be shot, but no one's volunteering," he said.

•

Mr. Ritter says "The Glory of Their Times" came out of a complex web of desires: to capture voices before they were stilled (Ty Cobb had just died when he began in 1961); to pay homage to his father—his "Daddy," as he always calls him—also recently dead; to cleave more closely to his own young son, whom he saw only on weekends, and with whom he shared little but a love of the game. So he hit the road, journeying from Baywood Park, Calif., to Milwaukee to Port Jervis, N.Y., to Bridgeton, N.J., avoiding players who'd been interviewed to death, seeking those good enough to have had long careers but obscure enough to have been largely forgotten.

Heard rather than read, "The Glory of Their Times" is more than a peek into a lost world; it is a clinic for anyone who ever wants to learn anything from anyone else. Mr. Ritter's questions are occasional, succinct, gentle, open-ended. "You saw some mighty good pitching, didn't you?" "What was McGraw like as a manager?" "How'd you get along with Connie Mack?" "What were the parks like in 1903–04–05?" Some weren't questions at all: "You must have seen Joe Jackson play, too."

Asking no more than he had to, Mr. Ritter listened, even when nothing was being said. He had to banish his then-girlfriend, who can be heard in some of the early interviews, because she was too prone to break the reverie. "It takes a long time and a lot of luck to get somebody to be living in 1912," he said. "So I wanted those silences. But she couldn't overcome her social graces."

His knowledge was deep—"Where'd you come up with all these things?" Goose Goslin asks him, amazed—but he did his homework. Still, feigning ignorance worked better than flaunting his smarts.

His manner with the elderly was natural and respectful, neither falsely familiar nor excessively deferential. He treated them like people, not as relics. He could be awed—listen to him pick up Chief Meyers's 48-ounce bat or punching the pocket of one of Ruth's old mitts—but he was no groupie. Broaching potentially sensitive matters, like the games in which Goslin hit into four double plays or Snodgrass made his famous flub, he

was empathetic. When his subjects embellished or dissembled, he let
them be.

Mr. Ritter, who describes himself as an orthodox Keynesian, left New
York University 11 years ago, after Reaganomics had taken over the
place. "I couldn't stand my students, and I certainly couldn't stand my
colleagues," he said. "I started to feel as though, 'Oh, Jesus, I've got to
get out of this place.'" Even though there's a room there named for him,
he's never been back.

Besides, by then "The Glory of Their Times" had started him on his
literary career. In another of his books, "East Side, West Side," published
in 1998, he tracked down many of the vanished landmarks of New York
sports. The book, he admits, is weighted toward baseball—like Washington Park, where the Brooklyn Dodgers played before Ebbets Field—
and boxing (the Madison Square Garden Bowl in Long Island City, Jack
Dempsey's restaurant) and gives short shrift to other sports: racing,
hockey, basketball. To him, the explanation is simple: his Daddy never
took him to see the horses, the Rangers or the Knicks, so they simply
don't count.

•

Mr. Ritter was always a bit of a recluse. When his mother pushed him
out of the house, he recalled, he invariably got no farther than the front
stoop. Now illness has made him still more of a homebody. He has
moved to a smaller apartment a few floors below his old place; it doesn't
have any of the random clutter that people of normal mobility usually
leave in their wake. The shelves look pruned and bare; Mr. Ritter has
given away hundreds of baseball books. Nowadays he gets his baseball
—at least one game every day they play—from television. "I don't like
the players, I don't like the umpires, I don't like the owners," he said.
"But I love the game."

His principal forays outside are to the sportswriters' lunches, which
began about a dozen years ago. At the most recent meeting, one of the
regulars, Lee Lowenfish, wore an Orioles T-shirt and a Giants cap. "Ah,
a tribute to Foster Castleman," said Marty Appel, another regular and a
former publicist for the Yankees, referring to an otherwise forgotten
third baseman who'd played for both teams in the 1950's.

The reference wasn't lost on anyone, including Mr. Ritter, who
laughed knowingly. And gratefully: he'd missed several sessions after his
stroke. With the help of Evelyn Begley, a baseball maven who helps tend

to him, he returned, tentatively but triumphantly, three months later. "Evelyn said they all loved me," he said quietly. "I didn't know that, but she could see in their faces something that I couldn't see."

For all his outwardly curmudgeonliness, Mr. Ritter is a sentimental, generous man. Unlikely as it seems now, at a time when every autograph costs, none of the old ballplayers ever asked him for anything. Even so, for 20 years he split all royalties with them and their survivors; each ended up with about $10,000, no small sum for people without pensions. For Snodgrass, who played center field in the Polo Grounds, Mr. Ritter dug up and sent off some turf shortly before the place was demolished. For Hans Loeber, a one-time Phillies third baseman (and perhaps the first major leaguer ever to bat against Babe Ruth), who was living out his days in a fleabag hotel, he bought a television set so he could watch ballgames.

For 30 years Mr. Ritter hadn't listened to his tapes. "I didn't like myself. I didn't like the nasal sound." But hearing them again four years ago, when they were released commercially, he was pleased. "I thought, 'Wow, what great interviews these are,' and I lost all self-consciousness," he said. "I think all of it is bound up with the love I had for all of the people involved."

One of those people was Jimmy Austin, the Yankee third baseman whose rear end dominates the classic Charles M. Conlon photo of Ty Cobb sliding into third. In his interview with Mr. Ritter, Austin recounted how he'd hit a homer off a half-drunk Rube Waddell one day in 1909 or 1910, and how Waddell fell on his own behind as Austin rounded the bases. "I will never forget it as long as I live," Austin joyously recalled.

Within a year, Austin was dead. Except, that is, on Larry Ritter's wondrous tapes, where he can still be heard, living, breathing, reminiscing. And laughing.

October 13, 2002

(*Editor's note*: Lawrence Ritter died February 15, 2004.)

The Collyer brothers' apartment. (Corbis/Bettmann)

29

The Paper Chase

The Collyer Brothers, Harlem's Legendary
Pack Rats, Offer a Gruesome Cautionary Tale.

FRANZ LIDZ

MY father never had much use for fairy tales. The fifth of five brothers raised in a one-bedroom tenement on the Lower East Side, he preferred real-life grotesqueries. And so at bedtime, I would listen raptly to his urban horror stories, tales that filled the dark with chimera, bogeymen, golems.

The most macabre was the tale of the Collyer Brothers, the hermit hoarders of Harlem. In lugubrious tones not unlike Boris Karloff's, my father described the vague aura of evil that had endowed the four-story brownstone on the northwest corner of Fifth Avenue and 128th Street for much of the 1930's and 40's. It was there, barricaded in a sanctuary of junk, that the blind and bedridden Homer Collyer lived with his devoted younger brother, Langley, the elderly scions of an upper-class Manhattan family.

And it was there that they amassed one of the world's legendary collections of urban junk, a collection so extraordinary that their accomplishment, such as it was, came to represent the ultimate New York cautionary tale.

The Collyer brothers' saga confirms a New Yorker's worst nightmare: crumpled people living in crumpled rooms with their crumpled possessions, the crowded chaos of the city refracted in their homes. It's not that Gothamites hoard more than other people; it's that they have less room to hoard in.

Even now, after more than a half century, the Collyer name still resonates. New York City firefighters refer to an emergency call to a junk-jammed apartment as a "Collyer." The brothers are recalled whenever a recluse dies amid an accumulation of junk; as a middle-aged woman snapped at her parents in a Roz Chast cartoon in The New Yorker: "You guys never throw anything out! You're starting to live like the COLLYER BROTHERS."

The elderly Collyers were well-to-do sons of a prominent Manhattan gynecologist and an opera singer. Homer had been Phi Beta Kappa at Columbia, where he earned his degree in admiralty law. Langley was a pianist who had performed at Carnegie Hall.

The brothers had moved to Harlem in 1909 when they were in their 20's and the neighborhood was a fashionable, and white, suburb of Manhattan. They became more and more reclusive as the neighborhood went shabby on them, booby-trapping their home with midnight street pickings and turning it into a sealed fortress of ephemera, 180 tons of it by the end. Children chucked rocks at their windows and called them "ghosty men."

My father recounted in great detail the rotting decadence of what had been a Victorian showplace. The Collyers had carved a network out of the neck-deep rubble. Within the winding warrens were tattered toys and chipped chandeliers, broken baby carriages and smashed baby grands, crushed violins and cracked mantel clocks, moldering hope chests crammed with monogrammed linen.

Homer went blind in the mid-30's and was crippled by rheumatism in 1940. His brother nursed him, washed him, fed him a hundred oranges a week in a bizarre attempt to cure his blindness and saved newspapers for him to read when he regained his sight. Hundreds of thousands of newspapers.

Langley was buried in an avalanche of rubbish in 1947 when he tripped one of his elaborate booby traps while bringing Homer dinner. Thanks to my father, I knew all the particulars: how Homer had starved to death, how Langley's body had been gnawed by rats, how the police had searched the city for Langley for nearly three weeks while he lay entombed in the debris of his own house. To my 7-year-old ears, the cruel twist was deliciously gruesome: Homer and Langley had been killed by the very bulwarks they had raised to keep the world out of their lives.

The shadowy world of Homer and Langley was resurrected this month in an exhibition at the Inquiring Mind Gallery in Saugerties, N.Y. In this show, Richard Finkelstein, a Manhattan painter, has reimagined the brothers' lives in 17 black and white drawings called "Love and

Squalor on 128th Street." One sketch depicts the brothers dancing in the debris before an audience of female mannequins, the women in their lives.

A murder mystery by Mark Saltzman called "Clutter: The True Story of the Collyer Brothers Who Never Threw Anything Out," opens next February in Burbank, Calif. And last year the Collyers popped up at the Gramercy Arts Theater on East 23rd Street in "The Dazzle," a period drama by Richard Greenberg that was loosely based on the brothers' story.

Very loosely. Like nearly everyone else who invokes the Collyers, the playwright acknowledged he knew next to nothing about them. Mr. Greenberg was less interested in historical accuracy than the "idea" of the Collyers; to him, they were just "two people propelled by the romantic possibilities of life, although perhaps not as we might conventionally define them."

"Some see eccentrics as 'the other,' and in terms of pure irrationality," Mr. Greenberg added in an interview published around the time the play was produced. "But I see such eccentrics as having a very pure logic, although their needs are different from most of ours."

•

New York has long teemed with pack rats who can't pass a garbage bin without lifting the lid. A few became legends.

In the 1940's, a woman named Theresa Fox was found dead in the kitchen of her three-room hovel—somewhere in Queens, according to one newspaper account—with $1,300 stashed in the ratty stockings she wore. Ms. Fox, who was said to have owned property in Brooklyn valued at $100,000, had 100 one-pound bags of coffee in her cupboard, and 500 cans of evaporated milk stuffed in her mattress. The drawers of her bedroom bureau brimmed with sugar, and dozens of loaves of bread were stacked against the walls in a fieldstone pattern.

During the 50's, a shabby, plucked sparrow of a man named Charles Huffman was found dead in a Brooklyn street with no money in his pockets; the police said his $7-a-week room was piled with bankbooks and more than $500,000 in stock certificates.

And in the 60's a realtor named George Aichele, who lived at 61 East 86th Street in Yorkville, was found dead in a dim catacomb of trash and cash. Amid the stacks of old newspapers, heaps of used razor blades, drifts of pipes and birdcages and zithers was a paper bag containing a single penny and a note explaining that it had been found in front of the house in December 1957.

"New Yorkers live in such tight spaces that hoarding gets out of control faster," said Kate Sherman, director of special projects at the New York Service Program for Older People on West 91st Street. She says if New Yorkers moved more, they might edit their junk more. "But with rent control," she conceded, "people tend to stay in the same place."

Last year Ms. Sherman gave a lecture at the center where she works, titled "I've Got Plenty of Nothing: The Dynamics of Hoarding," in which she cast the malady as materialism run amok. "Part of it is about living in this age and society where there are so many papers to keep track of," she said. "It is really hard to know what to throw away. And if you are having memory problems or do not have the energy to take bales of paper to the recycling area, it can easily get out of hand. But I think with extreme hoarders, there's a level of it that's kind of beyond rational explanation."

Social scientists disagree as to exactly what causes obsessive hoarding. In its December 1960 issue, the Journal of Chronic Diseases branded recluses like the Collyers "deviants who are often surrounded by mystery and violence."

It is a description that doesn't sit well with Randy Frost, a professor of clinical psychology at Smith College and a consultant to the New York City Hoarding Task Force, a group formed by the Weill Medical College of Cornell University to examine hoarding among the elderly.

"If, by deviancy, the researchers meant sinister, that's not true," Professor Frost said. "If anything, hoarders tend to be avoidant and afraid."

And violent?

"Only in situations where a hoarder's possessions are being taken away," he said. "What is true is that hoarders usually wind up isolated." He cited a Boston study of hoarders aged 65 and older. "Fifty-five percent of them had never been married," he said, noting that the figure for the general population is 5 percent.

Historical accounts of hoarding date back 5,400 years ago to the necropolises of ancient Egyptians. In those vast cities of the dead, rulers of the Memphite dynasties were buried in mastabas, oblong tombs with sloping sides and flat roofs. Huge storerooms above and below the late pharaoh were jam-packed with his possessions, a collection that typically included furniture, clothing, magical amulets, tools, weapons, game boards, jewelry, jugs of wine and lunch boxes laden with mummified ducks and geese.

"I wouldn't call it junk, exactly," said Peter Piccione, a Brooklyn-born Egyptologist who teaches at the College of Charleston in South Carolina.

What would he call it?

"Stuff," Professor Piccione replied. "The ancient Egyptians believed a pharaoh couldn't lead much of a life in the afterlife without his stuff. Basically, they thought you could take it with you."

All the Collyer brothers took with them were secrets. Though Homer's death and the search for Langley were front-page staples in New York City's 12 daily newspapers, not even the most tenacious reporter could explain why these sons of privilege had been subsumed by their stuff.

•

The brothers have haunted me ever since my father told me his cautionary tales, and presumably they also haunted the two congenital collectors who helped me tell the brothers' story.

One was Carl Schoettler, a feature writer for The Baltimore Sun and lifelong bibliophile whose apartment is a dark forest of thousands upon thousands upon thousands of books. Together we visited the infamous corner at 128th Street and Fifth Avenue, now a vest-pocket park that is home to a dozen sycamores. We made a pilgrimage to Cypress Hills Cemetery in Brooklyn, where Homer and Langley are buried along with Mae West and for a time, in a crypt, the heart of Paderewski, the pianist whose notices drove Langley from the concert stage. We talked to old Harlem residents who claimed to have actually met the elusive Collyers.

My other collaborator was my Uncle Arthur, 88, so habitual a hoarder that my mother used to call him the lost Collyer brother. Small, bent and eternally boyish, Uncle Arthur dresses in layers of Salvation Army overcoats kept closed with rusty safety pins. Like a Beckett tramp, he holds his pants up with bits of rope.

Uncle Arthur was a 19-year-old novice collector when he moved to a tiny tenement apartment in Harlem, only three blocks from the Collyer homestead. He already knew that Homer and Langley were the preeminent junk collectors. "I'd walk by their house and wonder what of value did they have," he said. "You got to have brains to collect that much stuff."

"I always wanted to get in touch with them," he added. "I always wanted to get in touch with anybody who collected as much as I did. They collected more. They had their junk up to the windows. I didn't have that much."

Uncle Arthur does, however, have quite lot, and he has turned squalor into an art form. Until his collection was "deaccessioned" three years ago, nearly every cubic inch of his one-bedroom apartment in Flatbush, Brooklyn, was full, and virtually every surface was covered with heaps of stuff that mounted toward the ceiling. Uncle Arthur hates a vacuum.

Tangled mounds of twine and electrical cord climbed up gentle rolling hills of newspapers still in their plastic sleeves. A riot of shirts and jackets slopped out of stained grocery bags and onto the grubby carpet. The stove and the kitchen counters disappeared from view, lost under a couple of feet of cans, bottles and Calder-like mobiles that Uncle Arthur had fashioned out of clothespins and coat hangers. The bedroom closet was packed with newspapers from the Carter administration; the refrigerator, with English muffins from the end of the Reformation.

He shares the apartment with Wagging II, his cat. "Collecting junk is my hobby," he said. "My junk is like a friend, another person, another cat."

An urban prospector, Uncle Arthur trails through the streets of Brooklyn, collecting the detritus of the New York night. He finds his booty in back alleys, subway cars, train stations. "Believe it or not, I've never bought a single piece of junk," Uncle Arthur said. "I found it all on the street. You'd be surprised what you find once you look. Pennies, nickels, dimes, safety pins, jacks, dice, mirrors, small bottles, dresser handles, screws, wire, cord, moth balls, cigarette packs, pens that say different things on them, bullets."

He envied the space the Collyer brothers had in their 12-room house. Although by the time he got to Brooklyn in 1975, he was doing pretty well, he never quite got over the feeling that he never met the Collyers' high standards of junk connoisseurship. "I save this, I save that," he said. "I mix it all together, the good and the bad. So it's my fault."

He particularly prizes first-edition magazines, bus transfers and parking tickets plucked from windshields. "People just leave parking tickets on their cars," he said wonderingly. "I must have found thousands of dollars' worth. Every day I could pick one up."

My father used to claim that Uncle Arthur's hoarding was his way of "channeling aggression and sublimating it." And there is perhaps a defensiveness behind Uncle Arthur's hobby. Like Langley Collyer, he builds barricades, and sets booby traps and nests inside his walls of junk. But he is incapable of aggression. The only time I've ever seen Uncle Arthur really get mad was when my father told him to give it up. The tiny folds that line his pale forehead are not engraved by anger but merely the result of squinting down at the sidewalk.

Uncle Arthur has his own theory as to what lies behind his hoarding. "Maybe it's something I missed in my childhood," he said. "Like something big. The thing is you don't have to pay for junk. It's free."

He's not insensitive. He knows that people sniff at his junk, and frequently. "My landlord doesn't like my hobby," he conceded. "But what can he do? I've got a lease."

October 26, 2003

The author in Union Square Park. (Michelle V. Agins/The New York Times)

30

The War Within

A Brand-New New Yorker, He Is Enchanted by the Storied City. But His Tour of Duty in Iraq Has Clouded His View of Himself and of His Adopted Home.

DAVID C. BOTTI

ARLY one morning last July, my rifle company boarded a convoy of trucks leaving Nasiriyah, an Iraqi city 180 miles south of Baghdad, bound for Kuwait. After tossing my pack onto a truck, I looked back at members of the Carabinieri, Italy's military police force, who were staying. They were made groggy and disgruntled by the early hour, and about to assume watch over the building we had shared for the past month.

Last Wednesday, I turned on the morning news and saw that that same building had become a charred skeleton. It was all chaos and smoke after a car or truck bomb exploded directly beneath the window where I had once slept. I listened to the grisly numbers: the dead, the missing, the wounded, Iraqis and Italians. But there were no faces, no names. I had no way of knowing who among them I may have known. I could only imagine that everyone I had known there had become a casualty. I was at a remove, trying to resume my life in New York.

The August night I returned to the city from Iraq, I found myself drunk in the bathroom of an East Village bar. As I steadied the wall, I wondered how this skin of mine, tanned brown from the Iraqi sun, could now soak up the atmosphere of a good, seedy city bar. Wondered how the people in line behind me could enjoy the night while their peers still slept with rifles, halfway around the world, where I had been just the week before.

I wandered back to my friends, and drifted out of the conversation as soon as I sat down. It was easy to leave the city once more, relive the past four months in the time it took for the next round to arrive. No one spoke to me. Perhaps my silence betrayed my thoughts; I was glad to be left alone. But at that moment I was not having flashbacks, or letting alcohol numb grief and pain. There was no nervous tick or trembling hands. My thoughts, my reverie, lay with the people I had known in Iraq, the soldiers and citizens still dealing with the violent reality.

As the fighting unexpectedly intensifies in Iraq, as the American body count rises, each headline strikes deeper, and I can still see it, still feel it: walking through a foreign city, looking to the rooftops, the windows, in alleys, behind me, in front, to the sides. One person thanks you for freedom, and the next stares through you as if you are already a ghost.

It is a forceful process, ingesting the news and carrying it with me through the day. There are moments when I want the rifle back in my hand, so I can return to Iraq and remain there, until the war ends in a solid conclusion. There is still a reluctance to forget my initial, unwavering idealism, the belief that leaving Iraq meant that things were improving, and that others would soon be following me home.

But sometimes, it's New York that feels like a foreign city. One night, in another bar, I read a note posted by the staff above the urinal that ridiculed the city's smoking ban and urged patrons to send Mayor Bloomberg hate mail in an attempt to change the law.

This was the city I had returned to: outspoken and opinionated, the center of freethinking. I want the inspiration and nurturing that New York can give young writers. I am not ashamed of my service, but am conscious that my past might overshadow what I want to accomplish. As my friends and I headed home from that Village bar last August, I allowed myself respite from the guilt of being safe and happy. I watched the blocks pass with the hopeful feeling that soon the city would cease to feel new again.

•

I first truly experienced New York in spring 2002, as one of those servicemen you might have seen flooding Times Square during Fleet Week —drunk and proud and hungry for urban excess. We arrived as a collection of reserve marines headquartered in Albany and Long Island, already mobilized four months in response to the World Trade Center attacks. Sept. 11 threw us into the stream of world events, and we deployed to Camp Lejeune, N.C., at the ready as our country faced uncertain times.

Three years before, I had been a college sophomore in upstate New York, discontented with the comfortable routine of academic life. An impromptu visit to the Marine recruiter during winter break seemed to provide a sadistic cure. I snuck out of the house and signed the papers that would fill my next two summers up with boot camp and infantry training, bringing me into the Corps.

After graduating from Skidmore, I moved home to Waltham, Mass., near Boston, and continued to train with my rifle company in Albany. We never gave a thought to the possibility of mobilizing. But those two weeks in New York in 2002 showed us how different life had become.

There were free subway rides and photographs with babies, women asking us questions about our ribbons. We were called heroes, even though this was New York and the fighting was then in Afghanistan. A police officer brought a group of us past the line of visitors at ground zero, onto the crowded viewing platform. I leaned against the wooden railing, feeling my uniform pulse at the moment. At the wall of names, I found a family friend and wanted to cry—but I remembered the uniform and held it in.

Fleet Week ended before I was ready to leave. I watched the skyline grow smaller above New York Harbor, and knew I needed to return when the state of the world allowed.

Seven months later my reserve unit was sent home. There was an epic apartment hunt, and half my savings depleted by real estate fees, before the rental truck finally sat packed full in my parents' driveway. My father and mother stood on the front steps in the cold night air, arms folded, looking on in brooding acceptance.

In the tradition of my grandfather moving into Mulberry Street by way of Ellis Island a century earlier, I had succumbed to the storied pull of the great city. I wanted to live in the center of progress, to write and join the masses of starving artists, hoping this rite of passage would one day lead to better things.

I answered the phone that night before I left home. A marine from my platoon reported that rumors were circulating among the ranks about possible reactivation and deployment to Southwest Asia. There was a choice to make, but my bedroom was empty, and I had rented a truck. I couldn't stay.

•

The new apartment, in Riverdale in the Bronx, was a rare find, spacious and nestled between the safety of two nursing homes and a highway. I had roommates, my friends were nearby, and the subway system began to make sense. I bought bookcases, pots and pans, towels and lamps, hoping that the more settled I became, the more I could ward off my fate unfolding in the headlines. I found a job to pay the rent, and enrolled in an N.Y.U. fiction-writing workshop.

With our apartment still in boxes and the refrigerator filled with take-out, my roommates and I prepared to celebrate our first weekend in the city. I could do nothing but acquiesce when I was suddenly given orders to spend that weekend getting the first in a series of anthrax shots.

After just one month of city living, the call to mobilize came. I was given the necessary information. And in an even tone, I replied that I understood, closing my eyes in my cubicle to contemplate the new phase of life I was entering. Word traveled quickly through the office that day. Friends and strangers approached me with words of encouragement and admiration. I left the office hours later, carrying a small flag signed by my co-workers that I would carry in the top flap of my pack throughout my deployment.

The city was beautiful my last night on its streets, the chill making me appreciate the inviting warmth in a corner cafe or the familiar rock of a heated subway car. I headed south on Park Avenue, February numbing my hand as I held the cellphone to my ear. There was a marathon of calls through chattering teeth. Friends and family were confused, wanted to know more than I knew myself. Then I found a park bench, and sat alone for the first time since the news came. I tried to remember everything I could, collecting memories for the times ahead.

As I stood and walked on, I saw the words "Stop Bush" spray-painted on a mailbox. Before I could reflect on this, I saw the same words again, scratched onto a beat-up basement door. For the first time, I felt the sting of the war's controversy.

I wondered whether people could see a difference between soldier and politician. I sought to find a stranger on the street and explain that I just wanted for my friends and me to come home alive, that I didn't care about politics. I was like everyone else, a kid who had come to New York seeking something better. I had everything in common with them. And nothing.

I watched the day end, the people returning home or preparing for a night out. When it got late, I headed home, wishing I could line up every person in the city, shake their hands, say, "Good-bye, I've had a good time, maybe I can come back again some day." I spent the bus ride home that night consoling my mother by cellphone. Telling her lies as I tried to persuade her they would never send a reserve infantry company into Iraq: we would only be asked to guard the supply lines throughout Kuwait. She didn't believe me, but pretended to.

After I hung up, a woman sitting in front of me turned and said she had heard the whole conversation. She promised to pray for me.

I spent my first night in country one month later, packed into the barracks of a defeated Iraqi Army division on the outskirts of Nasiriyah. I woke the next morning to the harsh sun.

In the next room I found myself facing a mural of the World Trade Center, rising over marines sleeping on their packs and in crude cots. The mural had been painted on a weathered wall by a marine passing through, soaring amid Iraqi propaganda images of tanks and barbed wire and fists thrust through cracked stars and stripes. Beneath the towers, a simple strip of blue brought to mind the cobblestones of South Street Seaport.

Often, we heard mention of New York, even in the Iraqi desert, from the occasional newspaper thrown from a passing convoy, its precious pages whipping in the desert wind, or from the coveys of reporters passing through in S.U.V.'s stuffed with trendy camping gear. They offered outrageous rumors of a smoking ban and subway fare hikes.

One reporter set out to interview another marine from New York, placing him where the camera would catch a dramatic view of the Euphrates River. The reporter asked what the difference was between New York and Iraq. The marine paused and looked at the reporter in disbelief, then smiled: "The sand."

Early on, I began interviewing the 30 members of my platoon, trying to fill my journal with thoughts other than my own. Among questions about protesters and the divided opinion on the war, I asked whether they had thought about Sept. 11 since arriving in Iraq. "Every day," one marine said, replying fast, as if he had wanted to answer the question before even hearing it. "I'm trying to relate it to here. I want people I know living in New York City to live, and not have to worry about things."

My service in Iraq felt like a lifetime, and an instant. There were moments I was scared; times when I thought myself lucky to live the experience or felt anger for having to stay in such a place. In the end, my

battalion flew home safe, with no casualties and 15 months of active
duty served since 9/11, including four months in Iraq.

•

Days after I returned to New York in August, I found a live bat in my
toilet. The next afternoon came the blackout. The routine of daily living
consumed me before I could fully comprehend where I was. When I
looked at the city during those early days back, it was often through the
eyes of the Iraqis I had known, who spoke of New York with mythic reverence. Our 21-year-old interpreter, who had taken to wearing a baseball
cap backward, recited youthful dreams of visits to America, to New
York, where he could leave behind the life in a country he despised.

First, it was simple things: How could a building rise so high? How
could women wear those clothes? How could I survive there? One
month's rent for my apartment would buy the dowry of his girlfriend,
who had talked about leaving him if the price could not be met.

I was eager to become anonymous again, to settle into the great glory
of a mundane life. At the same time I was curious to see how New York
was reacting to the war. I sought some kind of acknowledgement of the
suffering I had seen, some kind of change or traces of a collective mourning. The only real evidence of the war's impact seemed to be the scrolling
marquees in Times Square, still counting the casualties and the violent
incidents.

New York, even with its tradition of freethinking and global awareness, has a blurry sense of life beyond its gravitational pull. Set foot onto
the eternal pavement, watch buildings close out the sky, and the pace of
the city draws you in. It took time to realize that within the city's imper-
sonal pulse, most people wanted to understand what Iraq was like, without the mediation of the press and government. Talking to me, one
person said, was the closest he could get to having his own boots planted
in the desert.

The first time someone asked "How was it?," I froze. I mumbled what
he might have wanted to hear, themes he could relate to from the news reports: insane heat, unrest, whatever would make him nod and end the in-
quiry. But it never seemed right to discuss these things at a party or around
the office water cooler in between arguments over the pennant race.

Others went further: Did I ever think I was going to die? Was I emotionally scarred? And I could see in their eyes, the question that burned
brightest. Had I killed anyone?

At first I was disgusted. But after numbing myself to the routine questions, I understood that Americans had lived more closely with this war than with any before.

Everything changed last Wednesday. The guilty sense of complacency that I had adopted dissolved in a rush of vivid memories spurred by the destruction of the building where I had lived. I kept thinking about how we cringed at the Italians wandering about the building in nothing but Speedos, or how we begged for leftovers from their boiling vats of fresh pasta. To the rest of the world, the building is yet another symbol of terrorism; it will disappear from the headlines as quick as it arrived. For the platoon, it had been a home and a refuge. When the Italians arrived, it became a learning experience; two groups of young men with nothing in common but the will of their governments.

I've spent the three months since I returned home hoping that a day like last Wednesday would never come. But it did. And now life in New York seems more foreign to me than it ever has before.

November 16, 2003

The author with a child from the Bronx. (Joyce Dopkeen/The New York Times)

31

Uptown Girl

In Researching Her Book on the South Bronx, Adrian Nicole LeBlanc Absorbed Its Poverty, Its Toughness, Its Glacial Pace. She Also Rediscovered Herself.

ADRIAN NICOLE LEBLANC

IT seems significant that on one of my first outings to the South Bronx, I couldn't find my way back home. I lived in Chelsea then, and I was still new to New York. I worked days as an editor at Seventeen magazine and did my freelance reporting at night. The Village Voice had assigned me a piece on drug dealers' girlfriends. I borrowed a friend's clunking car to take some of the girls clubbing. Entering a pool hall on the Grand Concourse, I had my first experience of being frisked. It was after 4 a.m. when I dropped off the last girl. The rain dumped down.

Back then, in the early 90's, the South Bronx still seemed to me like the iconic ghetto it was purported to be; that night, as I drove up and down its desolate boulevards, the shapes of the ordinary world disappeared. All I saw beyond the fogging windshield was threat. No hint of the pace of well-lit, clipped Manhattan. Rain slashed the signs of unfamiliar streets. Elevated subway tracks loomed overhead. At a gas station, I anxiously left the car to ask directions, but my questions got drowned out by the pleas of the Indian attendant, barricaded in behind his bars, urgently waving me, please, away.

My own fear increased with the resulting chill. Eventually, I was flying by the Whitestone Cinema, headed east. Blessedly, I spotted the "New England Thruway" sign, a friendly highway green.

Originally, I come from Leominster, in northern Massachusetts. Absurdly, I seriously considered driving the four hours home. In a panic, one reverts to what one knows. At least from Leominster, I knew my way back to New York. What I wouldn't realize for another decade was that the homecoming would ultimately occur the other way around: the pull of the Bronx, and the connection to the family I found there, not the fear of it, would carry me home to my blood family.

Only now, a year after its publication, is the full meaning of the title of my first book, "Random Family," revealing itself to me. The book documents more than a decade in the life of one extended family from the South Bronx. Had I been asked midway through the reporting what the title meant, I might have answered, "The families my subjects inherited and those they chose" or "The family that teenagers create among their friends."

But from where I stand now, I'd say that a sense of belonging can also spring from a geographical affinity, the comfort we feel in places both known and discovered or, in some cases, the places that are within us even before we arrive, their streets coursing through our personal histories.

•

My strongest early memories of my father involve him driving away. Off he'd go, in the orange pumpkin, our nickname for the rust-colored American Ambassador supplied by the union when he left a chemical factory job and turned to organizing full time. My father drove to far-away destinations—Pittsburgh, Akron, Detroit—and returned with exotic tales infused with the urgency of the mundane world, compelling stories about regular people struggling to make ends meet.

Once we spent a family holiday at a roadside Ramada Inn in Delaware. While my mother sunned by the pool, I trailed Edie, an elderly maid whose gentle presence made my father's hotel room a home. Edie let me refill the vending machine with miniature toothbrushes, their silver tubes of toothpaste as slim and shiny as smelts. She let me push her tidy hallway cart. In the sweet-smelling laundry closet, which doubled as her office, we counted her tips.

As I was growing up, my mother liked to tell me that every woman needs an education and a car. (The education was something no one could ever take away from you, while a car could take you away from anywhere you suddenly didn't want to be.) After high school, I was always driving away—for college, for graduate school, on assignment, back to my apartment in New York.

Like my father's, my visits home were brief; I was using my education the way I was supposed to, to escape the working class that my ambitious mother had found herself trapped in. She devoted her life to making my escape possible, struggling to balance her love without letting me feel entirely at home. But if I wanted to succeed—whatever that meant —I couldn't stop moving. Irrationally, I worried that if I ever slowed down, or slipped up, I'd somehow end up on my father's old slot on the assembly line.

When I started my reporting in the Bronx, however, suddenly I was like my father with his union: I knew that this was the work I wanted to do. I felt a sense of purpose, energized and fully alive. The work drew on my deepest self, yet, unlike the elite worlds to which my education exposed me, didn't require that I bury my working-class alliances.

In fact, those initial nights of reporting—listening to music and watching the girls dress up to go dancing, hanging out in front of bodegas and in courtyards and on stoops, driving around as they shouted out of the car to the windows of the boys they liked—took me back to an earlier time. It was a lot like my teenage years with my hometown friends, aimless and open-ended, not about the things we didn't have, or some distant future, but about the vitality and wonder of the life that was already ours, and within our reach.

It turns out I wasn't the first of my relatives to do time in the Bronx. Not long after I began serious work on my book, I called my mother from the pay phone of a cafe in the Italian neighborhood of Belmont. "I don't know why," I told her, "I feel so at home here." I supposed it was the familiarity of the Italians on Arthur Avenue. My mother neglected to mention that her parents had lived there for a decade before moving to Leominster, where, not long after, my grandfather died. It would be years before an uncle, in an emotional moment after a family funeral, confessed that the greatest love story in my family's history had taken place in that neighborhood—perhaps the site of the loss of promise the most painful to bear.

My mother's father rented a room as a boarder from my grandmother's older sister, who had come from a neighboring village in Italy. He saw my grandmother's photograph, and they started corresponding; he dictated his letters because he didn't know how to write. Eventually, he helped pay her passage; her younger brother, Orazio, escorted her. There was a swoon after the first kiss in Central Park, another legendary kiss in the stairwell of the sister's house.

Six months later, on Oct. 8, 1905, the Rev. Thomas T. Lynch officiated at the marriage at St. Elizabeth's Roman Catholic Church in Washington Heights. My grandmother liked to tell my mother how she looked like a princess that day, dressed in white, perched atop a carriage driven by six white horses that delivered her to the church. She was adorned in jewelry, including a gold chain that my grandfather had given her, and a bracelet etched with a delicate scroll. Over her heart, she pinned a bird with four tiny pearls, two on each wing, and a ruby balanced on its beak.

It was a hopeful beginning, but things got harder quickly. As my grandmother began having children, nine in all, my grandfather took whatever work he could find—lighting lamps, maintenance, delivering coal. For a time, he was a superintendent in a building in Belmont, just two blocks away from Thorpe house, the homeless shelter on Crotona Avenue where, 90 years later, I would be spending my weekends and nights.

By then, I'd met Lolli, the young woman who would become one of my primary subjects (and who is identified as Coco in my book). In the restroom at Seventeen, I'd slip out of my black blazer and miniskirt at the end of my work day and put on a T-shirt and jeans. We happily explored her Bronx streets, pointing out our favorites among the trays of gold medallions and door-knocker earrings in the jewelry shops on Fordham Road, admiring the dusty baby shower cakes decorated with miniature pacifiers in the window of the cuchifrito-bakery on Burnside Avenue, watching the bright fake fish that paddled spastic laps in a plastic aquarium at the dollar store.

On Mount Hope Place, where her first love had lived before he went to prison, Lolli showed me the graffiti heart she'd etched into the wall of a stairwell where they used to kiss. One Sunday morning, on Tremont Avenue, we waved to a young bride and groom gleefully shouting from the sun roof of a white stretch limousine.

I gradually realized, however, that Lolli had never ventured the few blocks from her Puerto Rican neighborhood to the Italian section. So one day, when her 3-year-old daughter was hungry, I suggested lunch on Arthur Avenue. I was slowly becoming a familiar face on the street; the bakery clerk nodded hello, and the butcher at the Arthur Avenue Market tutored me about what to look for in a proper cut of beef.

Lolli was uncharacteristically reluctant as we stepped into a coffee shop where I'd been a few times. Helping her daughter climb onto a stool, she stood behind her, pressing her pregnant belly against the little girl's back so she wouldn't topple off. We waited while the waitress chatted with a customer at the far end of the counter. I asked for menus. It was 11 a.m. The short-order cook was flipping eggs on the grill. From

the opposite end of the room, without looking in our direction, the waitress said, "Kitchen's closed."

•

In the meantime, I had moved to SoHo. I didn't find it an easy fit. On
weekends, when it teemed with shoppers buying things I could never afford, I'd linger around the corner of Something Special, Lenny Cecere's
small store on MacDougal, just to hear the banter of Italian men. On the
rare days I didn't go to the Bronx, I'd head out to Coney Island, to stroll
on the boardwalk among the old Russians, or to Bensonhurst, to eat
panelle at Joe's of Avenue U. My apartment was rent-stabilized, so I
couldn't think of leaving permanently, but it was more like a hotel than a
home.

The parts of the Bronx that I was getting to know didn't require the
same stretching. Uptown, on the sidewalk, in the Laundromat, at the
Western Union office, my movements came naturally. What became tax-
ing were the transitions.

I remember the day I realized that I had to leave my Midtown job. I'd
spent a spate of nights out reporting in the Soundview projects, where
the elevator doors rattled and ached, and that tired morning I was struck
by the silence of my ascent at Seventeen. The bell for my floor gently
sounded, and I stepped noiselessly off the elevator onto the red carpet
that led to my office. I no longer knew what I was doing there.

Whenever I was downtown, which was less and less, I felt that life
was elsewhere. Uptown, I was learning to surrender to the slower
rhythms of my subjects' days. Ordinary acts absorbed me utterly. Even
the most mundane things—children playing, a trip to the grocery store,
watching an old dog sleeping—gave me a sense of discovery. After all, I
was supposed to spend hours hanging out, observing. I started to crave
the street. On the best days, I was keenly aware of the sensory environment but unaware of myself. I knew I was in precisely the right place, at
the right time. Doing my work meant remaining still.

Like that of a child shuttling between divorced parents, my behavior
changed with my surroundings: at a welfare office in the Bronx, I could
be endlessly patient, numbed. Yet if I had to wait in line at the Gourmet
Garage, I became irritable. Increasingly at ease in the places most white
New Yorkers thought of as impossibly dangerous, I'd tense up at book
parties and gallery openings. I preferred to brave the stairwell in a
housing project than walk into a roof-top party. A college friend, now a

psychologist, declared me counter-phobic. Possibly true, but what good do labels do?

But the greatest threat to my reporting wasn't the danger, which was erratic and unusual, but the frustrations and despair, which were relentless, pervading every task of daily life. In the Bronx, survival regularly felt impossible, escape unimaginable. Even hope became a risk.

Back in SoHo, I slept, a lot. I'm generally an early morning person, but I came to love the bed. I'd sleep a solid 12 hours after a prison visit, a whole day after a weekend in Lolli's mother's courtyard. One afternoon, one of the girls from the Bronx called to wake me; I used to be prompt, calling up to their windows, waking them. Now, I was late, I answered the telephone cranky. "You sound like my mother," she said critically.

Poverty is a climate. Within a few years, I had adapted to its weather's unpredictability: I stopped believing that institutions functioned in any reliable or useful fashion. I would be surprised, delighted, when anything went smoothly. I developed a sense of humor. I stopped wearing black, started wearing fuchsia. I became an optimist, and a fatalist. I cared more about my sex appeal. My downtown friends commented that I'd become more defensive, suspicious and sarcastic. My uptown friends told me I needed to gain weight and relax.

Surely some of this was a result of my immersion in my subjects' world, my experience of their profound economic and physical vulnerability. I wish I'd been strong enough to move to the Bronx and live in the spaces that, for 24 hours a day, filled my head.

•

My own family's crisis took me back to Leominster; my father was found to have cancer. During the 18 months that I cared for him, my city life receded; my hometown roots were renewed. Over the phone, my downtown friends expressed their worries about me: I needed to rest, I needed to eat, I needed to get back to New York. My Bronx friends told me to stay strong, to fight the terror, to try to make my father laugh, to fill the house with children. They'd shown me what my Italian ancestors had buried in their stoic formality. When it's not possible to protect the people you love and make things better, you grab onto the good moments when you can.

A Bronx friend, who had survived a spinal injury, coached my father through a similar trauma and gave me indispensable caretaking advice.

Another friend, who worked as a home health aide, prepared me for what to expect as my father moved closer to death. Lolli and her children came to visit. ("You mad skinny," said her 9-year-old, taking in my father. "That's for sure," my father said.) As I watched Lolli holding my father's bony hand, I felt the reconnection of something broken running through my life. When my father passed, Lolli's mother told me to take care of my own. "Your mother's the only one you've got," she said.

Not so long ago, I returned to New York and reintroduced myself to my apartment and my neighborhood. I walked to the Angelika, became a morning regular at Once Upon a Tart, swam laps at a nearby pool. Photographs got framed, dinners cooked, walls painted. I moved into my place, then I got restless again. Nights, I reported a story about a rapper and drug dealer who lived in Bedford-Stuyvesant. I was back at work. Absorbed, I watched him get his weekly trim among the men debating politics at his barbershop. Sitting in the passenger seat of his S.U.V., flying down the low Brooklyn streets, windows open, his music blasting, looking out at the new neighborhood, I felt life pouring over me.

To be where I am is to accept where I came from, to be both a visitor and an escapee. Maybe always leaving is my closest kinship, but I've learned to claim the life I live here, wherever that may be. The open invitation is what I cherish most about my work in this city—the righteousness of my ignorance, the job of getting lost again and again.

February 1, 2004

Lodovico Capponi, by Bronzino. (The Frick Collection)

32

My Friend Lodovico

Finding a Soul Mate on Upper Fifth Avenue.

DAVID MASELLO

TEN years ago, upon breaking up with someone after an embarrassing public argument in Central Park, I went to see Lodovico Capponi. I needed his approval and reassurance. He was also one of the first people I visited a few days after Sept. 11. Whenever friends are in from out of town, I often take them to meet him, and if I find myself in his Upper East Side neighborhood, I can rarely resist dropping by.

Lodovico lives in the Frick Collection, the mansion-museum on Fifth Avenue. He is a portrait, painted in the 1550's by Agnolo Bronzino, the celebrated Florentine artist employed as a court painter to the Medicis; the 500th anniversary of Bronzino's birth is being celebrated this year. In this four-foot-high oil, Lodovico is shown with wavy, red-brown hair, a flawless complexion and a wandering left eye.

I have known Lodovico for 23 years, as long as I have lived in New York. And after all these years, I keep asking myself the same question: Why do I continue to visit this mute, overdressed, imperious young man? Many people to whom I introduce him find him austere, even humorless. Others consider another Bronzino young man who hangs on a wall at the Metropolitan Museum of Art handsomer and more engaging.

When I was close to Lodovico's age, about 22, some people said I resembled him; my right eye wanders lazily in the way his left does; his nose appears to be equally ample and Italian. I suppose it's natural that we are attracted to those who remind us of ourselves. Years ago, after I sent a postcard of the portrait to my father in Florida, he called to mention that he had taped Lodovico to his refrigerator as a reminder of me. "He looks like you, only without your eyeglasses," my father said. "And get a haircut—you could be as clean-cut as this kid."

Lodovico was a constant in my early years in New York. I knew always where to find him, in the West Gallery of the Frick. Being a painting, he would never change or age. At a time when I still had few friends and a fragile self-confidence as a young man in a new city working in an office job for a book publisher, I admired Lodovico's regal bearing, his unblinking confidence and his solid ownership of a defined station in life.

Much has changed since we met. I am now twice as old as he is in the painting, I've had careers and I've been happily involved with a partner for years. Yet I need the unspoken advice that Lodovico still supplies. When I visit the Frick, his portrait is what I go to first, striding purposefully to the work, and leaving the museum after only several minutes, sometimes even before the coat checker has hung up my garment. I have never visited the Frick without spending some time with Lodovico.

He wears a high-collared, velvet-striped taffeta jacket over a white satin shirt, sleeves embellished with fisheye cutouts. A long swag of luxurious black velvet swoops from his right shoulder down to his billowing breeches, which seem fashioned from shimmering ribbons. In his right hand, he pinches a cameo with the mysterious inscription "Sorte" (fate, or fortune, in Italian), and in his left he clasps neatly folded brown gloves that I had long mistaken as a wallet until the audio-guide narrator enlightened me one day.

The space where he dwells is a retreat not only from Manhattan streets, but from all concerns in life, even though every passion, from lust and jealousy to murder and love, is on display. Even before reaching the galleries, some visitors are seduced by the trickling fountain in the interior courtyard where they wind up spending contemplative hours listening to the water instead of looking at the artworks. This is where I sat those many years ago after my romantic breakup; rather than confront Lodovico in tears, I collected myself beside the waters before presenting myself to him for consolation.

Despite his calm demeanor, Lodovico was living through trying times when his portrait was being painted. While on the job as a court page, he fell in love with a young girl, Maddalena Vettori, whom his employer, Duke Cosimo I de' Medici, had chosen as a bride for one of his cousins. Upon learning of their courtship, the duke forbade the couple to meet. The duke's wife, Eleonara of Toledo, empathized with the young couple and lobbied on their behalf. After three years, the duke acquiesced, but stipulated that unless the couple married within 24 hours, they would be forever separated. They wed immediately and produced eight children.

One reason I go to see Lodovico is because he is an expert creation. I marvel at the folds in the fabric and the resulting shadows, the shimmer of material, the smoothness of skin and the absence of brush strokes, an almost photographically flawless application of color. I love the literal cloak of mystery created by the green material. I can imagine a marble palazzo just behind the folds, corridors bustling with court pages, ladies-in-waiting lifting skirts as they walk, busybody Eleonara passing messages between Lodovico and Maddalena.

•

Lodovico and I have maintained an odd relationship. We don't speak, and when together, we stare each other down. Yet I can look at him indefinitely. And I miss him quickly if too many weeks go by without a visit. I break my gaze only when another visitor approaches.

He neither smiles nor frowns, seems judging or indifferent, appears happy or sad. Lodovico is just as he is. There is nothing else in the painting but him; no alluring snippets of late Renaissance cityscapes, beloved pets, fanciful furniture. He is simply a young, well-dressed, attractive man who has taken the time to stand for us over what must have been many weeks.

Lodovico is my Dorian Gray. Because he will never age or fade, neither will my memories of life in New York in my early 20's when Lodovico was one of the first figures I met and came to know.

If he could see me, he would have discerned over the years a portrait of me standing before him, alone, with various mates, as they entered and left my life, with friends (some of whom died in the 80's during our version of the black plague), and with strangers who share their thoughts about the painting. He would have seen me wearing ties as wide as napkins, later ones ruler-narrow, glasses in every style from granny to aviator.

I can't claim that an image in a painting became one of my first real friends in New York, but I can say that I visited the painting so often when I was new to the city that, as an object, it became friendly and familiar. The painting and the room where it hangs became, and remain, constants in my life.

Lodovico and I are equally removed from each other's time, and I worry, increasingly, about the growing gulf in our ages. Will his youth eventually intimidate me? Yet I know that if he came to life somehow, we would eagerly teach each other the ways of our time. I wouldn't know how to negotiate the intrigues of Renaissance Florentine court life, and he wouldn't understand whole-wheat pasta. But I'm sure our friendship would be an easy one. We would be, as they say in Italian, simpatico.

February 8, 2004

33

Fare-Beater Inc.

A Former Seminarian Found His True Calling in the Subtle Art of Sluggery.

JIM DWYER

The real thing.

O N fare-beating, the criminal cause and commercial activity around
which his life found meaning, Alan Campbell speaks softly, almost
monkishly. Far more than a simple acrobat who jumped turnstiles, or a
bottom-feeding hustler who sucked tokens out of slots, Mr. Campbell
worked on a scale of dizzying, historic proportion. He manufactured
slugs by the millions over years and years, but remained a phantom, hidden behind layers of distributors. Unable to hunt him down, the transit
system struggled to mount a defense. It deployed an army of police
officers. It tinkered with turnstile mechanisms. Even the design of the
token was changed over and over.

"Slugs have been around a long time, and if it worked, people passed
the word," Mr. Campbell said. "The general public tends to be larcenous
in certain areas."

The slug-making era is now just remembered twilight. The public pays
its fare with electrons bought and stored on magnetic stripes, not with
little discs rattling in the pocket or purse. At 64, Mr. Campbell is a slug
master in winter, self-critical but not self-flaying. This may be less a function of age than temperament. He entered Cathedral College High
School, a minor seminary in Clinton Hill, Brooklyn, at age 14, and
stayed eight years awaiting the grace of the Holy Spirit to summon him
on to the priesthood. He never heard it. Somewhere, slugs were calling.

He wandered toward the New School for graduate work in sociology
and philosophy, but never finished. Living rent-controlled on Clinton
Street in Brooklyn Heights, he read a pamphlet on how the ordinary,
cheap No. 14 brass washer could be used to make dime phone calls. It
was an epiphany. "You had to Scotch-tape over one side of the hole," he
said. "The phone could defend itself against the washer if the hole went
all the way through. The tape blocked the hole."

He discovered a supply house in a loft near Chambers Street that sold
fasteners, nuts and bolts, and, eureka, No. 14 washers. He bought loads.
His family of law-abiding, pious Catholics—"but not overly pious," he
cautioned—assumed that he was keeping body and soul with part-time
jobs at Mount Loretto on Staten Island, and with the Narcotics Addiction Control Commission. Certainly not with hustles like brass washers.

Moreover, he had turned to a more profitable opportunity: a slug that
worked in subway turnstiles. "The goal was more in saving money, originally," he said. "Then I heard, 'If you had more of them, I would buy
them.' If you can make slugs, it gets the costs way down." Around 1970

—the year the fare increased from 20 to 30 cents, triggering a mad run on all available slug supplies—he was introduced, by chance, to the wonders of the reciprocating press, an industrial-strength hole puncher. He bought his own.

"The metal is slipped into long coils—really big ones are 300 pounds —and fed through the press," he recalled. "I believe it was Russians who figured out that a submachine gun could be made from a reciprocating press. Making a slug is the easiest and simplest use of the reciprocating press. You could make up to a million if you kept the machine going."

How many was he selling? "As far as the total, I didn't want documents like that in my possession," he said. "Sometimes I used newspaper articles to track it." In those early years, one could read that 2,000, 8,000, 10,000 slugs a day were being collected from turnstiles. On his prices, he is vague—"variable rates; at one point I raised it to 15 cents" —and while he has a diary somewhere, he believes any figures would sound deceptively large.

"For many years, I was living mostly off the income from the slugs, partly because I didn't need much money," he said. "I didn't have a wife or family. And in part that was because of the slugs. A woman left me over them."

It seems that a slug customer had been nabbed, then named his supplier, resulting in Mr. Campbell's arrest in 1974 and the forfeiture of his press, at Union and Henry Streets in Carroll Gardens, Brooklyn. Mr. Campbell got probation.

"The woman was with me when I first got caught, and she was upset when I went back into it," he said. "I was even doing it on probation. You can always say about a relationship, 'It's for the best.' People wouldn't do it"—manufacture slugs, he means—"if they had families, children. It's not that crime does not pay. The social costs are the real problem. The key motive was perverse, to be getting up to something." He even used slugs himself, a reckless act, he concedes, but was never caught.

Even so, he decided to step back and become a wholesaler. He succeeded wildly. By 1985, the turnstiles were collecting 13,000 slugs per day, roughly the equivalent of all public transit ridership in Kansas City. "Middle-class people," Mr. Campbell said. "Street people would just rush the turnstile."

A great deal of his fortune came from his association with Kim Gibbs, whom Mr. Campbell met in the late 70's through a tennis partner and slug customer. Mr. Gibbs, who had a messenger business on West 47th Street, formed a distribution ring he called the Ministry, designated himself the commander in chief, named a prime minister, and sent his crew to peddle token slugs by the tens of thousands. Mr. Campbell churned them out from a new factory in Paterson, N.J., and deposited bags of slugs at self-storage places around Brooklyn. A day later, Mr. Gibbs or one of his men would collect them.

In 1986, around the time the fare went to a dollar, the transit system took its boldest anti-slug action by switching to the bull's-eye token, with an alloy center. The slug take in the turnstiles quickly dropped to about 400 per day, a 97 percent decrease, then gradually climbed. "It slowed me down," Mr. Campbell admitted.

Mr. Gibbs was arrested in 1988, and during his journey through the courts, the number of slugs dropped by half. Under stern questioning, he refused to name his supplier. Released, he returned to the Ministry. An agreeable young guy who called himself Ray Santiago showed up looking for work in early 1991. He was an undercover police officer, true name, Ralph Diaz.

"I should have said, let's get out, call it a day," Mr. Campbell said. "The psychology was very much like gambling, or stock speculation—you know in one part of your head it would make sense to get out. It makes sense for a criminal to call it off, but most criminal enterprises don't work that way. There is a denial."

The police tailed Mr. Campbell for weeks, but he drove at the speed limit in the left lane, or stopped for 10 minutes to fill up his gas tank. One day in the summer of 1991, he bought groceries, then disappeared into the factory for two days. When he emerged, the police grabbed him. Inside, besides his reciprocating press, they found reading material on the promised MetroCard system. He pleaded guilty and served 19 months.

His life of transit crime has come to an end, he says. The MetroCard, he said, "is not spoofable. You could pick someone's pocket, but you couldn't counterfeit it."

He has helped a friend manage a coffee bar, gives tennis lessons, and draws a small Social Security check, having barely paid any tax over his years in sluggery. "The phenomenon is not all that rare," the former seminarian said, "where people become monsters."

March 28, 2004

34

The Ballad of Sonny Payne

The Subway Is Filled With Panhandlers. But
Perhaps None Is as Beloved as the Man With
the White Beard and Gentle Eyes Who
Moves Through the F Train.

STEVEN KURUTZ

Sonny Payne at work. (Karen Gordon/The New York Times)

WITH the exception of the mayor and a stray actor or two, the subway trains are generally bereft of public figures. It's an anonymous
journey. This is not the case on the F train, however, where every day a
luminary rides alongside the commuters in the form of a small, sweet-
natured old panhandler named Sonny Payne.

Sonny has worked the F train so long and with such success that along
the Brooklyn stretch of the line, from Avenue X in Coney Island to the
Jay Street/Borough Hall station in Downtown Brooklyn, he is considered
an esteemed part of the commuting. "He's like something out of
'Cheers,'" one passenger said. This makes him feel good. Every so often
he'll go unsighted for a few weeks, causing some riders to worry that he
has died. When he appears again, their faces lift with relief and they greet
him even more warmly than before.

"I've been upstate," he likes to say after one of these periodic ab-
sences.

Sonny, the name he prefers and the one by which he is universally
known, is black with a scruffy white beard, and his wardrobe reflects the
thrown-together style of the rootless: loose-fitting pants, a blue spring
jacket worn year round, an outdated sweatshirt, all topped with an old
ball cap. He is either 65 or 67, depending on his mood when you ask
him, but he has a slight frame and a childlike air. "I went to the Bronx
Zoo this past summer," he once noted proudly. "All by myself."

Although his name has a certain theatrical ring, Sonny is most famous
for his introductory speech, which he recites upon entering each car. Delivered in a honeyed, singsong voice as the train buckets along, he says:
"Pardon me, my name is Sonny Payne. I'm homeless and I'm hungry. If
you don't have it, I can understand, because I don't have it. But if you
have a little change, a piece of fruit, something to eat, I'd greatly appreciate it."

So catchy is the speech that it's sometimes posted verbatim on the Web
site Craigslist, and a less imaginative panhandler named Marty adopted
it for his own use. Sonny doesn't feel slighted. "In a way," he said, "I
take it as a backhanded compliment."

The subways, of course, are filled with tired, sallow people asking passengers for money. Most are viewed as a nuisance and are lucky to get
spare change; if they catch riders in a foul mood, sandwiched together
on an evening's commuting, they may get nothing. Even if someone is in-
clined to donate, the parade of beggars worsens their own odds. There

are the doo-wop singers, the sad-eyed women, the drunks, the preachers, the guitar-strumming bandoleros, all with a hand out.

For Sonny, the jostling over spare nickels has long passed. He is above the fray. Through salient charm and learned observation, he has solved the mystery of what makes subway riders, already taxed, give to a beggar. He isn't even a beggar but an old friend, and in place of loose change he is often given bills. One evening not long ago he made $136. He took the money and booked a hotel room for two nights. "I treated myself," he said. "I really enjoyed it."

Although there are other familiar figures who troll the subways in search of a livelihood, Sonny may be the most beloved panhandler in New York.

•

I first saw Sonny five years ago, while riding the F train. I was living in Park Slope, writing nightclub reviews, and I would run into him some evenings on my way into Manhattan. Whenever I saw him, he brightened my day, and I always made it a point to give change. Eventually, quarters no longer seemed adequate, and I upgraded to dollar bills.

For a while, I thought Sonny was simply the beneficiary of my own whims. I liked that his name recalled that of an old blues singer and felt that his speech had a regal quality. But the more I mentioned him to other people who lived along the F, the more it became apparent that I wasn't alone in my affection.

"I made it a habit to not give money to anyone," said Lisa Langsdorf, a onetime F train rider who now lives in Williamsburg. "Sonny was the exception. I felt like everything he was saying was so truthful. And when I moved to Park Slope, it was my first job out of college. I had no money. I think Sonny had more money than I did."

Sonny's success is owed, in no small part, to consistency. Each morning, he boards the F train at Avenue X in Coney Island and panhandles to the East Broadway stop. In the evenings, when people are returning from their offices, Sonny is back in his, collecting for dinner. Sometimes he rides all the way to 34th Street, but he prefers to stay in Brooklyn. "People in Manhattan are busy," he explains.

His appeal is also due to the way his presence magically alters the mood of a car. There is another panhandler on the F, a stout man who speaks in a clipped, agitating manner, and he sweeps through the train like a violent windstorm. Sonny, by contrast, is like a cool breeze that gently brushes by, leaving you lighter for having had the experience.

Both because he is old and because he belongs to an earlier time, one in which a job was done with care and resolve, Sonny moves slowly through the train. His approach could best be described as courtly. He introduces himself. If someone is fishing through a pocket for change, he waits patiently. Then he thanks the person and says, "Get home safe."

Although Sonny's approach seems lackadaisical, it is highly considered. His routine, for instance, is arranged so that if he takes a train from 34th Street in Manhattan to Jay Street in Downtown Brooklyn, he can move from car to car, panhandling the entire way, with only one more stop than there are cars. He then rests and counts his change before the subway reaches Jay Street, where he exits and waits for the next Avenue X-bound train.

These are things unknown to a majority of passengers. To them, at best, he is simply a fellow rider. Yet he is a rider who never goes unnoticed, one who exudes a halo of intrigue. "It seems like everyone wants to know what his story is," Ms. Langsdorf said. "I've always wondered about him."

•

On a bright morning last spring, after years of wondering myself, I had breakfast with Sonny at a diner near the Jay Street station. We had agreed to an earlier meeting, but he had stood me up. And so when I saw him on the train this time, I proposed an interview then and there. He agreed, and explained that he hadn't made our previous meeting because the trains had been delayed. He seemed pleased for the conversation.

He was also plainly hungry. Up close, his face looked gaunt, and except for one lone incisor, his upper teeth were missing; his lower teeth were intact but yellowed. I offered to pay for his breakfast, and he quickly ordered scrambled eggs, ham and home fries with toast, and a large glass of milk. He wore a gray sweatshirt, his blue jacket, a backpack he said contained clothes and a Bible, and a wool hat that said "F: Brooklyn to Queens."

I asked him how he accounted for his popularity.

"Well," he said, "I say my name for one. Most people don't ever say their name. I don't shake a change cup, either. People don't like that. That irritates me."

He seemed to enjoy talking about his panhandling style and went on unprompted. "When I first started," he said, "I was ashamed to ask for change. So I thought, if I'm going to do this, I'm going to be straight. You got to be honest and straight with people. Also, you can't make them feel bad. You can't say too much about your life. People don't want to hear that. It depresses them. If you're long-winded, you're dead."

Sonny's daily goal is to bring in $30, enough to buy that evening's dinner and the next morning's breakfast. On average, he makes $7 a trip panhandling between Avenue X and Jay Street, and he keeps the change in separate pockets, using his front left pocket for quarters, his front right for dimes and nickels, and his backpack for pennies. By night's end, he said, he can tell by the weight of his pack how much money is inside.

When he has collected enough loose change, he generally goes to a Pathmark in Brooklyn, where a Coinstar machine turns the coins into bills. Two or three nights a week, he exchanges his quarters at a Popeye's at Stillwell and Surf Avenues, where he also eats. This particular morning, as Sonny finished his breakfast and took a big drink of milk, he looked as if he could consume three meals and still not be filled up. I asked if he wanted a cup of coffee. "I can't have coffee," he said. "Gives me the shakes."

Although his sleepy, gracious manner suggests a childhood in the South, Sonny said he was born in Trinidad and came to Washington as an infant. "My father was named Howard Augustine Payne, and my mother was Georgetta Payne," he said. "I was born St. Augustine Des Sales Payne. They divorced when I was young, and I lived with my mother in Corona, Queens. I used to ice skate right where Shea Stadium is now. But I haven't been to Queens in nine months now. In Queens, if you don't have access to public transportation, it's rough."

Sonny said that before he was laid off, he worked for 23 years as a printer. For the past year, he added, he has stayed at the Church of the Greater God on Neptune Avenue in Coney Island. "The reverend, we call him Brother Jack," he said. "You can almost feel him when you talk to him, he's so real."

The conversation lasted a while longer, ranging over sports, cellphones, which Sonny called leashes, and the coming of warmer weather, about which he had mixed feelings. "I like this time of year," he said, "but you have to be careful. All the kids are coming out of school. They tease homeless people. You can't respond. If you respond, then you have to debate. Then they gang up on you." He sighed, "When you're homeless, there's a lot of stress."

Sonny became homeless, he said, after a string of bad luck; he was laid off, his apartment caught fire, he didn't want to bother friends. Early on, he stayed in city-run shelters, but he stopped, he said, after he was robbed. Now he prefers to stay in small churches where he can secure a safe bed.

Ciara McElroy, the director of social services at Peter's Place, a drop-in center on West 23rd Street that serves the elderly homeless, said it is common for older people to avoid the shelters. "There is a lack of community in a shelter," she said. "There is more violence and theft." The number of elderly homeless like Sonny has increased over the past year, she added, because of the rising costs of housing.

Ms. McElroy remembered Sonny from the years she lived along the F. According to her, someone like Sonny, who is independent and has been homeless for years, survives by establishing a routine and developing contacts that may be helpful. In Sonny's case, he seems to be allowed to panhandle, although the activity is officially illegal.

Sonny appears in remarkably good shape for having been homeless many years now. He never appears drunk or disheveled. Yet he exhibits a prominent trait of living on the streets, which is secrecy, and trying to explore his world outside the subways is like tracking a storybook character.

One windy afternoon I took the F train to Avenue X in search of the church where Sonny said he stays. I hoped to speak with Brother Jack, but what I really wanted was to take away the random quality of my interaction with Sonny. I was in search of a fixed location, a place where I could always find him.

There was no Church of the Greater God, but after walking for some time, I happened upon a squat, windowless brick building with a sign out front that read: "Coney Island Gospel Assembly, Jack A. SanFilippo, founding pastor."

According to Constance Hulla, who is Mr. SanFilippo's daughter and the current pastor, the church does indeed run a homeless outreach program, but neither Ms. Hulla nor several of the residents recalled Sonny. And although Ms. Hulla's father was known as Brother Jack, he died two decades ago.

Even Sonny's name is a mystery. Sonny Payne was, of course, the name of a big-band drummer in the 1950's who played with Count Basie and who died in 1979.

•

One night not long ago, I ran into Sonny on the F train. It had been some time since I saw him, and his beard was a little thicker and whiter than usual. On his finger I noticed a ring with a crescent and a star, a symbol of Islam. A passenger had given it to him, he said, and now whenever the man sees Sonny, he gives him $5 if he is wearing the ring.

Sonny was panhandling to collect money for dinner, and I rode with him from Jay Street to 34th Street, where we turned around and headed back towards Coney Island. As usual, he was doing quite well. A woman who lives in Park Slope gave him the uneaten contents of her daughter's lunchbox: an apple, yogurt and a child-size box of juice. Others gave change or dollar bills.

When the train pulled into Avenue X, the last station, Sonny walked down the stairs and bought a MetroCard for the next day. He put $2 worth of nickels into the machine, getting rid of the bulkiest coins, and then headed for Popeye's.

I found it strange that someone as seemingly intelligent and personable as Sonny has remained homeless for so long. I asked him if he would stay homeless if he had the chance to get off the street. "I want to be back living in an apartment," he said. "I know some homeless people prefer the street because they're afraid of responsibility. But that goes against how I was raised. When I was in the shelters, I saw a lot of young guys in there. If I was 30, there's no way I'd be homeless. I'd find a job. I know how to do a lot of different things."

Inside, Sonny ordered four pieces of chicken and emptied his pocket of quarters, carefully stacking them on the counter in groups of four. There was over $25 in all. "Where do you get all this change?" the counter asked.

"From gracious people," Sonny replied.

Then he took his order and went outside. "I'll see you later," he said. "I'm taking a cab to the church." In a flash, he hailed a taxi, hopped in and drove off.

May 16, 2004

Part IV

City Lore

El Congo Real at 111th Street. (Angel Franco/The New York Times)

35

The White Baby

In the Botanicas of Spanish Harlem, the Spirits Are Asked to Grant Prayers. But Long Ago, a Visitor Learns, the Gods Cruelly Mocked One Man's Wish.

ERNESTO QUIÑONEZ

IN the 1970's, my three sisters and I would go to El Congo Real at 111th and Lexington, the largest botanica in Spanish Harlem, to buy fotonovelas. These comic-book soaps were corny love stories. The women in them were always being dumped by their boyfriends, but then, pages later, the man would see the light and marry the girl right before the word FIN appeared in big block letters.

Back then, El Congo Real didn't have the huge wooden counter that now divides the religious artifacts from the public. It was just one big open space where on the floor, next to life-size statues of the crippled San Lazaro, were boxes and boxes of comic-book soap operas. My sisters would sift through all the boxes looking for the fotonovelas they hadn't yet read. For 50 cents, they'd buy a couple and maybe, if they had left-over change, a candle to go with it.

My mother, a Jehovah's Witness, hated the botanicas. She warned all her children, "If you go inside those botanicas, se te puede pegar algo," something dark will follow you home. To my mother, this dark thing was bound to come in, curl up in a corner of our house, wait until we were sleeping, then uncoil itself and roam; maybe open the refrigerator, take the phone off the hook, leave the faucet dripping. It would hover over our dreaming bodies at night, hissing and murmuring unintelligible sounds.

To Mami, botanicas were places where evil spirits lived. To her, these religious stores full of candles, beads, oils, herbs, cauldrons, plaster statues of Catholic saints and tons of religious paraphernalia were not

holy places but dens of darkness. People went there to ask for consulta-
tions on supernatural matters, things that should be left alone. All I knew
was that's where the stories were.

The dark, heavyset woman who owned El Congo Real was always
very nice. She would even let my sisters trade in their old fotonovelas for
new ones. She read them herself, so she'd advise my sisters on the better
stories: which had the most wicked men, which had the most romance,
or women who got back at their men and had them on their knees.

My sisters loved betrayal, deceit, vengeance, as long as the ending was
a happy one. So they'd ask the owner for recommendations. And sometimes she would tell us real stories she had heard inside her botanica.

Like the one about the widow who had four fat, ugly, bumbling sons
whom no girl would marry. So she placed all her hopes on the youngest.
She blew her life savings and bought him a new car in hopes of some girl
marrying him, at least for the car. The car was stolen, and so the widow
went to El Congo Real for a consultation to ask the Orishas—the Black
Gods of Santeria, the religion slaves brought to the New World 200 years
ago—to help her find the car. "Grandchildren," she pleaded. "I need
grandchildren."

There was also the story about the man who would hear his dead uncle
open the refrigerator at night and make himself a sandwich. When he visited the botanica for a consultation, he was told that his uncle was angry
at him for letting him die hungry. In another version of the story, the man
hears the refrigerator opening at night, and so he wakes up and turns on
the light, only to see it closed. When he opens the door, a slice of Kraft
singles slaps him in the face.

But out of all the stories there was one, especially, that has stayed with
me all these years. It was the one I heard when I was 10, about a dark
man who enters El Congo Real and asks to have a consultation. He is escorted to the basement where the babalawo, the high santero, awaits.
The dark man is now in the Ile, the house of the Black Gods. He wants
his son to be born with white skin, he tells the babalawo. He wants his
son to have blue or green eyes. The babalawo thoughtfully nods. The
dark man asks what kind of offering he must make to the Orishas for
them to grant him a white baby. He tells how he doesn't want his kid to
be discriminated against because of the color of his skin. How he was
passed over for promotions at his factory job because he wasn't white.

The story of the dark man asking for a white baby didn't take hold
just of my imagination but of the entire neighborhood's, and like a pit

bull, it never let it go. To this day, some people still talk about it. It was a statement not only about race and discrimination, but also about the belief that the Orishas have the power to grant anything.

Because to many residents of Spanish Harlem, the Black Gods are as real as poverty. They are as essential and as timely as the welfare check that arrives every 1st and 16th day of the month. The Orishas are like family. They are loved, respected and feared as a child would his father, who can hug and kiss you one day and chastise and brutally punish you the next.

And just like families rich or poor, neighborhoods have their idiots, their black sheep, their clowns, their little stars. Neighborhoods also have their urban legends. With this in mind, I went to the botanicas of Spanish Harlem to track down a story I had heard 25 years ago.

•

On the bus going back to the old neighborhood, I wonder why this man would think that the Black Gods would grant him something white. Didn't he know the origin of Santeria, which was brought to Cuba, Haiti and Brazil by enslaved Africans? Aboard those slave ships the babalawos carried in their heads an entire religion: hundreds of prayers, potions, spells, healing plants, divinations, songs, the entire language of the Black Gods.

These poet-priests, yanked out of their beloved Africa, were denied their rituals by their white Roman Catholic masters, and so they cunningly disguised their African gods inside Catholic saints. The masters were fooled, believing the slaves had embraced Catholicism, but no, the slaves worshiped the saints with the same songs and dances they performed to their deities, the Orishas, the Black Gods. It is this instinct of survival that lives on to this day in las botanicas.

When I reach El Congo Real, just a few feet away from the red brick Methodist church the Young Lords took over in the 60's, I walk down the steps to the basement. Two women are ahead of me. In the small waiting area are four folding chairs and a few magazines thrown on a small table.

"I never seen you here," one of the women says, but she doesn't give an opportunity to talk. She tells me: "This padrino is good. He told me I was going to hit the number." She claps her hands. "I hit it the next day."

Two men come in and pick up some boxes and leave. They are stocking the religious merchandise sold upstairs. I wait. I'm thinking about what to say, how to ask about something that might not have happened. Because it's hard to grasp what is true and what is fiction in Santeria when its beliefs have been passed down by oral tradition.

My turn arrives to enter the Ile, the house of the Orishas. It is a magnificent room, with fresh flowers, fruit offerings at the feet of many statues of saints and emblems of the Orishas. Nailed to the wall are bows and arrows, spears, stalks of sugar canes, white flags, altars to every Orisha, ribbons, silk scarves, candy and drums.

The babalawo is a tall dark man with white hair and a white mustache. He tells me in Spanish to sit down, calls me mi negrito, my little dark one. I sit where he tells me.

Next to me is a small statue of the regal-looking Santa Barbara, wearing her golden gown, lifting a royal goblet in hand. It is the Catholic saint in which dwells the Orisha Chango, god of thunder and lightning, supreme being of divine justice.

The babalawo takes out a ledger and asks me my name. He writes it down. First is the derecho, the fee, a right of the Orishas. He instructs me to fold the two twenties and cross myself with them, my shoulders, then stomach, then forehead, kissing the money at the end. I give him the money and we begin.

Let's see, mi negrito, what the Orishas have to say to you. He picks up a necklace made of tortoise shells, about 40 inches long. He blesses me with the necklace by touching my shoulders, abdomen and forehead. He casts the necklace on the table and writes down combinations of numbers. He asks me to pick up some objects and hold them in my hand.

A bone. A stone. A shell. He writes more numbers down. I don't ask him anything about the white baby, at least not yet.

After he finishes writing all the combinations, he reads them to himself, carefully, and then looks up at me and smiles. No one wishes you ill, mi negrito. No one has used the Orishas' powers to bring you harm. Then he looks me squarely in the eye and tells me that two women are coming into my life. One is dark, the other white. The dark one will give me children, he says, correctly pointing out that I don't have any. But the white woman will love me. It is up to me to choose.

He instructs me to buy a small statue of la Caridad de Cobre. Hidden inside her is Ochun, goddess of love and beauty, mother of marriage. Listen to her, he says. She will show you the way.

He tells me to make an altar for Ochun. At the feet of the small statue of la Caridad de Cobre, I am to place five yellow candles, because her number is five and her color is yellow, and a peacock feather, because that is her bird. I am to buy five cakes and place them in front of Ochun's altar for a night. Then I must offer the five cakes to the Ochun by tossing them in the East River. And she will help me with my decision on the two women.

Before I go upstairs and buy what I need for my offering, I ask him about the dark man who came here many years ago hoping the Orishas would grant him and his wife a white baby. Does he know anything about it? His eyebrows collapse. He wants to know why I want to know. He frowns. I'm writing something on it, I tell him. He says he can't discuss anything that happens in the Ile. I ask only if the story is true. He says yes. Then he points a finger at me and smiles, shaking his head. I know you, you are one of those people that leaves before trouble begins. That's good, mi negrito, because that means someone is looking out for you. Some spirit tells your spirit to leave before the hot water comes.

Then he says that if I really want to know more about the white baby to go and see a barber named Hipolito at the barbershop at 104th and Lexington, the one right next to another botanica called Justo. What happened with the white baby, he says, happened at Justo.

Of course it had to be Justo, I'm thinking as I make my purchase upstairs, because while El Congo Real might be the largest botanica in Spanish Harlem, Justo is the oldest. It's been serving El Barrio since 1930.

I know Justo botanica real well because it's right in front of P.S. 72, the grammar school I attended. I know the barbershop, too. It's right next door to the botanica. My father would take me there as a little kid and I would cry thinking that the haircut would make me shorter.

•

I walked to 104th Street and decided I might as well get a haircut. Barbers are more willing to talk if they are cutting your hair.

I also like barbershops because there is always someone walking in and out trying to hock something. Once at Tunito's Barbershop at 110th and Lexington (no longer around), this junkie walked in and said that the pack of darts he was selling for only $5 was a collector's item. That people who collect darts would pay $1,000 for them. Gold points, he said. Collector's item, gold points, mi panas. And we all laughed at him.

Hipolito the barber was working on someone, so I waited. He was an old man, with just a little hair on both sides. He was short and had a mustache and he somersaulted between perfect English and Spanish. In one corner a radio was playing a Spanish station on low volume. In another corner a dusty fan was lazily spinning.

When it was my turn, I took my seat in the barber's chair.

Hipolito wasn't very talkative, but he told me enough. A guy went in the botanica to ask a santero for his son to be born white, he told me, and sure enough, his son turns out white, with blue eyes and blond hair. Six months after the baby is brought home, the lights go out. All over the city. It was the blackout of '77.

So the father goes down to Justo to buy candles. Everyone was buying candles. El Barrio looked like a botanica that night, candles here and candles there. When the guy comes home from the botanica, Hipolito says, there's a cop in his house. At first he thinks maybe the cops are making sure everyone is all right, something like that. But no. That Irish cop was the real father of the baby.

The cop thought the Russians had dropped the bomb but had missed New York, and so they had knocked out all the lights. He was so worried, he drove to see his woman to make sure his kid was all right. And the guy who thought he was the father?

Hipolito shrugged. The guy went to the Orishas, the Black Gods, to ask for something white, he says. So the Orishas spat in his face.

There, at least, was the first version. I got others. At Justo a woman told me that the Orishas did grant a white baby but a daughter, not a son. Someone else said the baby was an albino. Another babalawo I visited in a botanica on 116th Street between Madison and Park told me that sometimes you play the wrong number but it's that number that hits, and sometimes you play the right number but that number doesn't come up. I didn't know exactly what he meant, but I had an idea.

Taking the bus back to the West Side, carrying a plastic bag filled with a small statue of a saint, five yellow candles, a peacock feather and five sweet cakes I bought at a bakery (for I will not offend the Orishas and will do as told) I thought about El Barrio looking like a botanica that night of the blackout, with candles here and candles there. It was the biggest altar ever built for the Orishas.

But when I think about it now, what is most vivid to me about that hot night in July 1977 was that it felt as if everyone in Spanish Harlem had left their apartments to go out to the streets and look up at the heavens. The New York City sky looked the way it does in Puerto Rico or Santo Domingo or Ecuador, or any of our Latin American countries, filled with galaxies of magic. We were all amazed. We had forgotten the planets, the moon, the stars. The night sky above us seemed so close you could touch it.

What I didn't know that night was that somewhere in another part of the neighborhood a comic-book soap like the ones my sisters read was being played out. A real-life drama full of betrayal and deceit. Angry words must have been exchanged. Corny sentences that might be dismissed as clichéd, unless you are the one who's saying them at the moment. A man finding out that his child was not his and that the Orishas, like their Greek counterparts, could play jokes on Man. I choose to believe that is what really happened.

Whether what I had heard was true or not never really mattered. As those who follow Santeria never doubt the power of the Orishas, I never doubt the rumors that come out of Spanish Harlem. They happened to someone at some time in some form.

And who's to say? Maybe it was the Orishas, the Black Gods, who had a hand in what occurred that hot night in '77. Maybe it was them telling the neighborhood: We demand an altar. You build us one and we will show you the heavens. And you will see that you are all a people once again. Because regardless of all the darkness of that night or what happened soon after—the looting, the fires, the federal troops—it was the only time in Spanish Harlem we all emerged to see, once more, the stars.

June 4, 2000

Looking north from SoHo. (James Estrin/The New York Times)

36

New York, Brick by Brick

The AIA Guide, That Admiring, Classic Work
on New York's Ad Hoc, Additive Architecture,
Offers Its First New Edition
in More Than a Decade.

PHILLIP LOPATE

I N Borges's story "The Aleph," the narrator opens the trapdoor of a cellar to find himself staring at "millions of acts both delightful and awful," all of which simultaneously "occupied the same point in space." So a newcomer might feel, arriving in New York City for the first time.

How does one begin to "read" New York, to make sense of that limitless, cabalistic text? The best single gloss I know of is the AIA Guide to New York City, by Norval White and Elliot Willensky, about to appear in a new edition, the first in 12 years. Covering each borough almost block by block, building by building, it is an extraordinarily learned, personable exegesis of our metropolis. No other American or, for that matter, world city can boast so definitive a one-volume guide to its built environment.

The first edition appeared in 1967. A svelte 400-plus pages, written by two young architectural enthusiasts who paid for its first printing, it was given free to the members at the American Institute of Architects convention in honor of that group's 100th anniversary.

Changes in the city fabric necessitated expanded editions in 1978 and 1988. Now, after nearly 33 years in print and 185,000 copies sold, the fourth edition tips the scales at 1,056 pages. You can still walk around with the AIA Guide in hand, but strong wrists are required. I confess I have taken to ripping pages out before exploring a new neighborhood, then guiltily reinserting them at home. Heaven, for me, would be a loose-leaf edition.

Though I've never met either Norval White or Elliot Willensky, their pithy, opinionated viewpoints have become as familiar to me as Gilbert and Sullivan's. Gateway Plaza's towers are "the scullery maids of Battery Park City"; the Upper West Side's Calhoun School suggests that a "modern-day Gulliver must have been here and left behind his giant-sized TV." Since the entries are unsigned, one can only speculate who contributed what. Mr. Willensky died in 1990, at a youthful 56. I imagine him the more unbuttoned of the pair, partly based on a reading of his warm, schmaltzy book, "When Brooklyn Was the World." Mr. White seems more formal and circumspect, given certain word changes in this fourth edition. For instance, the breezy "Get a load of those rusticated marshmallow columns" has been trimmed to "Savor those rusticated . . ." For the most part, thankfully, the guide has not been rewritten, merely added to, with hundreds of new entries, 2,000 new photographs and 80 new maps. Mr. White has also reinspected on foot almost all of the 5,000 buildings, to ensure that the information is still accurate.

The Necrology section on perished New York treasures, which was ghoulishly fascinating, has been dropped, regrettably, for space reasons, but the AIA Guide remains saturated with ghosts and demolitions. We learn what once was on this site and is no more, what utopian proposals came to naught.

In a city famous for historical amnesia, destroying and remaking wherever there was profit to be made thereby, this volume is an Ancient Mariner recounting Gotham's actual transformations. Take an entry, at random, about one Clason Point in the Bronx:

A protuberance into either Long Island Sound or the East River, depending on your geographical alliances. It has, over the years, been labeled after its successive occupants: Snakipins (the native American settlement), Cornell Point (after Thomas Cornell, 1642), and finally Clason Point (after Isaac Clason). Between 1883 and 1927 it was the home of Clason Military Academy, operated by a Roman Catholic order. Before the trolley came, in 1910, public access was via boat, launch or steamer from Long Island, Mott Haven, and Manhattan. The waters were not polluted then. The attractions were dance halls and hotels, picnic grounds and a bathing pier, restaurants, a salt water pool, and places with names like Dietrich's, Gilligan's Pavilion and Killian's Grove, Higg's Camp Grounds and Kane's Casino. (Kane's Casino held out until it caught fire in 1942.)

Between 1923 and 1938 the city operated a popular ferry service to
College Point, in Queens. Tragedy came in 1924 when a freak wind
squall blew down the Clason Point Amusement Park's Ferris wheel (on
the site of Shorehaven Beach Club, now endangered), killing 24. Prohibition, pollution and competition (from filtered pools like easily accessi-
ble Starlight Park in nearby West Farms) finally doomed the resort area.

An entire resort about which I knew nothing, and now I cannot get
that freak wind squall out of my mind. But fine as it is to learn about
some obscure metropolitan corner, it's just as irresistible to look up
familiar places, and see what judgments W & W will render. Kane Street
Synagogue? "Originally a brick and brownstone Romanesque Revival,
its present stuccoed exterior is bland but waterproof." Fair enough. The
World Trade Center? "When completed, these stolid, banal monoliths
came to overshadow Lower Manhattan's cluster of filigreed towers that
symbolized the very concept of 'skyline.'" I guess they're right, even if
I've grown perversely attached to the Twin Towers over the years.

What needs to be grasped is that the AIA Guide to New York City is
not only usefully descriptive but influentially, if controversially, prescrip-
tive. Indeed, I would place it on that short shelf of postwar urban clas-
sics, like Jane Jacobs's "Death and Life of Great American Cities,"
Robert A. Caro's "Power Broker" and William H. Whyte's "City," that
have profoundly altered the way we looked at cities, and taught us to appreciate their messy, ad hoc, additive nature. Where garden-city planners
had seen chaos in mixed usage, these authors saw diversity and neighborhood vitality; what architectural purists regarded as a retrograde and
degraded melange of styles, these authors defended as rich historical lay-
ering. A single block might have eight consecutive buildings of differing
height and period styles and still feel unified to the viewer's glance—provided, say, all the buildings lined up at a continuous street wall.

By drawing attention to what likably blends in or antisocially sticks
out, the AIA Guide has applied a communal, city-making standard to
the often narcissistic art of modern architecture. Beyond that, it has
taught us to appreciate the amazing one-thing-after-anotherness of New
York, which is its true, distinguishing aesthetic.

The guide reflects the sea change that began in the 1960's, part of
which involved a revaluation of the city's heritage. Not surprisingly, Mr.
White and Mr. Willensky were among those young architects picketing
the demolition of McKim, Mead & White's magnificent Pennsylvania

Station in 1962, as they proudly tell us in the guide. The razing of Penn
Station led to the passage of the Landmarks Preservation Act, and to
a widespread consensus about the principles or premises supporting
urbanism.

Among these principles, which found articulate enunciation in the
AIA Guide, were: that whatever architecture from previous periods was
still attractive and functioning should be protected and preserved; that
one could learn from this past (the way Battery Park City's promenade
unashamedly speaks the same design vocabulary as the Brooklyn Heights
promenade); that mixed use and density might not be such bad things after all, whereas voids introduced into the urban fabric, like unused corporate plazas, tend to be boring; that the integrity of the street wall
should be maintained wherever possible; that the public realm (streets,
parks, transportation) should resist privatization; and that new buildings
should fit into their immediate surroundings, the principle of Contextualism.

Certainly, Contextualism can become, as this paper's architectural
critic, Herbert Muschamp, has pointed out, a rigid ideology supporting
a failure of artistic nerve and imagination. When he criticizes the Giuliani administration's new zoning proposals as a conservative effort that
would seek to freeze the city's skyline in an "Art Deco contour," and, he
argues, freeze out edgy new architecture that might challenge the street
wall, he is partly assailing the sensibility enshrined in the AIA Guide.

Frustration with the scarcity of daring contemporary architecture in
New York is certainly understandable. On the other hand, New York
has never been an architectural mecca, if what we mean by that term is
genius-designed, innovative buildings that stand forth as art objects.
Chicago has more great textbook architecture than New York, but New
York has a thicker, more continuous, livelier urban fabric. New York
excels in the creation of places, urban spaces that achieve a sense of
identity. For instance, Times Square, known the world over, was never
much architecturally, nor is it now, but it's had the knack of concentrat-
ing energy, desire, imagination in a single site.

Another New York specialty is its production of decent background
buildings that perform like good role players in the urban weave. Such
reliable New York types as the brownstone row house, the six-story bar-
bell walkup, the 12- to 15-story apartment buildings like those found
along West End Avenue or Sutton Place, even the tenement, don't require
brilliant architects to make their successful contribution to the mix.

Certainly, New York can boast of some architectural masterpieces, all duly noted in the AIA Guide, by masters like Stanford White, Cass Gilbert, Louis Sullivan, Mies van der Rohe, Frank Lloyd Wright, Gordon Bunshaft and Eero Saarinen. But what gives the city its pizazz is that lively, eclectic synchronicity that makes the whole so much greater than its parts. Hence, the AIA Guide's love of Rockefeller Center, which many snootier architectural critics have criticized as mundane. To Mr. White and Mr. Willensky it is "an island of architectural excellence," "the greatest urban complex of the 20th century: an understated and urbane place that has become a classic lesson in the point and counterpoint of space, form and circulation."

Conversely, the guide seems a bit too skeptical about some of the newer efforts to perpetuate innovative, surprising architecture. The LMVH Building by Christian de Portzamparc (which I happen to love) is summarized as: "Folded planes create a sleek but aggressive glass curtain wall punctuating dour 57th Street. Its high style may soon be last year's. French Champagne does those things." Then again, you don't go to the AIA Guide for its hip enthusiasms but for the avuncular back story on some richly detailed facade you've found on a walk.

New York is jam-packed with these visual grace notes: chromatic terra cotta inlays, ornate second-story grilles, fanciful water towers, staid buildings that end in grandiloquent Mayan or Babylonian crowns, cast-iron fronts with elegant patterns. This city's streets are aburst with fragments of greatness (or oddness: it almost comes to the same thing), and the AIA Guide, dedicated as it is to an aesthetic of modest delights more than knockout masterpieces, does a wonderful job of pointing them out.

Mr. White and Mr. Willensky are especially helpful in unraveling the story of New York's unsung heroes who contributed mightily to the city's texture. So we learn of Clarence F. True, an architect and developer who bought up property along lower Riverside Drive and built "idiosyncratic" mansions, many of which still exist, in an "Elizabethan Renaissance" style; Alfred T. White, a pragmatically idealistic businessman whose philosophy, "philanthropy plus 5 percent," led him to put up well-constructed, low-rent housing in Brooklyn and Queens; Herbert Johnson, "a sainted parkie" under Robert Moses "whose vision and incredibly hard work transformed the dunes and marshes into an invaluable public accommodation" at Jamaica Bay.

We also encounter Frank Freeman, "Brooklyn's greatest architect," whose 1892 City of Brooklyn Fire Headquarters on Jay Street is "a building to write home about"; the Three Musketeers of the 1920's and 30's, Ralph Walker, Raymond Hood and Ely Jacques Kahn, whose stepback skyscrapers helped define that entertainingly moderne style Rem Koolhaas has labeled "Manhattanism"; and the Chanin brothers, two developers from Brooklyn who taught themselves architecture and insisted on the best Art Deco craftsmanship in their Central Park West and 42nd Street buildings ("Look back on such distinguished self-improvement, Mr. Trump").

Since the guide's focus is relentlessly New York, it makes no amends for its local-insider tone, as in this critique of Riverside South's high-rises: "A heavy hand here from the virtuoso," Philip Johnson, "but after what happened at the Trump International Hotel, what could you hope for in a Philip and Donald act?"

There are many thoughtful, measured assessments of the work by architectural firms that have been rebuilding or restoring New York in the last few decades, like James Stewart Polshek, Davis-Brody, Hardy Holzman Pfeiffer, Ehrenkrantz-Eckstut, Giovanni Pasanella, Gruzen Samton, Richard Dattner, Cesar Pelli. What's surprising, though, for a volume ostensibly dedicated to architecture, is how much of the guide's information is not professionally oriented, but gathers in the lore, traditions, casual institutions and events that collectively define New York's spirit. Here you will find asides on Edgar Allan Poe's pre-tavern strolls and the Gotham Book Mart's strengths, Citarella's fresh seafood, the 1920 anarchist bombing of J. P. Morgan's headquarters and poor Kitty Genovese's unanswered screams.

When push comes to shove, the AIA Guide sees that what matters about buildings is not solely their window treatment or spandrels, but the life lived in and through them. The best city architecture is that which makes possible the world of the street.

June 18, 2000

37

Memory's Curveball

Thick With the Glaze of Age, the Baseball Evoked Thoughts of a Legendary Team. But It Was Not What It Seemed.

DAN BARRY

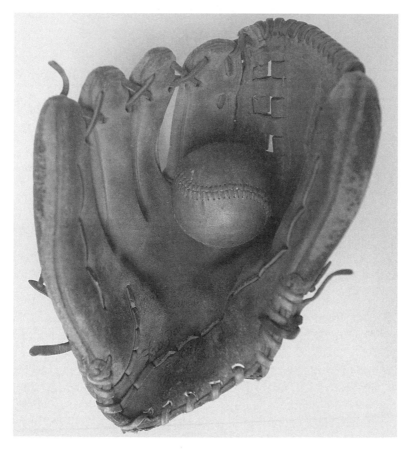

The author's baseball glove. (Tony Cenicola/The New York Times)

HERE was a baseball that never soared from a swinging bat. It never plopped into the webbing of an outstretched glove. It never skipped across wet grass, got caught in a rosebush or smacked against a strike zone painted on a school's brick facade. Here was a baseball that may never have brought joy.

And now Barbara Appelbaum, a conservator who specializes in the odd, was holding it in the cradle of her fingertips. She held the yellowed ball close to her face and turned it slowly, along the seams, studying the almost inscrutable signatures of long-ago vitality in its desiccated hide.

She placed it down on a small pillow and then gave me the same searching look that she had just given the ball. The worth of an object is difficult to determine, she said. How does one define worth? And what is the worth of memory?

I smiled. Depends on the memory, I thought.

Ms. Appelbaum, 53, is in the business of determining memory's worth. She and her business partner, Paul Himmelstein, work in an Upper West Side office that is cluttered with old and damaged objects in varying stages of restoration. On a table is a mangled marionette. Near the window, a broken hockey trophy. In the dark room, a centuries-old portrait, slashed long ago across the eyes of its dour, white-wigged subject.

Over the years she has worked on everything from mummies ("We had some mummies up here for a while. Some of them are really smelly.") to a costume that appeared in a Woody Allen movie ("I treated one of those sperm suits."). In describing her career, she said, "My main area of expertise is odd things." And that is what brought me to her. Me and a baseball.

•

When I was a boy, my family would travel from Long Island to Stuyvesant Town on the East Side of Manhattan to visit my Great-Aunt Betty. A retired schoolteacher, elegant and learned, she spoke with what she called "a lateral emission of the S sound." To my siblings and me, she sounded a little like Sylvester the Cat, but we loved her. On our birthdays, she always sent us cards depicting a clown juggling 10 real dimes.

She was also generous enough to allow a grown nephew, Ronnie, to live with her. He was in his mid-30's and was said to be brilliant but sensitive; which, in our family, was sympathetic code language for wounded and lost. It meant he was unable to function Out There.

We were squirming one day on Aunt Betty's uncomfortable furniture, drinking ginger ale and staring at framed photographs of strangers said to be relatives, when a gangling specter walked in. He was gripping a paper bag by the neck of the bottle inside.

Say hello to Uncle Ronnie, children.

A vague recollection of social graces kept Ronnie in the parlor. He sat mute during the talk of dead priests and hard times, but snapped alert when my father mentioned my love for baseball, a passion so intense, he explained, that I saved the box scores of meaningless practice games played during spring training.

Ronnie looked at me as though to size me up for the first time. He put his drink down and abruptly left the room. He emerged a few minutes later clutching a baseball in a trembling hand. "Here," he said.

The ball was covered with autographs of professional baseball players from another age. The names were of a New York baseball team that through the fog of memory I have remembered as the Brooklyn Dodgers. Specifically: Robinson, Reese, Snider, Hodges, Campanella and the rest of the 1955 World Championship Dodgers.

I held the ball as though it were an egg. Overwhelmed, I looked up to Ronnie, whose rheumy eyes were reading my face for that glimmer of connection he found so elusive in life. "Keep it," he said.

Then I saw my father, standing behind Ronnie and solemnly shaking his head. This is not open for debate, the gesture said. The reasons are beyond you, beyond the ball. I handed the ball back to Ronnie. It was too valuable to accept, I stammered, but thank you anyway thank you very much. Ronnie nodded a little too vigorously and left the room. He did not return.

A decade passed before I saw Ronnie again, this time at Aunt Betty's funeral. I was a young man now, just out of college. He was in the final stages of alcoholism, with legs so weak that a kid from a liquor store on First Avenue had to deliver his daily quart of vodka. The Stuyvesant Town apartment of Aunt Betty, once so well appointed, now reeked of cigarette smoke and despair.

Soon after, I visited him in an East Side hospital. He was strapped to a gurney, his belly bloated from a distended liver, his mind too addled to muster even fear. He had no idea who I was. An intern walked by, pointed to Ronnie's twiglike arm, and advised me to take my father's watch before it disappeared. I corrected the man a bit too quickly.

Ronnie died the next day. He was 45. He was buried in a coffin so cheap that I could see the staples in the velveteen covering.

•

Several weeks later, the Barrys returned to the apartment in Stuyvesant Town to remove the last possessions of an old, refined lady and a young, brilliant drunk. I went into Ronnie's dank room and drew open the curtains heavy with dirt, inviting the long-forgotten guest of sunlight. There, piled about the rumpled and stained mattress, was his legacy: books of Latin poetry; collections of Pogo comic strips; decades-old programs from the Metropolitan Opera; dozens of opera albums; a few bottles emptied of cheap vodka. An image came to me: Ronnie, hunched by the hi-fi, glass in hand, finding that elusive sense of connection in the songs of wounded soldiers and dying peasant girls.

The baseball sat on the dusty dresser. The smoke of countless cigarettes, smoldering in the room's never-ending darkness, had gradually coated the signatures of heroes in a mustard-colored glaze that obscured their names.

It was agreed that I would keep the ball. I stuck it in the pocket of an old baseball glove and for years used it as a bookshelf prop, a conversation piece. I told people that the faint scribbles belonged to famous Dodgers from one of the most celebrated teams in baseball history.

I even said as much in an essay for another newspaper about a decade ago. I concluded the essay by imagining that some day I would toss the ball in the air and smash it so hard with a bat that it would burst into dust. That never happened; the ball remained in the glove, forgotten and remembered and forgotten again.

About two months ago, I remembered Ronnie's baseball again, and wondered whether its amberlike sheen could be removed or lightened somehow. Even with the ball's awful condition, I thought, it would still be exciting to make out Jackie Robinson's name on its hide.

The American Institute for Conservation of Historic and Artistic Works in Washington directed me to Ms. Appelbaum, a recognized expert in peculiar items. She sounded enthusiastic when I called, but she expressed some caution. She confessed to knowing almost nothing about baseball. Also, she said, ink tends to seep gradually into a baseball's porous hide, leaving blurs of black or blue.

One more thing, she said: the task of a conservator is not simply to wipe away the grime of the years. "We don't want a 100-year-old painting to look new," she explained. "We know it's old, but it's O.K. if it looks old. I suppose if you want to get poetic, there's the question of how much the fading has to do with memory and nostalgia."

The worth of items like this baseball—and coins and cards and Beanie Babies—is best determined by the person, she said, not by the market. "You have to understand the context in which these things have value," she said. "They have value because people think they have value." I said that I understood. I left the baseball, still nestled in a glove, at her office and made an appointment to watch her attempt to solve its mysteries.

I returned one afternoon with a photocopy of the Dodgers roster from 1955. Ms. Appelbaum had already examined the ball, which now sat on a small pillow. She showed me a faint signature—the best there was, she said—with a last name beginning with ST and ending with Y or G. But no Dodger surname came close to that.

"You know what the other possibility is," she said. "It's another team from another game."

When I expressed my doubts, Ms. Appelbaum muttered something about "Great-Aunt Fannies" and "family myths," then returned her attention to the ball.

After some more inconclusive examination—"I wonder if this is Pee Wee Reese right here," she murmured at one point—Ms. Appelbaum brought the ball into a room crammed with the tools of her craft. Cotton swabs in a Chock Full o'Nuts can. A wooden mallet. A saw. A few wooden stamps, including one that said, "Do Not Expose to Direct Sunlight." And an ultraviolet light, used to increase the contrast between materials that might look the same under normal lighting.

She brushed back her straight white hair and put on a head loupe: a high-powered magnifying lens, often used by jewelers, that is placed over the eyes. "The awful thing about wearing the loupe is you get loupe hair," she said, with eyes now appearing three times their normal size.

The conservator placed the ball under the light's blue cast and turned it this way and that, holding it as though it were as fragile as the man who had once owned it. "Hello, Mister, Mister—who?" she said. "Sometimes you think you see something, and then . . . ." The thought went unfinished, and she switched off the ultraviolet light.

Frustrated, Ms. Appelbaum returned the ball to its pillow and reached for two of her most essential supplies: a bag of cotton and a 10-inch bamboo skewer, one of dozens bought from a restaurant-supply store. She rolled a piece of cotton around the skewer's end, dipped it into a jar of homemade cleaning solution and began dabbing gently at the ball's yellowed veneer.

It gradually occurred to me that she was peeling decades of nicotine residue from the ball, residue absorbed from cigarettes smoked in the closest quarters by my uncle. "Cigarette smoke is very greasy," she said, removing a cotton tip stained orange with nicotine and replaced it with a fresh twist of white. "You can see why it's hard to breathe with this stuff in your lungs." She paused, then said: "But it's a relic. It's a piece of somebody's life. The smoke was part of his life."

After she had discolored a half-dozen swabs of cotton, Ms. Appelbaum removed the loupe from her head. "We're basically making things up out of a few black dots," she said. "And a few more black dots makes up the difference in figuring out who it is and who it is not."

We returned to the ultraviolet lamp. This time I held the baseball under the bluish glow, although I was resigned to not learning anything that I hadn't known for decades. Dead uncle's ball, covered with illegible Dodger signatures.

It may have been the ultraviolet light, or it may have been the spotty cleaning that the ball had just undergone. Whatever the reason, I suddenly saw the ball more clearly. And the signature that Ms. Appelbaum had first noticed—the ST with the Y or G—became obvious.

"This says Ed Stanky," I announced.

"Uh-huh," Ms. Appelbaum said.

Not being a baseball fan, she could not have known that Eddie Stanky, also known as Muggsy and the Brat, was a second baseman who played for several teams, including the Brooklyn Dodgers. But here was the problem: Stanky played for the Dodgers in the late 1940's, not in 1955.

Here was the possible solution: Stanky also played for the fabled 1951 New York Giants, participants in what may be the single most famous game in baseball history. On Oct. 3, 1951, the Giants won the National League pennant when Bobby Thomson hit a come-from-behind home run against the Dodgers in the last inning of a playoff game at the Polo Grounds. That home run was so dramatic it earned a nickname: "The shot heard round the world."

I turned the ball slowly under the ultraviolet light, looking for other clues that might help to strip away memory's glaze. I could not find Willie Mays, who had played well into my own childhood, or Monte Irvin, or Al Dark. I thought I saw a Robert Thomson (whose nickname,

"The Staten Island Scot," never really caught on), but I could not be
sure. The signature might also have been that of Hank Thompson, who
shared third-base duties with Thomson that year.

•

As I studied the ball, I wondered whether my mind was playing tricks
again. Was I willing myself to see certain names, the way that I had
once willed myself to believe this ball had been signed by the 1955
Dodgers? And what difference would it make: the Dodgers, the Giants,
the Twelve Apostles? The ball was still worthless, the memory still
painful.

Then I saw the name Lockman: Whitey Lockman, the Giants first
baseman that year. A minute later, another name came into focus under
the ultraviolet glow: Herman Franks. In past years, Franks had been a
little-used catcher; in the years to come, he would be a scout and a manager. But in this year, 1951, he was the third-base coach for the New
York Giants.

Stanky, Lockman, Franks: I had triangulation.

I looked up to tell Ms. Appelbaum what I had determined. I even told
her that this team, the 1951 New York Giants, had recently been in the
news. A few months earlier, The Wall Street Journal had reported that
the 1951 Giants used a spyglass and an elaborate electrical buzz system
to steal the signs of opposing players in games at the Polo Grounds. The
system gave Giants batters an advantage by alerting them to the pitch—
fastball, curveball—the opposing pitcher was about to throw.

The implication was that the sign-stealing had helped the Giants to
win 37 of their last 44 games, enabling them to catch the Dodgers and
force a three-game playoff, a playoff that the Giants won with Thomson's home run. In those final weeks, The Journal said, Herman Franks
sat in the Giants clubhouse, just beyond center field, with a spyglass in
his hands.

"Yeah, whatever," Ms. Appelbaum said.

She seemed to have misgivings about the process and its effect on me.
She seemed to think that I had harbored hopes of restoring the baseball
to its original luster so that it would have market value. "Trying to figure
out an object's worth distracts from what families own things for," she
had told me earlier. "Finding out that what you own isn't worth much
on the open market destroys a family's feeling that they own something
special."

But selling the ball had never been my intention, I replied. I simply wanted to know more. And now I do.

Ronnie had probably been given the baseball in 1951, when he was a boy of 14, not in 1955, when he was a young man of 18. Only four years, but an eon in adolescence. For me, Ronnie becomes more than an alcoholic dying on a gurney; he is also a 14-year-old, with heroes and hope still intact. This dual image only deepens the sorrow.

I also know that I altered the memory of my unsettling childhood encounter with Ronnie. For a young boy, apparently, the names on an autographed ball were not nearly as memorable as the encounter with an adult in quiet agony. How the Giants became the Dodgers, I cannot say.

Finally, there is the baseball. Not only is it a relic of a lost life, not only is it worthless memorabilia, but now it bears the signatures of men who stole signs in baseball games played half a century ago. Their autographs will continue to fade, the way memories do. That is why I will keep this valuable baseball: to summon, now and then, the delights of ginger ale, the sounds of a beloved aunt and that fleeting flash of light on a troubled man's face.

June 10, 2001

38

My Neighborhood, Its Fall and Rise

Safe But Dreary in the 50's, the West Farms Area of the Bronx Had Grown Desolate in the 70's. Now It's on the Mend.

VIVIAN GORNICK

East Tremont Avenue in the 1950's. (Arthur Brower/The New York Times)

I WAS born and raised in the West Farms section of the Bronx in the kind of working-class neighborhood that was then, by definition, either Jewish or Irish or Italian. Most of the raising got done in a small five-room apartment on the second floor of a narrow brick apartment house around the corner from the Bronx Zoo, on a street inside a quadrant bounded to the north by Bronx Park, the south by East Tremont Avenue, the west by Southern Boulevard and the east by Boston Road.

The park was then—this was the 40's and 50's—an open expanse of green in which we walked and rode our bikes daily, clambered over the rocky embankments of the Bronx River, and in the goodness of time defended our virginity in all weathers and every season. But the hub of the world was East 180th Street between Boston Road and Southern Boulevard. Here we did everything: shopped for food, did the laundry, took the buses; went to the bank, the drugstore, the shoe repair; met our friends, hung out at the candy store, stood talking on the corner far into the summer night, late into the winter afternoon.

Here, also, when I was 10, Dorothy Belinsky's father put his arm around me in the candy store and showed me a pornographic postcard; when I was 12 (now a widow's child) the butcher put a half pound of lamb chops on the scale and charged me for a pound; and when I was 13 the teacher in the Yiddish school above the cleaners pressed his fingers into my shoulder and told me that ideas were everything.

It was a world complete with minor villains and even more minor heroes; above all, it was a world devoted to working-class respectability. The five-story brick and stone apartment houses we lived in stood ranked in overpowering uniformity, block upon block upon block, without a break and without an end. The streets before them were shabby, clean, silent, charmless. All was of a piece: on the one hand life was joyless, on the other it was coherent; either way, you were safe. But inside the apartments every straphanging father knew a weariness that hovered repeatedly at the breaking point, and every dissatisfied mother translated her deepest complaints into a habit of anxiety applied indiscriminately to either a cut knee or the outbreak of war.

It was the bleakness of expectation, the stultified vision and resented courage, that dragged us—the children—down, and made us hate the place. Our longing to get out of the Bronx was intense, and it induced, paradoxically, a solidarity that many were to carry well into other lives: the inevitable mixed legacy of the ghetto. For that's what the Bronx was for us: a working-class ghetto destined to be deserted by its young. By the time I graduated from college, nearly everyone I'd grown up with was gone, and the neighborhood itself was on its way down into the kind of urban defeat that has, over the last three decades, made headlines.

•

I went back just once, in the early 70's. The changes I found were enormous and, at the time, struck me as surreal. Never in all our years of dreary safety here could we have imagined these streets becoming a war zone. East Tremont Avenue—the busiest, liveliest, most interesting business street in the entire neighborhood—was now a place of terrible disintegration: boarded-up storefronts, gated windows, broken sidewalks, junky clothing set out on the street, the narcotic sound of salsa pouring from every storefront doorway, a falling-down restaurant plastered over with "Vote" signs across which was scrawled in indelible black ink, "All politicians is a whore."

At Southern Boulevard I turned back, walking up Vyse Avenue toward home; burned-out buildings, garbage overflowing the sidewalks, teenage boys dealing dope. When I reached East 180th Street—again, boarded-up fronts, broken-down stores, defaced signs—an added sense of disconnect overcame me. O.K., Simon's Grocery had become Melendez's Groceria, and the synagogue had become the First Highway Church of Jesus Christ; but Jack's Appetizing was now Rivera's Auto Parts, the shoe repair Bar-B-Que Chicken, the hardware store a pawnbroker.

I got to my own street—181st between Vyse and Bryant—and stood looking down it for a long moment: garbage strewn all around the houses, windows and doors broken, sidewalks full of holes, chalked obscenities, ground-down newspapers. My own once solid building now looked shrunken and terribly old. The glass in the front door was splintered, the iron banisters had been ripped from their brass ball sockets and the walls were covered with graffiti.

A chunky Hispanic woman came into the hall behind me. She stiffened, then asked if she could help me. "I grew up in this building," I said. "In 2B. I thought perhaps I could see the apartment once more. Do you happen to know who lives there?"

"I do," she said, as startled as I. She looked me over. "Sure. You can come and see the apartment. But I better tell you first, my kids are all over the place!"

I laughed and we walked down the hall together, exchanging names. Hers was Rita Garcia. Nine people were living in Apartment 2B, as opposed to our old, crowded four, so of course there were stacks of things everywhere: clothes, toys, appliances. They barricaded the windows, narrowed the doorways, filled the hallway. Everything looked painfully rundown and given up on. The light and air that had once characterized these rooms seemed permanently gone. I stared and stared, lost in an orgy of remembering.

Rita Garcia took me to the door. I looked at her, and held out my hand.

"Thanks," I said.

"I got to get my kids out of here," she said.

•

A few weeks ago I went back to the Bronx for the first time in 30 years. I got off the No. 2 train at East Tremont Avenue and started walking. To my persistently nostalgic eye, much looked as it had the last time I'd been here. East Tremont Avenue was still boarded-up storefronts, blaring salsa music, discount stores, pawnbrokers, empty lots.

On 180th Street, worse: empty lots everywhere interspersed with random sections of stores: a groceria, a drugstore, a church; a stretch of emptiness and discard; an auto repair, a video store, a beauty salon. At the park, again a dismal sight met my eyes: the benches that had once lined Bronx Park South are gone, a high wooden fence closes the park off from view and the old entrance is sealed up. This whole side of Bronx Park now belongs to the zoo, whose entry fee is $8 every day but one.

That is what I saw, walking around on my own, for a few quick hours one day back in the old neighborhood. But things were not as they had been 30 years ago, not by any stretch. It was only that an educated rather than a naked eye was required to see the enormous change that had taken place here. This time I hung around for a while, got myself a Virgil to lead me through the Bronx beneath the Bronx, and came away with a renewed respect, a deepened affection, even, for how social recovery occurs.

When I looked again, I saw that the streets were actually clean, entirely cleared of burned-out buildings, garbage and rubble; that many old apartment houses had been beautifully restored and new ones built from the ground up; that whole blocks were now occupied by neat two-story houses with front yards.

And when I was taken into some of the new and restored buildings, I learned that inside almost every one of them is a set of community workers (teachers, counselors, social workers) offering services meant to ease hard-pressed lives: day care, job instruction, tenant information, classes in English. I also learned that the largest empty lot on 180th Street—the one that pained me the most to look at, as here had once stood our candy store, drugstore and shoe repair—was becoming a park. The neighborhood voted on it, the city owned the land and approved the plan, and Henry J. Stern's Parks Department was making it happen. As Ronay Menschel, my Virgil, quietly remarked, "What is not visible to the naked eye is the investment in people that is being made here, one by one."

It turned out that my old neighborhood is a participant in an extraordinary effort that was put in motion more than 30 years ago—the Comprehensive Community Revitalization Program—to rescue five Bronx neighborhoods from the devastation that had overcome them all. In each neighborhood a community development corporation was founded to facilitate a plan meant to involve residents and local business people in their own rescue work. The community development corporation of West Farms (my neighborhood) is Phipps Houses, one of the oldest and largest of nonprofit developers in New York. Ronay Menschel has been its president for the last eight years.

According to a 1995 Phipps report, 1,700 apartments were lost in this neighborhood in the 1970's as a result of fire, neglect and abandonment, and the population dropped by 44 percent. Phipps came in, cleared several blocks along Boston Road and Bryant Avenue, and built the Lambert Houses, a set of low-rise buildings composed of 731 apartments with courtyards and community rooms. Then, one by one, Phipps (raising, of course, lots of private and government money to do so) went about either renovating or putting up one building after another: the Lee Goodwin Residence (33 units), Mapes Court (91 units), the Sojourner Truth Houses (62 units) and most recently the Daly Avenue Apartments (84 units).

Joining with Phipps in this sizable effort has been the church-owned Aquinas Housing Corporation, also responsible for renovating and restoring many buildings in the neighborhood (mainly for the elderly), and the New York City Partnership, which put up the two-story houses and helped first-time homeowners buy them.

The tenants in these buildings are a mixed population, mainly Hispanic or African-American, whose incomes range from medium to low to very low; many are on public assistance, some among the recently homeless; all have limited job skills and little education. But everybody's paying rents that range typically (at the brand new Daly Avenue Apartments, at least) from $676 to $808 for a two-bedroom apartment and from $806 to $1,007 for a three-bedroom.

All the Phipps buildings come with built-in social services because the agency's mission is to create decent housing and help put people on their feet. At the Career Education Center on 178th Street at Boston Road, classes are intended (in collaboration with the New York City Board of Education) to prepare high school dropouts for the G.E.D. exam. Over on Southern Boulevard, at the Sojourner Truth Houses, where half the residents are formerly homeless and half are homeless in transition, a group called Women in Need struggles to help them negotiate the world once more. At the Daly Avenue Apartments, the Head Start program is the jewel in Phipps's crown; here the rooms are beautifully appointed, the teacher in charge full of skill and imagination, and the children look smart and happy.

The community workers in these buildings spend their days developing workshops, programs, special events that will involve not only tenants and local business people but the schools, the Parks Department and the public library as well. For Phipps, the organizing never stops.

Ronay Menschel, a tall, slim, elegant-looking woman with a quiet manner and a long history in public service, spends a good part of her working week up here in West Farms. Everywhere she is greeted with affectionate respect. "Hi, Ronay! Good morning, Mrs. Menschel, nice to see you!" I heard repeatedly as we moved swiftly from building to building. For me, she was Virgil, but for the Bronx she's Lillian Wald.

Indeed. The Bronx that Phipps Houses began working in 30 years ago bears a strong resemblance to the Lower East Side that the famous social worker labored in 100 years ago.

In 1990, in a book written to celebrate the centennial of the Educational Alliance, one of the first great community-building organizations in New York, Adam Bellow reminds us of what Lillian Wald walked through every day of her working life:

> The squalor of the neighborhood infamous. . . . The streets were noisy, dirty, overflowing . . . strewn with garbage thrown from windows . . . gangs of ragged children roamed everywhere . . . pestilential odors legendary. . . .

Disease . . . ravaged the ghetto as well. . . .

Crime also flourished in this atmosphere; brothels and 'dancing academies' operated openly, protected by grafting policemen and their political bosses in Tammany Hall.

Every neighborhood produced its ethnic gangs, and many youths were involved in street fights, larceny and organized extortion.

•

The neighborhood was looked upon as a blight. Uptown, the immigrant Jews of the Lower East Side were considered a source of antisocial behavior that threatened the entire city. When a complaint was made in 1900 about street crime, the police commissioner supposedly said, "What can you do when you have a hundred thousand young Hebrews running around the streets?"

My mother, who would be 98 if she were alive today, was a child on those very streets. She survived the tenements, grew up, got married out of her mother's house and, in 1930, with her infant son (my brother) in her arms, she and her immigrant husband went north to start a new life in the Bronx. We'll never know to what degree Lillian Wald and the Educational Alliance were responsible for that move.

The scorn and humiliation that New York levels at its dispossessed—those born into the wrong class, race or sex—is of a remarkably high order. At the same time, so is the generosity that surges up repeatedly from the city's never-failing love for starting all over again: it is, in fact, its trademark.

Throughout my life I have watched New York neighborhoods rise and fall and rise again; and never is the energy higher, the spirit more inventive, existence less static than during the period of rescue work. When it's all over, the neighborhood is once again civil—the streets either peaceful or elegant—but the exhilaration of who-knows-what-will-come-of-this has died down.

Ronay Menschel and her army of smart, cheerful workers in the field are having the best of it, as are the countless other nonprofits like Phipps that, even as I write, are laboring all over desolated New York neighborhoods to excavate buried human treasure. Between the chaos of yesterday and the respectability of tomorrow lies the perfectibility of man. This is their moment. My old neighborhood probably never had it so good.

June 24, 2001

Joe Governali at the Tiffany Street Pier. (Richard Perry/The New York Times)

39

Ship of Dreams

In 1780, H.M.S Hussar Sank Near Hell Gate. Joseph Governali Was in Hot Pursuit, With Good Reason: Legend Says the Frigate Was Laden With Gold.

TOM VANDERBILT

TO begin to look for the fortune in lost Revolutionary War gold said to lie at the bottom of the East River, one must first get to the river. On the back streets of Hunts Point in the Bronx, the water is almost a fiction, a gray and ghostly shimmer barely visible past the hulking warehouses and factories that have colonized the waterfront: a New York Post printing plant, a Con Ed plant and, as announced by a putrescent gust, a waste transfer station.

Driving with Joseph Governali, a 41-year-old actor, real estate agent and aspiring treasure salvager, and Lloyd Ultan, the genial and official factotum of Bronx history, we are having trouble even finding a suitable vantage point for the purported resting place of H.M.S. Hussar, the British frigate that sank along with a rumored fortune off what was then Port Morris on Nov. 23, 1780. Those few streets that do lead to the water end in fences and concrete barricades. Rain and the wary glances of watchmen add to the unease.

Finally, down Tiffany Street, we find the Tiffany Street Pier, a recently remodeled municipal pier where Mr. Governali occasionally meets his fellow treasure hunters if he does not feel like going to Long Island. There is no docking access, so he simply "jumps down into" the boat. The pier is closed for the winter. To the right, however, is a remarkably open patch of landscape.

We descend upon the sand and rocks. Before us lie the churning waters of Hell Gate, the turbulent confluence of the Harlem and East Rivers. Looming through the haze are the squat buildings and razor wire

of Rikers Island. To the right, on North Brother Island, are the ruins of
the hospital that once housed Typhoid Mary. Mr. Governali, standing
astride a rock, points to a crumpled folding chair nearby. "Lloyd, look!"
he shouts. "I found the chair where the captain sat on the Hussar!"

Returning to the car, a woman waiting out the rain in an adjacent ve-
hicle looks at Mr. Governali, a waterfront noir figure wearing a fedora
and raincoat with raised collar. "He must be some kind of movie star or
something," she cackles.

•

Mr. Governali, who has appeared in scores of commercials and in bit
parts in films like "Die Hard 3," is still waiting for his star turn. In that
he is no different from the untold legions drawn by New York's perpet-
ual incandescence and visible wealth. Yet for the last few years, Mr. Governali has been looking for another kind of fortune, another brand of
celebrity. In this he has joined a smaller procession of New Yorkers who
have, over three centuries, spent many hours and dollars, and risked
their lives in the capricious waters of Hell Gate.

The object of their search is a ship that may or may not be there and
that may or may not contain millions of dollars in gold. Somewhere beneath the black roiling water—and Mr. Governali is the latest to think
he knows where—sits the Hussar, a ship that has proven even more elusive than fame or fortune.

As a ship, the Hussar was a minor player amid the might of the Royal
Navy, a 28-gun, sixth-rate Mermaid class frigate. Built at Rotherhithe on
the Thames River in 1763, the Hussar was 114 feet long by 34 feet wide,
with a crew of around 100. It engaged in skirmishes off Ireland and
Portugal before being summoned to America as part of a nearly 100-ship
"Cork" fleet.

As a legend, however, the Hussar has loomed like a massive galleon in
New York's imagination, the flagship of the city's desire and mythmak-
ing. The tale, like the ship, lies buried in the detritus of history, every so
often glittering again like the edge of a gold coin through a scrim of silt.
As with any story, time has etched many imperfections in the tale of the
Hussar, and the truth is often no more visible than the waters at the bottom of Hell Gate. The basic events, however, can be charted as follows:

With British control over New York looking increasingly tentative
and the crown's troops long owed payment, the Hussar arrived in Manhattan in early November, said to be bearing a payroll and 70 American

prisoners of war. It was soon after dispatched, most accounts say, to Newport, R.I. Some say the Hussar picked up gold from the British pay office (then on Cherry Street) or from another ship in the harbor, or that it had it all along. All agreed that as the ship sailed upriver toward Long Island Sound, entering Hell Gate, it struck a reef known as Pot Rock and began taking on water.

Hampered by the violent currents, the Hussar's captain, Maurice Pole, struggled to steer toward shore, but the ship sank somewhere between Port Morris and Montressor's Island (today North Brother Island). Most of the crew survived, and the masts, it was said, jutted above water for days before being swept away.

The Hussar, one claim reported, had taken on a slave named Swan as a pilot to navigate Hell Gate. Swan's widow is quoted as having "frequently heard Mr. Swan in his lifetime say that there was a large quantity of money on board the ship when she sunk." At an inquest, however, Captain Pole denied there was any treasure aboard the ship. The first mate testified they had unloaded the soldiers' payment before going upriver. There the story might have died, save for a lingering suspicion that the British were covering up the treasure so that they might later retrieve it. So, beginning as soon as three years after the ship's sinking and continuing to the present, enterprising men have gone in search of the Hussar.

The would-be salvors ranged from George M. Thomas, an itinerant street preacher turned patent medicine vendor, in 1880, to Simon Lake, inventor of the modern submarine, who wrote in his autobiography: "No one now knows precisely where the old hulk rests, and my explorations early in 1937 were unsuccessful. I have not given up the idea, but other things are more pressing."

Thomas Jefferson financed an early expedition, and in 1823 The New York Evening Post reported that a Samuel Davis had invented "a machine for raising sunken ships" and was about to "commence operations" to raise the Hussar. Most recently, a Cape Cod treasure hunter named Barry Clifford whose reputation was secured with his discovery in 1986 of the pirate vessel Whydah along with a reported $14 million in gold, announced in 1985 he had found the Hussar. (Mr. Clifford is currently salvaging Captain Kidd's ship off Madagascar.)

In the Herman Melville Library of the South Street Seaport Museum, a file on the Hussar contains a forlorn sampling of telephone messages and letters from various people claiming to have found the ship. While there seems to be more evidence that the Hussar did not carry treasure than that it did, one reported fact that has encouraged Hussar seekers is that the British themselves mounted at least three expeditions in search of the ship. "In the spring of 1794 two brigs were dispatched from England to undertake the recovery of the lost treasure," The New-York Daily Times wrote in 1856. "They came fully equipped with men, a large diving-bell and other equipments for sub-marine explorations."

The Times also wrote of an 1856 expedition during which a number of bones had been found, "showing, evidently, that a part, if not all the American prisoners on board, were manacled and chained."

•

One morning at an East Side Starbucks (about as close as one can get to the legacy of Melville in New York these days), after changing tables to avoid being overheard, Mr. Governali looked left and right, hunched his shoulders and said with hushed urgency: "The British sent three expeditions here to locate the ship. They had sunken ships all over the world. Why come here for that one ship?"

Craig Leckner, a casting agent and friend of Mr. Governali's who has helped him with his research, says he began as a debunker. Trolling through the paper trail, however, he says he has seen enough to make him think there might be something to the rumors. "There's not a treasure hunter in the world who doesn't know about the Hussar," he said. "What's great about Joe is that here's this average guy who has a chance to change history."

While Mr. Governali, who is divorced and has no children, has long been a diver, he is hardly the weather-beaten, salt-encrusted Jacques Cousteau character one might expect of a treasure hunter. He looks more suited to play, and indeed is often cast in, one of Hollywood's most enduring roles: a Mafioso.

"I hate mob parts," he said. "We've got royalty in our family. A Governali sits in Parliament in Italy. My father's cousin, Paul Governali, played for Notre Dame." The associations die hard, though. "We're from Corleone, Sicily," he said, pausing for the expected reaction. "People say: 'Where you from? Corleone? No way.' It's that kind of thing."

As much as Mr. Governali loathes Mafia stereotypes, he wields even more opprobrium for stereotypes of the Bronx. "People don't know that a major battle of the Revolutionary War was fought here," said Mr. Governali, a lifelong Bronxite who now lives in Throgs Neck. So several years ago, in an effort to restore luster to the borough's image, he began working with Mr. Ultan on a documentary provisionally titled "Hidden Treasures of the Bronx." He saw the Hussar as its opening salvo.

As a diver, he had long heard about the Hussar ("Every diver knows about these legends"), but for the film he plunged into its history. In the Rare Book Room of the New York Public Library, however, Mr. Governali found a document a few years ago that turned his research into practice: a map by the commissary general showing the location of three wrecks, including the Hussar. The map was noteworthy, he said, because "it showed the wreck to be a place that nobody had looked."

Nor will anyone be finding the map anytime soon. "It was misfiled," he added with a smile. As one might expect, he did not alert the librarian, but did take the time to trace it onto a series of later maps.

Mr. Governali regretted that he could not show me the map. Here one enters into the competitive, suspicious world of underwater salvage, which is as much about plowing through dusty archives as about sonar and scuba.

After several diving attempts on the Hussar in the last few years, he has retrieved several artifacts. He showed me several stills from underwater footage, which admittedly were rather Rorschachtian. "It's very hard to see," he said, "but this is part of the ballast, this was an iron nail we found, and this is a 10-pint pitcher." Determining ownership of a wreck involves navigating a jurisdictional and legal maze, but Mr. Governali was sufficiently convinced to file a claim in Admiralty Court for possession of the wreck.

James Sinclair, a marine archaeologist from St. Augustine, Fla., who has worked on the Titanic, among other projects, began advising Mr. Governali after Mr. Governali sent him some artifacts, including the pitcher.

"Pottery's one of the best tools for dating a site," Mr. Sinclair said. "A piece from ancient Egypt is probably in just about as good a shape as a piece from yesterday. This piece was intact, a lovely little pitcher probably used for serving beer out of a keg." He describes it as a "very standard sort of stylistic piece that fits into the latter half of the 1700's."

Elsewhere, the pitcher might prove he had found the Hussar. But this is Hell Gate, which in the 18th and 19th centuries, before it was effectively demolished, was one of the most treacherous bodies of water in the United States.

"New York Harbor may be full of such pieces," Mr. Sinclair said. Dozens of pieces, from anchors to cannon, reputed to be from the Hussar have been brought up over the years. "In investigating any sort of crash, you're looking at lots of little bits and pieces of evidence," he said, adding that much more must be assembled to draw any conclusions.

The ship's age adds complications. "Much of the evidence has gone the way of a lot of organic matter under water," Mr. Sinclair said. "It's pretty much gone."

"Joe's heart is in the right place," he added. "But he's caught between two worlds. On the one hand, he has to make money. In his spare time he is trying to get the project together. It's a tough way to make a living."

•

There was a time, not long ago, when this port city was closer to the sea, when wrecks loomed larger in memory. As Joseph Mitchell wrote of Gotham's underwater ruins in his 1959 book, "The Bottom of the Harbor," "Some are close to shore, in depths of only 20 to 30 feet; around noon, on unusually clear, sunny fall days, when there is not much plankton in the water and the turbidity is low, it is possible to see these and see schools of sea bass streaming in and out of holes in their hulls."

Whether or not it contains a fortune, most people agree that the discovery of the Hussar would be a landmark achievement. "Finding it would give, if nothing else, a great time capsule of the Revolutionary War," Mr. Sinclair said, "and the end to an ages-old mystery." A layer of skepticism is added with every failed attempt on the Hussar. Mr. Governali is nonplussed. "A lot of people believe it's underground," he said. "It's not underground. Let me put it this way: Nobody's crazy enough to go into a court of law and claim a wreck that's not there. I'm crazy, but not that crazy."

Yet there must be some mania at work to explain those who plunge into the violent murk of Hell Gate, looking for a ship that may be nothing more than a splintering of worm-eaten wood. Mr. Governali, who insists he is not a treasure hunter, sees in the ship a chance at redemption for his hometown borough, a glittering prize returned to the civic mantle.

One also gets the sense that he enjoys this role, that the search for the ship is a series of auditions for the final stardom. Only in a city where life proceeds with cinematic pomp would a shipwreck seeker be an actor. Mr. Governali, who says he studied with an acting teacher named Joe

Paradise, has learned his lessons well. "He gets into the nature of every-thing," Mr. Governali said of Mr. Paradise. "It's not about acting. It's about the emotion behind the person, what he feels, what he wants, what he needs. His spine, he calls it."

Mr. Governali wants this ship. He says he has asked the British gov-ernment for permission to salvage. He says he wants an Anglican bishop on board to administer last rites when the ship is found. If further proof were needed of the extent to which the search for the Hussar has penetrated his character, he offers a small confession. "My stage name is Joey Treasures," he says sheepishly. Then he shrugs, as Tony Soprano would after revealing some inner moment to Dr. Melfi. "You know us Italians. We gotta have nicknames."

February 17, 2002

After the plane crash in Brooklyn. (UPI)

276

40

The Day the Boy Fell From the Sky

Decades Later, a Park Slope Nurse Remembers.

W E N D E L L   J A M I E S O N

ON a winter afternoon, the light in Snooky's Pub in Park Slope, Brooklyn, is almost the color of Scotch and water. Outside, the baby stroller army rolls down Seventh Avenue. Inside there is cigarette smoke, a Dennis Quaid movie playing silently on TV, and murmured talk and laughter around the polished bar, the light glinting on the upside-down glasses.

Some days, you can find Barbara Lewnes here, after her morning errands, having lunch, talking with a few of the regulars. A widow with sharp, strikingly youthful features and white hair, she has friends at Snooky's. Not long ago, when she didn't come in for a while, Michael the bartender worked the phones to track her down. He wanted to invite her to a benefit for a victim of the World Trade Center, but he was also a little worried.

Those who know Barbara Lewnes know that she has two grown children, that she lives nearby on Prospect Park West, and that she has been around Park Slope since the late 1950's. They know that her husband was a doctor, that her son is a physical therapist in Arizona, and that her daughter lives in Manhattan and has written a book about the city's street kids. And they know that she was there the day the plane hit.

"I guess you want to talk about the plane crash," one of the bartenders said recently to a caller looking for Mrs. Lewnes.

The plane crash. A DC-8, clipped in a midair collision, tumbled from low clouds in December 1960 and came to rest in shattered pieces at Seventh Avenue and Sterling Place, six blocks north of Snooky's. Mrs. Lewnes was a young nurse then at Methodist Hospital of Brooklyn, 13 blocks south of the crash site, and she cared for the plane's only survivor, an 11-year-old named Stephen Baltz.

Many old-time Park Slopers remember that boy, the picture of him sitting dazed in a snowbank with a blackened face. They remember how the entire city seemed to pray for him that long Christmastime night. And they remember, of course, that he died the next morning.

But time has a way of burnishing stories and smoothing over the rough edges, of pulling legends and heroes out of horrors. When newspaper articles remember that day, as they have rather more often since Sept. 11, the writers frequently describe a heroic effort to save Stephen by doctors who worked until dawn. Barbara Lewnes, reading her newspaper in Snooky's on a chilly afternoon, remembers it differently.

•

Barbara Lewnes was Barbara Stull then, 22 years old. She briefly wanted to be a singer. She had been on the radio and had sung "at every hospital and church and school function that ever was" in Jersey City, her hometown. But after graduating from high school, she followed a friend to the nursing school at Methodist, where she was accepted in 1957. A photograph from that time shows a pretty brunette with an intense gaze, wearing a pointed nurse's hat.

She joined a lively community of young women who worked a few years as nurses before quitting and being married, often to doctors. In December 1960, six months after graduating, Barbara Lewnes was doing her part to carry on the tradition: she was dating four doctors.

There was one in particular, Dr. George Lewnes, an internist whose family was an institution in Park Slope, having owned and run two ice cream parlors known to local teenagers as Loonies.

She worked in the hospital's Buckley building—prepping patients for surgery, caring for those with heart ailments—and had her own place on Prospect Park West. She remembers it as a fine time: dates in Manhattan with George and the other doctors, Broadway shows, drinks at Trader Vic's. And being a nurse. "I loved it," she said not long ago, sitting at a back table in Snooky's. "I loved the contact with the patients, knowing you could do something to make their lives easier."

Her sweet but sometimes vague memories of those days click sharply into focus on Dec. 16, 1960. First, the weather: freezing, spitting rain flecked with snow and hail, the streets piled with snowbanks from an earlier blizzard.

Before her shift, which started at midnight, she had a date with Dr. Lewnes at the Hamilton House restaurant in Bay Ridge. She decided to spend the morning at the hospital, helping other nurses trace Christmas drawings on a window in the pediatrics ward.

At 10:30 a.m., when she was walking down Sixth Street, half a block from the hospital, she heard the sirens. First one, then another, then more than she could count, enveloping her and rising from the gently ascending streets, mixing with the snow and rain that swirled around the tops of Park Slope's many church steeples.

At the hospital, she passed the emergency room, and that's where she heard the words.

Like all hospitals at the height of the cold war, Methodist had a disaster plan, not just for plane crashes, but also for nuclear attacks. Routine surgical operations were canceled, nursing classes suspended and rooms cleared for the influx of patients sure to arrive.

Seconds later, it seemed, Miss Stull was crowded into a doctor's car, racing through red lights down Seventh Avenue to the crash. A block from Sterling Place, she saw a surreal image that has since been printed in her memory like a photograph: the triangular tail section of a jetliner, disembodied and scorched, the word "United" clearly visible. Several buildings were burning furiously.

She and other medical workers set up cots inside Grace Methodist Church at St. John's Place and Seventh Avenue. But when the patients came, they were not from the DC-8. They were police officers and firefighters, their faces masked by soot, their soaked uniforms starting to ice up.

There was talk of a survivor from the jet, a little boy found terribly burned in a snowbank and taken to Methodist in a police car. One fireman told the young nurse that the boy had been flying without his parents and had lived because he'd been sitting on a stewardess's lap in a jump seat. When the jet hit, the fireman surmised, the back door had popped open and the child had been thrown out. Miss Stull looked over the snowbank: the plane's door was still open.

Hours later, she headed back to Methodist Hospital. She needed to prepare for dinner, and saw little to do at the crash scene or the hospital. Around 6 p.m., she stopped at the security office to remind the director of nursing, Edith Roberts, that she would be back for her shift at midnight. There was a pause. Miss Roberts said to wait, and she went to talk to someone. "I walked over to the chapel for a minute," Mrs. Lewnes remembered, "and then I walked back, and she said: 'Barbara, we'll use you. You'll special him tonight.'"

"Special." One nurse for one patient. That terribly burned boy would be hers.

The next few hours were oddly calm, a comforting memory of a long-ago date with her husband-to-be. She remembers the evening clearly: Dr. Lewnes picking her up, the two of them driving out to Bay Ridge in his father's black Chevy, sitting in a booth at the Hamilton House, eating lobster. George was quiet. Looking back, she thinks he knew what she was in for.

Around the city, candle-lighted churches hung with Christmas decorations were filling up for Friday night services. Many who attended that night, some with crumpled copies of afternoon newspapers under their arms, at least one of which had a picture of Stephen Baltz on the front page, remember prayers for that little boy.

Back at the crash site, the fires were long out and flatbed trucks were backing in to take away the first pieces of the DC-8. The bodies were all recovered and lined up. The firemen sipped coffee or dozed in the darkness of the church. At Michel's restaurant on Flatbush Avenue, they gathered wearily around a buffet of sandwiches and soup donated by the proprietor.

Even closer to where Miss Stull and Dr. Lewnes sat, on a field on Staten Island, lay the remains of the other plane that had fallen, a propeller-driven T.W.A. Super Constellation that had been cut into pieces by the faster DC-8. None of the 44 people on the Super Constellation survived. In all, 128 passengers and crew members from both planes died that day, as did 6 people on the ground in Park Slope, making it the worst air disaster in history at the time.

As Miss Stull headed home with Dr. Lewnes, she became nervous. "I couldn't even imagine the nursing care that he would need," she said of Stephen.

The child had been placed in a glassed-in nursery and was surrounded by doctors, nurses, equipment. The doctors spoke quietly, each weighing in on his area of expertise: the head of orthopedics saying he wanted to set Stephen's broken leg, but could not because of the burns; the plastic surgeon speaking of skin grafts. The chief of pediatrics, of surgery. They were all there.

Then she saw him. He was so badly burned, she could not tell what race he was. A bone stuck out of one of his legs. He was covered only by a small, sterilized sheet on his groin. "They couldn't even cover him with a sheet because of the bacteria factor," she said. "He was just open wounds all over. I've never seen someone burned like this."

She was put somewhat at ease by the experts milling around.

"They all kind of worked together; they had to," she said. "It was just a case that I don't think many people get to see in a lifetime."

As each doctor noticed Miss Stull, he updated her briefly on Stephen's condition and what could be expected during the night. She started to have a sickened feeling.

One by one, their orders given, the doctors headed out the door, and not long after 12:30 a.m. the nurse realized that she was alone with two young nursing students and Stephen Baltz. "When I got there, every chief of every service was on the floor, and I thought, 'It's not going to be too bad, all the people here to help me.' Because, you see, decisions had to be made that nursing usually doesn't do. But everyone disappeared."

Silence, except for Stephen's halting breaths.

•

Her training kicked in. First, check his respiration by watching his chest gently rise and fall. Next, his fluids, his blood and urine. Every 10 minutes she updated her logbook. She stood the whole time. There was only one chair in the room, and a nursing student was asleep in it.

Stephen had also been sleeping when she got there, but a little later, he suddenly chirped up with the bell-like voice of a healthy child. He wanted to know where he was, he felt fine, he wanted a television.

"You stood there looking at this little boy," she said, "and he was saying this, and you know to me it still is the weirdest thing that I've ever seen."

She couldn't explain that the need to keep the room sterile prevented her from bringing in a television set. "Maybe tomorrow," she said gently. "I don't think we have one right now. I'll see about finding one."

They looked at each other, eye to eye.

Then he dozed off.

That happened again and again.

Stephen had been alone on the plane because his mother and sisters had flown east from Chicago a few days earlier to spend Christmas with his aunt, but he had been delayed by a sore throat.

When his parents arrived at the hospital, they were given a room nearby. Every hour, Stephen's father, William S. Baltz, vice president of the Admiral Corporation of Chicago, which made television sets, came to the room. Calmly, he leaned over his son.

"I remember how he was with Stephen, and how he was able to come in and talk to Stephen as if nothing was wrong," she said. "I never saw him break down, and that was amazing. I didn't have children then, but you could just imagine."

It was one of the longest nights of the year. The boy's breaths continued, and grayish light filtered in from the windows. Around 7 a.m., a doctor reappeared. Soon, the room was crowded. The administrators filed in. So did more doctors, students from around the hospital to see this unique case, and her own replacement. A feeling of euphoria came over Miss Stull.

"I felt wonderful, and he seemed more alert," she said. "I decided, you know, he's going to make it. Three-quarters of your patients die in those midnight-to-8 a.m. hours. Everyone was quite surprised, even pleased, and they said it's beginning to look like things are settling down a bit." She headed back to her apartment. It was going to be a beautiful, clear winter day.

Stephen Baltz died at 10 a.m. The hospital never called her to tell her. She learned about it from the radio when she woke up that afternoon. The announcer said the death toll from the crash had gone up by one.

At Methodist, Mr. Baltz himself told the reporters that his son was gone. As he and his wife left the hospital, he slipped the four dimes and five nickels that had been in Stephen's pocket into the donation box.

Barbara Stull went on to become the night supervisor and a few years later married Dr. George Lewnes. The wedding reception was at the restaurant where the firemen had warmed themselves the day of the crash. She quit the hospital and raised her two children, Alexia and George Jr., occasionally returning to the hospital to fill in for vacationing nurses. She also spent some time there in 1994, when George Sr. died.

She has traveled a good deal, but has never flown United. For decades, she thought of the crash mostly around Christmas, when a gallery on Seventh Avenue would display a picture of the wreckage in the window, but in recent years, she said, she has been drawn back more and more to that day, and to that long night with Stephen, although she is not sure exactly what is tugging on her memory. She imagines her 22-year-old self, scared to death, and wonders how on earth they could have left her alone and in charge.

•

Forty years later, she got her answer.

The assistant nursing supervisor running Methodist's nurses that Dec. 16 was a tough, blunt-speaking Flatbush native named Eileen Bonner. It was she who designed the hospital's disaster response plan, and it was she with whom Edith Roberts consulted before specialing Barbara Stull to Stephen Baltz. Ms. Bonner went on to work in the Reagan White House and was commissioned a colonel in the Army Reserves, but she kept in touch with the young nurse from Jersey City, with whom she felt a rapport.

"She was an excellent nurse, No. 1," Ms. Bonner said not too long ago, sitting in her apartment in Bay Ridge. "She was clinically excellent, and she also was very outgoing. And if you asked her a question, you'd get a straight response. She didn't look at you like, 'I wonder what she wants me to say?' Dependability, common sense, she had all of that, and she was available."

Ms. Bonner also remembers that long day and night, but not in the same minute-by-minute, second-by-second detail as Barbara Lewnes does. She knows that Mrs. Lewnes was with Stephen, but does not recall other staffing specifics. Nor do Mrs. Lewnes's precise notes survive. Hospitals do not keep records longer than 24 years. All the specialists who stood around Stephen's bed have apparently since died.

In December 2000, a group of those who recall the crash gathered at Sterling Place and Seventh Avenue to remember that day. It was the only memorial to mark the 40th anniversary of the disaster, at a street corner where the only reminder is a vacant lot amid rows of million-dollar brownstones. The only official memorial to the collision is in the hospital chapel: a tiny plaque that includes Stephen's coins.

After the outdoor remembrance, Mrs. Lewnes and Ms. Bonner were invited to speak at Grace Methodist. Mrs. Lewnes told of her night with Stephen, when she was "literally secluded" with him, and was briefly overcome by emotion. Ms. Bonner spoke in the gravelly, matter-of-fact tones of a retired Army colonel, and described how Stephen was terribly burned, not only outside but inside, in his lungs. Then she said something that stunned the retired nurse. "We all knew that he was too badly burned to live."

Everybody but Barbara Lewnes.

"I never thought that," she said later. "I had never heard that expressed. It was never said in front of me. I just thought, the longer a person lives, the better the chance that they are going to make it."

That, she suspects, is why the doctors left. There was nothing they could do. That is why no one thought to call her the next day. Why call to tell someone something they must have already known?

"I was probably the only person who thought he might make it," she said. She, and that 11-year-old boy.

March 24, 2002

ABOUT THE CONTRIBUTORS

ANDRÉ ACIMAN, a professor of comparative literature at the City University Graduate Center, is the author of "Out of Egypt: A Memoir" and "False Papers: Essays on Exile and Memory," the editor of "Letters of Transit" and, most recently, the editor of "The Proust Project."

TARA BAHRAMPOUR, a reporter for The Washington Post and a former reporter for the City section of The New York Times, is the author of the memoir "To See and See Again: A Life in Iran and America."

DAN BARRY, the About New York columnist for The New York Times, is the author of "Pull Me Up: A Memoir."

THOMAS BELLER, editor of Open City magazine and the New York-centric Web site mrbellersneighborhood.com, is the author of two works of fiction, "Seduction Theory: Stories" and "The Sleep-Over Artist: A Novel." An essay collection, "How to Be a Man," was published this spring.

DAVID C. BOTTI, a corporal in the Marine Corps Reserve, served for four months in Iraq during the summer of 2003. He lives in New York City and is at work on a collection of short stories.

JEROME CHARYN, who runs the film studies program at the American University in Paris, is the author of more than 30 books, including a series of novels about a New York police chief and "Gangsters and Gold

Diggers: Old New York, the Jazz Age and the Birth of Broadway." "Savage Shorthand," a short biography of Isaac Babel, will be published later this year. He is working on a book about Quentin Tarantino.

LAURA SHAINE CUNNINGHAM, a novelist and playwright, is the author of two memoirs, "Sleeping Arrangements" and "A Place in the Country," along with the novels "Beautiful Bodies," "Dreams of Rescue" and "The Midnight Diary of Zoya Blume." She is at work on a new memoir/novel, "The House of Special Purpose."

JIM DWYER, a reporter for The New York Times, is the author of "Subway Lives: 24 Hours in the Life of the New York City Subway," and the author, with Kevin Flynn, of "102 Minutes: The Untold Story of the Fight to Survive Inside the Twin Towers."

JILL EISENSTADT, editor at large for BKLYN magazine, is the author of two novels, "From Rockaway" and "Kiss Out." She is currently writing film scripts with her sister, the actress and filmmaker Debra Eisenstadt.

VIVIAN GORNICK is the author of eight books, including the memoir "Fierce Attachments" and the essay collection "The End of the Novel of Love." Her most recent book, on Elizabeth Cady Stanton and feminism in America, will be published in the fall of 2005.

MEL GUSSOW, a culture writer for The New York Times, is the author of the biography "Edward Albee: A Singular Journey" along with books about Harold Pinter, Tom Stoppard, Samuel Beckett and Arthur Miller.

IVOR HANSON is writing a book based on his experiences as a New York City window cleaner.

MOLLY HASKELL is a film critic whose books include "Holding My Own in No Man's Land: Men and Women, Films and Feminists."

SIRI HUSTVEDT is the author of a book of poetry, a book of essays and three novels: "The Blindfold," "The Enchantment of Lily Dahl" and "What I Loved." Two more collections of her essays will be published this year.

WENDELL JAMIESON is an assistant metropolitan editor at The New York Times.

SUKI KIM is the author of "The Interpreter," a first novel that was the winner of the 2004 PEN Beyond Margins Award.

CHUCK KLOSTERMAN, a columnist for Esquire and a senior writer for Spin, is the author of "Fargo Rock City," "Sex, Drugs and Cocoa Puffs" and the forthcoming "Killing Yourself to Live."

STEVEN KURUTZ is a reporter for the City section of The New York Times.

DAVID LEAVITT is a novelist and short story writer whose works include "Martin Bauman; or, A Sure Thing" and, most recently, "The Body of Jonah Boyd." A former New York resident, he teaches creative writing at the University of Florida.

ADRIAN NICOLE LEBLANC is the author of "Random Family: Love, Drugs, Trouble, and Coming of Age in the Bronx," which was a nonfiction finalist for the National Book Critics Circle Award. She teaches at Columbia University Graduate School of Journalism and is currently working on a book about New York comedians.

DENNY LEE, a regular contributor to the Escapes section of The New York Times, is a former reporter for The Times's City section.

FRANZ LIDZ, a senior writer at Sports Illustrated, is the author of the memoir "Unstrung Heroes: My Improbable Life With Four Impossible Uncles," and "Ghosty Men: The Strange But True Story of the Collyer Brothers, New York's Greatest Hoarders."

ROBERT LIPSYTE, a longtime sports columnist for The New York Times and the Coping columnist for The Times's City section for six years, is the author of 16 books, including the memoir "In the Country of Illness" and the young adult novel "The Contender." In 1966 and in 1996, he won Columbia University's Meyer Berger Award for distinguished reporting.

PHILLIP LOPATE is a novelist and essayist whose works include "Bachelorhood," "Against Joie de Vivre," "Portrait of My Body," "Waterfront" and "Writing New York: A Literary Anthology." He teaches at Columbia University, Bennington College and Hofstra University.

FIELD MALONEY is on the editorial staff of The New Yorker.

DAVID MARGOLICK, a contributing editor at Vanity Fair, was for many years a reporter at The New York Times. His books include "Strange Fruit: The Biography of a Song" and the forthcoming "The Fight," about the Joe Louis–Max Schmeling fights.

KATHERINE MARSH, a former contributing editor at Rolling Stone, is senior editor of The Washington City Paper.

DAVID MASELLO is a senior editor at Country Living magazine and a regular contributor to Art & Antiques magazine. He is the author of two books, "Architecture Without Rules: The Houses of Marcel Breuer" and "Art in Public Places: Walking New York's Neighborhoods to See the Best Paintings, Sculptures, Murals, Mosaics, and Mobiles."

GLYN MAXWELL, a poet and playwright from Hertfordshire, England, is poetry editor of The New Republic. His most recent book of poetry is "The Sugar Mile."

ED MORALES is the author of "Living in Spanglish: The Search for Latino Identity in America" and "The Latin Beat: The Roots and Rhythms of Latin Music From Rumba to Rock." He is working on a collection of essays called "Latin From Manhattan."

JAN MORRIS has written three books about New York, including "Manhattan '45." Her most recent book is "The World: Travels, 1950–2000."

RICHARD PRICE is the author of seven novels, including the Dempsy trilogy "Clockers," "Freedomland" and "Samaritan," and the author of numerous screenplays, including "The Color of Money," "Sea of Love" and "Ransom."

JOE QUEENAN's books include "Balsamic Dreams," "True Believers: The Tragic Inner Life of Sports Fans" and, most recently, "Queenan Country: A Reluctant Anglophile's Pilgrimage to the Mother Country."

ERNESTO QUIÑONEZ is the author of the novel "Bodega Dreams" and, most recently, the novel "Chango's Fire."

JIM RASENBERGER is the author of "High Steel: The Daring Men Who Built the World's Greatest Skyline."

WITOLD RYBCZYNSKI, the Martin and Margy Meterson Professor of Urbanism at the University of Pennsylvania, is the author of "A Clearing in the Distance," a biography of Frederick Law Olmsted that won the J. Anthony Lukas Prize.

TOM VANDERBILT, a contributing editor at ID and Print magazines, is the author of "Survival City: Adventures Among the Ruins of Atomic America."

SUZANNE VEGA is a singer-songwriter from New York.

PATRICIA VOLK is the author of "The Yellow Banana," "White Light," "All It Takes" and "Stuffed: Adventures of a Restaurant Family."

MEG WOLITZER's seventh novel, "The Position," has just been published. She is also the author of "The Wife" and "Surrender, Dorothy," and her short fiction has appeared in "Best American Short Stories" and "The Pushcart Prize."

ABOUT THE EDITOR

CONSTANCE ROSENBLUM is the editor of the City section of The New York Times, a post she has held since 1999. Prior to that, she was editor of the paper's Arts and Leisure section from 1990 through 1997. Previously, she was culture editor of The Philadelphia Inquirer, and, at the New York Daily News, a feature writer, features editor and deputy magazine editor. She is the author of "Gold Digger: The Outrageous Life and Times of Peggy Hopkins Joyce." She has been an adjunct professor at the Columbia University Graduate School of Journalism, teaching courses in urban affairs reporting and cultural reporting.